Music
for
Young
Children

Second
Edition

Music
for
Young
Children

Vernice Nye
University of Oregon

wcb
Wm. C. Brown Company Publishers
Dubuque, Iowa

Contents

Preface

This book is directed to teachers, aides, parents, and those preparing to work with young children. It is designed to answer some of the questions concerning how young children learn music and how music becomes a foundation for learning in all areas of the curriculum, as well as indicating what musical experiences should be provided and how to guide learning in that subject.

The major emphasis is on the young child and his developing abilities. Some knowledge of child psychology is helpful for complete understanding of the material presented here. The use of this volume as a textbook should be supplemented by observation and experience with young children, by discussion and analysis, and by additional reading, especially of the authors indicated. Local and state curriculum guides for preschool and kindergarten may also be employed in supplement.

"Mainstreaming" is incorporated into this second edition of the book. Discussion of teaching special children (physically and mentally handicapped, emotionally and socially disturbed) in the regular classroom music programs can be found in three of the six chapters. This edition includes additional traditional song material, and there is general updating. Chapter Six, which deals with parents, has been expanded. The reader will notice that the teacher is referred to in both feminine and masculine terms while the child is usually identified as "he." The author realizes that the spirit of these times is to avoid use of the masculine or feminine gender, but believes that their use in these pages seemed to present ideas more clearly, if traditionally.

Music is viewed in this textbook as an independent subject yet one that contributes concurrently to all of the other subjects. However, the full intent of the author is to show that all other subjects contribute to music as well as to each other, because the early childhood program described is almost totally integrated. And for those aspiring to teach music as a subject of itself, there are ample suggestions and materials for that approach. Thus the book serves both types of music teaching. It is recommended that the suggested materials be chosen selectively in order to provide a rich, stimulating, integrated base for the learning of music by children ages three to five in a meaningful setting.

The relation of the teacher and the child to music is discussed first; then the planning of an environment for musical growth is described. The structure of music as a discipline is stated, together with the objectives of music instruction for this age group. Chapter IV, "Realizing Music Goals and Instructional Objectives," develops in detail the teaching of music as a school subject; it is followed by Chapter V, "Music in an Integrated Curriculum," which reveals the relationships between music and the curriculum as a whole, and describes how music can compliment other subjects. The position of parents in the music program is outlined in the final chapter, and suggested ways to involve parents are listed. Appendix A presents exemplary teaching plans. Suggested activities and references are included as part of every chapter.

How suitable is this approach for children who are culturally and educationally different? In the author's opinion, all children, including both the gifted and the educationally impaired, can profit from working with the musical ideas developed in this book. Certainly all children need to have musical experience in which they can feel genuine accomplishment and enjoyment, regardless of what their cognitive, emotional, and affective abilities and levels are. They all need to find joy in learning and to develop wholesome and positive self-images. When differences in economic, cultural, intellectual, and physical abilities or emotional stability present difficulties that impair the realization of basic needs, an approach that provides for their satisfaction is necessary. Also, emphasis on music can be of special value to the culturally different children since the customs and values of a culture are conveyed through its music.

The author is aware of the fact that many who address themselves to the exceptional child and to the problem of mainstreaming, do so by the organization of a chapter or a book on this topic. But she, realizing the developmental characteristics of young children and the necessity for individualizing instruction for all children, feels that when individualization has been effectively done, most mainstreaming problems will be solved. The characteristics of the handicapped are often synonymous with those of the young child, even though the handicapped are frequently older. Therefore, in this book mainstreaming of the exceptional child is intertwined throughout, with major emphasis given in chapters 2 and 6.

While this volume presents many specific ideas, it is not a "cookbook." It is an invitation to understand children's musical learning problems and to devise appropriate approaches and procedures to solve them. These teaching procedures in turn are based on different psychological approaches. Therefore, the recommended general approach is to diagnose, then use specific learning tasks. The teacher works with the child in his total experience world.

Music for Young Children is unique not only because it describes music for young children ages three through five, but also because it places music in a substantial position within the curriculum as a whole, while at the same time introducing it into the routines of the school and the home.

The book can be used as a textbook for college classes with titles such as

Music for Young Children
Creative Arts and Literature for Young Children
Workshop in Music for In-service Teachers
Workshop in Music for Parents of Young Children

It can serve as a supplementary textbook for classes such as

Developing Programs (or Curricula) for Young Children
Music for Children
Language Arts and Communication for Young Children
Physical Education and Movement for Young Children

Vernice Nye

1 Music and Early Childhood Education

The Teacher and Music

Since the middle and late 1960's there has arisen much interest in music for the young child. For many years, however, there has been a controversy concerning the position of the arts in the classroom. The question has occasioned healthy debate, compelling those who believe in the arts to re-examine them in relation to their purposes and to the teaching strategies involved. Some educators find the arts central to their concept of good education; others find them only peripheral. A recent emphasis on cognitive development sometimes ignores cognitive learnings in music; this has caused some to place less emphasis on the arts, at least as they have been taught in the past. However, many educators question the validity of programs that emphasize cognitive skills to the neglect of creative, psychomotor, and affective aspects of learning. Cognitive learning is considered by some to be confined to the left side of the brain, while the arts, dealing with spatial learning, develop the right side of the brain. There is research that indicates that some children need a right-brained approach in their learning to ensure optimum development. The teacher needs to be aware of the issues involved, for she must defend sound principles of learning and the methods used to implement those principles in the classroom.

Variations in adult intellectual achievement are now known to be traceable to what has occurred by the age of five. Similarly patterns of emotional, linguistic and cognitive conduct are associated with early socio-economic backgrounds. Research shows that the preschool child acquires skills, knowledge, and notions about the world and people at an extremely rapid rate. A German investigator (Michel 1973) summarized the findings of a number of research studies, stating that "the musical achievements of children particularly of pre-school age, have, up to now, been considerably under-estimated, and that the age 'levels' of musical development hitherto accepted as being rigidly fixed, could, given suitable development conditions, be to a great extent, anticipated, even proved to be spurious." Michel further concluded that the optimum potential figures in the first years of life are significant not only for the general education of all children, but al-

1

so for early identification of those who are highly gifted in music; that the ages between three and six are particularly important to musical development; and that musical activity during the pre-school years should be planned in order to facilitate musical development.

Numerous researchers have emphasized the importance of planning experiences to encourage musical growth of young children. Studies have indicated that pre-school children possess the potential to advance in their control of music skills such as matching pitch, keeping time with the beat, imitating rhythmic patterns, and singing accurately on pitch songs of limited range. Writers in the field of music education conclude that early musical experiences must develop musical percepts in order that musical concepts can be acquired. Research bears this out.

The emphasis in music for young children is placed on the satisfaction and enjoyment it brings to the child. Complete mastery is not the goal; but the teacher knows that in order for these children to enjoy music, they must also learn musical skills and concepts at their maturity-interest level. Children need space in which to move, adventures and experiences to express, time and opportunity to explore and create, a variety of percussion instruments to play, music to listen to, and different types of songs to sing, compare, and contrast.

Music for Young Children is concerned with assisting individuals, through the medium of music, to respond to many stimuli and to express such responses in recognizable form. The teacher may utilize musical sounds to stimulate interest, curiosity, imagination, and to arouse feelings. Suggestions such as "Show me how you feel when you listen to this music" are essential in helping children grow through music. Responding to and producing music are and always have been a vital part of human experience; it is entirely logical, therefore, that music should have an essential place in early childhood education.

Music activities in nursery school and kindergarten are more closely related and interwoven with every part of the curriculum than they are at any other period of a child's educational experience. At this age, music greatly stimulates and enhances the intellectual, physical, affective, and social growth.

An effective music program depends upon the teacher's understanding of this age group and of music's importance in giving meaning to every facet of children's experiences. Obviously, a teacher's musical capabilities and interests are essential ingredients. The teacher must form a clear and workable philosophy of music and movement education to use as a basis and guide for selecting and organizing appropriate learning experiences, as well as for implementing a balanced and well organized music program.

In music more than in any other area, the teacher looks to spontaneous individual expressions of children as a starting point for the expansion and enrichment of their musical learning. The teacher must reinforce each child's musical efforts in a positive manner. Each child is encouraged to use his own creative ability in rhythm, sound, and movement. However, the teacher continues to identify the specific musical objectives for each child in terms of his level of performance and then selects and organizes appropriate learning experiences, materials, and media to realize these explicitly identified and stated objectives.

The early years of a child's life are extremely important ones both for learning and for establishing a base for future learnings. Hess (1973) states that what is learned first stays longest and is the most difficult to extinguish. Because they are novel experiences, whatever we learn first is likely to make the greatest impression on us. Also, once we learn something and establish patterns of behavior, it is more difficult to learn to do the same thing in another way. The major task involved in the teaching of music to children of this age is first to provide sufficient experiences to develop the child's perceptual background as a prerequisite to learning musical concepts, giving the children ample time and space to experiment with and explore all types of sounds—to listen to and interpret sounds with their bodies, voices, and instruments. Satis Coleman (1922) was probably the foremost exponent of music for children in the early 20th century. Her contention was that children feel the joy of creating and to that end she experimented with procedures in singing, rhythmic responses, instrument-making, and composing that released the child's power to create. Spontaneity and feeling were fostered before stressing attention to technique, which grew as the child's interest and enthusiasm demanded skill development. Her music program included dancing, singing, pantomiming, rhythmic speech and instrumental sounds. Music making, she asserted, was the process by which the child could express feelings and emotions. Mrs. Coleman's aim was child growth through musical experiences.

Music time can and should be any time throughout the day when there is a chance for music to enhance learning. Although it is true that music is a discipline in its own right, it is most meaningfully taught to children as an integral part of all activities in the educational program—science, social studies, language, health, safety, values, and mathematical concepts. Music interprets feelings that arise and moods that emerge during the day—happiness is a raindrop splashing on a window pane, a fluffy cloud racing through the sky, a bird building a nest; sadness is when mother leaves you in the morning, when you are left alone, when you want to play with someone; anger is when that boy won't let you play with his wagon; jealously is when Susie likes Mary better than me,—they play house together.

As someone has said, "At these ages music is better caught than taught" because young children first learn by imitation. If the teacher enjoys music and engages in it in varied ways, the children will usually imitate the teacher's attitude. Children need experiences in listening to mothers, fathers, brothers, sisters, and teachers sing. They should have available well-chosen recordings and tapes to which to listen. Many of the quality books for young children have been recorded with artistic and appropriately related music to accompany them.

From the standpoint of a child, music is almost always an experience in which he participates *actively* through observing, experimenting, selecting, interpreting, moving, and evaluating the stimuli of his environment. Leavitt (1958) writes "When pleasant sounds and strong movements are the stimuli the many senses are alerted. The ear becomes keenly attuned, the sense of touch is activated, and the pleasant sounds and strong movements are transferred to each muscle and nerve fiber in the child's body. The result is a deep (affective and cognitive) experience. It may be a quiet feeling, a pleasurable feeling, even a tingling feeling. It is a feeling that enhances the activity of the moment. A child, unlike a conditioned adult, cannot suppress feeling. Whatever is felt must be transmitted in some physical manner. When the sensory perception is especially acute the feeling is compulsive, and the level of response moves from talking to singing and from jerky walking to dancing. Thus, for the two- to six-year-old the essence of music is an intense inner feeling and active physical expression."

The young child's existence in the world has been comparatively brief, and hence there are continually new and exciting things and situations for him to explore and manipulate, so that he is usually more free to try new and creative experiences than are older children and adults. Taylor (1964) states that "At its brightest and most responsive, one finds the supreme sensibility in the young child, where as yet the capacity to respond to life has not been dulled or tarnished by a set of verbal symbols in which it is customary to find one's expression. Thus in the young child we find a natural poet, a natural musician, a person who is accustomed to responding to aesthetic values by his very own nature."

Cognitive learning takes place directly by virtue of aesthetic stimuli and nonverbal experiences with sound and movement. Aronoff (1969) suggests that "The freedom to respond (within given limits) will develop the child's imagination, flexibility, and fluency in his musical thinking, and perhaps in his general attitude as well. Considerable insight into the nature of music can be achieved by experimenting with musical materials, and encouragement to explore is an essential part of learning by discovery. Through moving, singing, and playing alone and with his classmates, the young child can demonstrate his accomplishments and thereby achieve the human dignity born of being productive."

Music literally permeates the entire learning environment of young children. It is an outpouring of human feelings, of fear, hate, aggression, jealousy, love, friendship, acceptance, joy, happiness, and feelings of artistic sensitivity and awareness. Children sing at work and as they reenact their world through play. They create songs, rhythms, speech patterns, poems, stories and instrumentation of sounds about the things they experience in their immediate surroundings—the trip to the pet shop, the visit to the farm or dairy, the stop at the post office, the birthday party, the planting of seeds, playing house, falling leaves, snow, rain, sounds of machines, animals, pets, and their make-believe ideas. Thus music is an important aspect in all areas of a curriculum for young children.

The Child and Music

Young children are eager to hear, see, taste, touch, and smell everything that their newly discovered world contains. A feeling for the subject matter and content of music is acquired through the many and varied opportunities to make discoveries through the use of the senses. Such discoveries form the basis of all learning.

Children who have had many opportunities to experiment with sound and to use music in their daily activities have usually acquired a helpful background for classroom experiences. A primary factor in learning music is the feeling of security and freedom achieved when expressing oneself musically. Children need a teacher who can encourage maximum musical development by assessing individual needs so that continuous growth occurs.

Young children have limited facility and verbal skills for communicating with others, and have had little experience in relating in social situations; therefore, their best point of reference is logically that of "self." The egocentricity of children is appealed to through the use of their bodies in physical-rhythmic-exploratory movements, through songs involving their names, clothing, food, and the like, as well as through individual playing of instruments and even recordings. An innate awareness of the need for skills to use as tools for further learning causes children to enjoy and to seek repetition in song, movement, and playing.

Children are sensitive to vocal tone qualities; a stern voice can frighten, whereas a pleasant voice can lead them to trust and cooperate. Rudolph and Cohen, (1964) remark that "We need only to hear children's spontaneous chants and melodic taunts, listen to the strong rhythms and precise rhymes that go with ritual games, and observe the delightful playfulness and inventive pantomime in original dancing to recognize that children are inherently musical."

The world of children is filled with music not of their own making. They hear it on television and radio, from stereo sets and other sound sources. They may have their own cassette or record player to play favorite recordings. Obviously, young children live in a musical world that may be a confusing one; thus it is important that music become an understandable and useful medium of expression for children. For this to occur, teachers develop guidelines for children's activities within which each child will have the freedom to learn. Cherry (1971) writes, "These guidelines are important. They keep a child from exploring beyond set limits, and they keep group activities from disintegrating. Guidelines offer comfort and build confidence because they give the inexperienced child a starting point, and help him in learning to discriminate between random and meaningful experiences. A child does not ordinarily want to be told 'Do whatever you want to do.' This only leads to confusion and frustration. He responds best to gentle guidance in which he is encouraged to interpret his ideas in his own way."

Music and Human Values

Children must first know who they are and value themselves before they can appreciate and value others, whether in the family, school, neighborhood, or the increasingly widening world community.

A child and his music are one as he interacts with everything and everybody in his environment. If free to do so he begins to create and perform music. As the teacher accepts the child's musical efforts and reinforces them in positive ways, the child's self-image is enhanced; he is motivated to increase his interest and efforts. When a child comes to school he brings with him the types of music to which he has been exposed in the home, on television, radio, and in the neighborhood. A teacher must accept the child's level of interest and share with him his kind of music. After analyzing his level of musical understanding and musical background exemplified in his chosen or identified type of music, she uses these data as a basis for introducing in sequence carefully identified musical learnings and for extending his interests to various types of music.

The child should never be told that his type of song is a bad one, nor should he be forced to take part in music activities. However, a competent and sensitive teacher knows and continues to explore varied ways of interacting, extending a child's interests in music and encouraging each of his music efforts until he readily joins in music activities. His taste in music as well as his desire and ability to enter into music will increase as his efforts are accepted, extended, and appreciated. If he is continually corrected, forced to fit into a type of organization that is unreal to him, he soon begins to dislike music or any activities related to it. Moreover, through music the child learns to relate in various ways with other children, to appreciate and value likenesses and differences in people. He learns to cooperate, and through these interactions in music, builds positive feelings toward others, and they in turn accept him for his own worth. A child's self-concept is primarily derived from the acceptance and reaction of others toward him and what he does. In this sense, music performance affords opportunity to demonstrate behaviorally who he is and some of the things he is able to do.

Suggested Activities

1. Indicate what characteristics teachers of young children should possess.
2. What attitudes about children and about the teaching of music should teachers of young children possess? Why are these attitudes of great importance?
3. During observations in preprimary programs, make record of the music objectives, activities, and materials of instruction.
4. During a classroom visitation, observe the individual differences, capabilities, interests, and needs present, and notice how the teacher has taken these factors into account in the teaching of music.

References

Andress, Barbara L. et. al. *Music in Early Childhood.* Washington, D.C.: Music Educators National Conference, 1973.

Aronoff, Frances W. *Music and Young Children.* New York: Holt. Rinehart and Winston, 1969.

Ashton-Warner, Sylvia. *Teacher.* New York: Bantam Books, 1964.

Chukovsky, Kornei. *From Two to Five.* Edited and translated by Miriam Morton, Berkeley, Calif.: University of California Press, 1966.

Erikson, Eric. *Childhood and Society.* New York: Norton, 1950.

Flemming, Bonnie Mack et. al. *Resources for Creative Teaching in Early Childhood Education.* New York: Harcourt Brace Jovanovich, Inc., 1977.

Fowler, Charles B. "Discovery Method: Its Relevance for Music Education," *Journal of Research in Music Education* 14 (Summer 1966): 126-34.

Greenberg, Marvin. "Research in Music in Early Childhood Education" in *Council for Research in Music Education Bulletin No. 45* (Winter, 1976), pp. 1-20.

Hess, Robert and Doreen Crott. *Teachers of Young Children,* 2nd ed. Boston: Houghton Mifflin Co., 1976.

Music of Young Children, 5th printing. Santa Barbara, Calif.: Pillsbury Foundation for Advancement of Music Education, 1978. Reports of research.

Nye, Robert and Vernice T. Nye. "Music in Early Childhood." Chapter 15 in *Music in the Elementary School,* 3rd. ed. Englewood Cliffs, N.J.: Prentice-Hall, Inc., 1970.

2   Music and Learning

Music for young children derives its content and inspiration from a carefully organized environment in which the child participates. This environment should be designed for the realization of the identified goals and instructional objectives included in the various aspects of a planned program for young children. The environment should be so organized as to provide opportunities for the child to listen to music and, through his enjoyment of it acquire basic music-related concepts, understandings, skills and attitudes which set the stage for a life-long enjoyment and pursuit of music. An environment that encourages the development of this goal must provide the child with various types of music, both in informal and in structured organizational plans. Even though the young child will seldom be able to discriminate between each type of music (rock, folk, country, classical, spiritual), he will develop an awareness of changes in rhythm and sound. While few of these children can respond correctly to the beat, they can move to music in their unique ways.

The musical environment is so designed that structured music activities are used to further enjoyment in music while simultaneously providing for the learning of specific music concepts and skills on the child's level. A knowledgable, skilled and flexible teacher is essential to the success of a program that is organized to teach enjoyment and music concepts, skills and appreciations in both non-structured and structured environments. The teacher must be able to accept the children's individual responses and to reinforce them by imitating them. For example, "See how John is moving to the music! Let's see if we can all move as he moves." It is important that young children hear a musical selection repeatedly, for it is through such repetition that they memorize the words and melodies of songs in preparation for singing them. After a musical selection has been learned, repeated singing or playing on an instrument provides the positive feedback and feeling of success that this aged child so greatly needs and seeks.

Hemispheres of the Brain

The brain is known to have left and right hemispheres. The left hemisphere tends to specialize in analysis, sequential learning, speech and mathematical abilities; the right hemisphere specializes in visual-spatial abilities. Thus, cognitive learning is centered on the left side, and psychomotor and affective learning are centered on the right side. A resultant theory is that the arts are concerned with the right side of the brain, and one's mental powers could therefore be limited when the type of education encountered emphasizes the traditional subjects and neglects the arts. Educational experiments in elementary schools that involve an arts emphasis indicate that when the arts are in the curriculum not only for their own worth but also for the purpose of assisting learning in the other subjects, children are not only better adjusted learners, but learning in all areas of the curriculum improves. This type of curriculum requires that teachers understand both the old "basic" subjects and the arts; she should show the two areas can be integrated in order to produce better and more enjoyable learning.

The arts provide a basis for cognitive learning; experiential learning is essential in acquiring symbolic competence. Some authorities state that if children are given the appropriate environment and equipment, they will naturally discover order and sequence. Others say that this theory gives the arts, when rightly taught, status as the new "basic" subjects. Thus, both hemispheres of the brain are to be given attention, and exclusive emphasis on either is to be avoided. Some say that the crux of the situation is the role of the arts in developing human capacities rather than simply assisting learning throughout the curriculum. It is claimed that traditional education which emphasizes communication and the three R's neglects one half of the brain.

The young child learns primarily by using the right side of the brain, which controls psychomotor activities, spatial orientation, feelings, imagination, and intuition.

Piaget's Stages of Development

Other theories in education and psychology have been advanced as to how the young child learns. Jean Piaget, a developmental psychologist, has had a notable influence on the content and organization of programs for young children, especially in the English infant schools. Substantial emphasis is being given to his four sequential stages of cognitive development, which provide teachers with a meaningful framework for the child's development. These stages are:

Sensorimotor   This is a preverbal stage in which information is assimilated through the senses of hearing, sight, taste, touch, and smell as the child interacts with the objects, people, and conditions of his environment. This stage in which percepts are developed dominates learning up to two years of age and is action-oriented.

Preoperational   The child can utilize symbols and acquire labels and names for his experiences, can reenact his known world through symbolic play, and through these symbols can reconstruct prior experience from the first stage. Near the latter part of the preoperational stage the child's play becomes more socialized and involves rules. This stage lasts from two to seven years of age.

Concrete operational   There is a decline in symbolic play. The child is able to classify, order, number, and discriminate more easily. He shows facility in the use of concepts of time and space, and has the ability to think logically. This stage is from ages seven to eleven.

Formal operational   Beginning at about the age of eleven and into adulthood, the child becomes able to reason on the basis of the abstract; he can hypothesize and organize his thinking to relate between and among ideas. He can practice higher level cognitive thought processes.

Theoretical ages of the children, as stated above, are *mental* rather than chronological ages. The mental growth of individual children does not always relate reliably to their chronological ages. Also, these stages are not rigid partitions in the learning process; they overlap, and no one of them is ever completely culminated. In daily living, elements of all four stages are found in the learning of older children.

Piaget's theory as related to the teaching of young children two through five years old means that these children are primarily at the preoperational stage, though some are still at the latter part of the sensory-motor perception stage. The teacher who heeds Piaget's theory would therefore make provision for the young child to be involved, as an individual or as a member of a small group, in exploring music in many different ways, including the use of symbolic play activities. His music would have as its source activities, events, people, and things present in his immediate environment.

The child learns music through the use of his psychomotor skills. Nonverbal ways of communicating through the use of the body are essential to the effective learning and teaching of music. Movement is basic to understanding all forms of music—a conclusion that leads us directly to the theories of Dalcroze, who espoused this belief. The child sings nonsense syllables before he sings words to a melody. At these stages of growth, his understanding of spoken and written concepts of music is limited, but he can comprehend them through physical interpretations and explorations.

"Mainstreaming"

Recently a controversy has arisen concerning the use of special segregated classes for handicapped children. As an outgrowth of this controversy educational research authorities insist that use of special classes for these children increases rather than decreases discrimination and thus hampers rather than encourages the special child's educational and social advancement. From this controversy has come the idea of "mainstreaming," which is predicated on the principles of educating the majority of "special" children in regular classrooms; there these children are accepted on the basis of their learning needs while the specific handicap they possess is taken into account. "Mainstreaming" fosters more individualization, not only with handicapped children but with all children.

Since music provides for more flexibility at both concrete and abstract levels than other subject fields, it has been designated as an area in which "mainstreaming" can readily occur. It further lends itself to various cognitive, affective, and psychomotor (physical) involvement levels. Music activities can be provided to include a variety of responses and levels of difficulty that encourages successful participation by all children. As exceptional children participate freely both socially and individually in music with "normal" children, their ability to interact with others is advanced. Since most handicapped children lack faith in their ability and possess poor self-images, successful participation in music, even though it may be slow, is obvious to the child himself and others. Thus his attitude toward himself and others' acceptance of his ability motivate him to further learning in all areas. Obviously, the teacher needs to know the characteristic problems of the exceptional child as well as those of the normal child. Martha L. Peters (1970), in making a comparison of the musical sensitivity of mongoloid and normal children, found that little difference in awareness and response to music was shown between younger normal and handicapped children, but that the difference increased with age. Thus, work with "mainstreamed" groups should begin when the child is young, preferably ages one through five, since responses are usually more consistent at those ages.

In an article on "mainstreaming," Janet Perkins Gilbert (1977) includes Robert Smith's list of problems that educable mentally retarded students face. There appears to be a marked similarity between this list of problems and Piaget's first two stages of learning—sensory motor, ages birth to approximately age 2, and the preoperational stage, ages two to approximately seven. Refer to the details of Piaget's two stages above and compare them with the following list presented by Robert Smith (1968):

1. a short attention span
2. difficulty in using abstractions
3. failure to discern similarities and differences
4. failure to perceive causality

5. difficulty in generalizing experiences
6. poor verbal communication skills
7. inappropriate emotional reactions to confusing situations
8. poor memory
9. oversensitivity to incidental cues
10. reluctance to participate in new activities

After the music program goals are identified and stated, attention must be devoted to identifying goals to be included in other areas. These secondary goals usually are in the areas of personal social development, skill development in the language arts—speech, vocabulary, listening,—mathematical and scientific concepts, and space and motor development.

As children with special learning problems are integrated into the regular classroom their chances for musical growth are increased. But the so-called normal child also benefits from this combination in most aspects of social and affective learning—emotional acceptance and expression, and understanding and acceptance of differences.

Gilbert (1977) applies Smith's list of problems to music learning. Special children learn best when the teacher plans for a slower pace, frequent changes of activities, more structured routines, more direction, more teacher modeling, and for use of simple materials and activities; all of this to help solve problems resulting from *short attention span*. When these children manipulate suitable materials and view appropriate visual aids, they are assisted in clarifying music concepts (*abstractions*). They need more concrete stimuli. Music is an excellent vehicle for learning to discern different levels of discrimination (*same-different*) with the same musical experience. Since these children generally have difficulty in perceiving *cause and effect relationships*, the teacher must give specific and skilled attention to immediate reinforcement so as to facilitate their increased competency in this. To learn to *generalize from experience*, the student is aided by the teacher's planning to use common elements within an activity and to indicate the transition between experiences. The special child's learning is often in minute steps in which sequence is highly important. *Communication skills* are aided by the use of hand puppets, visual aids, song lyrics, and body movements. Verbalization and creative thinking may be improved by responses to open-ended questions. *Inappropriate emotional reactions* to confusing situations can be reduced or eliminated by precise directions and expectations, the teacher's ignoring such reactions, and by the learner's use of the music class to test various behaviors in a controlled situation where he has adult support. *Poor memory* can be ameliorated by activities that are carefully sequenced, one element at a time, and by repetition. Students can learn to isolate *relevant cues* when one cue is emphasized and extraneous stimuli are minimized. These children learn best when the teacher knows them well enough to plan activities in which they can succeed. In this way old patterns of failure can be changed into patterns of success and confidence, by enhancing the students' self-esteem through appropriate music activities. This should result in more willingness to *participate in new activities.*

The old slogan "Music for Every Child" is now a legal reality, and the teacher is to instruct children at the two ends of the spectrum, the handicapped and the gifted. In some instances teacher aids will be necessary. A flexible schedule will permit having handicapped children in separate groups as well as in the regular class. For more detail on teaching music to the special child, see Chapter Five, "Self-Awareness."

Developmental Characteristics of Young Children

Although some psychological researchers have challenged the concept that chronological age should indicate when children are taught various concepts and skills (Bruner, 1964; Gagné, 1968), it is still frequently admitted that children go through developmental stages in a sequential order (Mussen, Conger, Kagan, 1969; Sutton-Smith, 1973). According to Piaget and Inhelder (1969) children progress through logical and sequential chronological steps in physical, social, affective, and cognitive development. Children usually sit before they crawl, crawl before they stand, and stand before they walk. However, even though certain general characteristics are common to a specific age, this does not mean that these characteristics will be found in all children of a particular age level. Since each individual has his unique way and rate of development, a given characteristic may appear at an earlier or later date. The teacher's familiarity with the general characteristic growth and behavior patterns of the various chronological age levels is of value in organizing music programs. To identify levels of abilities and unique growth patterns of each child, the teacher must know the general growth and performance behavior of a particular chronological age group and utilize this as a point of reference for diagnosing differences.

One of the teacher's major tasks in teaching the very young is to first develop the child's perceptual background as a basis or prerequisite for teaching musical concepts, since musical perception leads to the formation of musical concepts. The young child's musical growth is the result of his various experiences and explorations in music, leading to "the apprehension, naming, and gradual classification of significant musical concepts" (Leonhard and House, 1959).

At the age of three through five years, children are complicated beings. As they grow older they become increasingly complex. At these ages, children grow and develop at a fast rate. Their vocabularies and language development advance noticeably, and their physical skills improve and become more coordinated. Some children suddenly become very social. Their cognitive abilities expand. Children of this age cannot be placed into rigid categories of common characteristics since there is great variance among them in kinds and degrees of behavior.

Characteristics of Young Children

The typical two-year-old has learned to walk, rock, sway, roll, jump, move up and down, clap hands, run, and gallop. He is almost constantly moving. The teacher encourages spontaneous movement and follows the child's tempo and rhythm with her voice by clapping hands, or with a percussion instrument. (The term *percussion* gives the teacher much flexibility since the piano and the tambourine are both percussion instruments.)

The typical three-year-old is learning to move rhythmically, and responds when the teacher delineates his movements with an accompaniment. The child is almost continually involved in walking, running, jumping, rolling, galloping, rocking, and clapping, and can do some of these things in time with the music. He can accomplish sudden stops or "freezes." To develop these movements, the teacher first stimulates free movement exploration and dramatization by encouraging and supporting the unique movements of each child. Then the teacher follows the child's tempo and rhythm with her voice, while clapping, or playing a percussion instrument. She selects or improvises short and simple action songs based upon the experiences of the child. Such songs should reflect the motion in terms of tempo, ups and downs in pitch, and the rhythm of the motion. These become musical games or pantomime songs.

Children of this age can listen to recorded music and dance by doing whatever they feel like doing in response to the music. Sometimes they imitate motions of the teacher as she joins them in their dancing. The alert teacher notices when a child begins a new motion, imitates it, and uses it to expand the child's and the group's rhythmic development. Todd (1970) lists three essentials for the teacher who guides preschool children, ages three, four, and five, in rhythmic movements. She:

1. is a leader who moves from one kind of movement to another, pacing the interest of the children.
2. uses a minimum of spoken suggestions.
3. shows a feeling of appreciation.

The typical four-year-old usually learns a given movement by moving at a fast tempo. The teacher provides such tempos, then assists the child to expand his control by gradually moving to slower tempos. This age group enjoys adding to the movements learned earlier by marching in a straight line or in a circle; forming square or rectangular patterns; sliding, hopping, whirling, stamping, crawling, swinging, bending, shaking, nodding, flopping, and walking on tip-toe. Movements of animals, machines, and space objects are imitated. When these children listen to recorded music they sometimes dance as they feel or sometimes follow the teacher's instructions. The teacher introduces new movements when children are ready for them and when they have not initiated them independently. Songs that are longer and more dramatic can be used in pantomiming activities. The old favorite "Eensy Weensy Spider" can have simple finger motions made to it. The swing can be the center of a musical game when simple chanting tunes are improvised to describe rhythmically what the swing does.

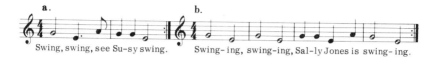

Dramatic play can be enriched by adding music, costumes, and additional stories. These children should not be pressured into keeping time although their ability to do so is greater than that of the three-year-olds. This ability depends more on maturity and innate ability than on practice (Read, 1971), thus the pleasure of moving freely should not be interrupted.

The typical five-year-old becomes able to move rhythmically to the regular beat; he can keep time with music. This age group can perform the basic locomotor movements with a good sense of balance. Their rhythmic activities are a natural extension of those of the four-year-olds. However, they are able to incorporate changes of direction and movement such as run and stop, walk and jump, whirl and fall. Changes in tempo and dynamics can be dramatized more easily; music and costumes can enhance dramatic play. These children are able to follow rules for playing and handling instruments. They are able to reflect, in their movements, the teacher's improvised accompaniments that have changes in tempo and dynamics: fast and slow, heavy and light, loud and soft, short and long. The child begins moving by himself, then moves with a partner, and eventually as one of a small group. The teacher expects that each child will respond in his own way. She understands that there will not be uniformity in responses and that some children may not want to be part of a large group. She knows also that skipping cannot be done by all children, but that the development of this skill can be assisted by providing accompaniments that stimulate it. The chants and songs of the four-year-olds can be extended.

There are indications that the five's are becoming more socially-conscious and more interested in group games that do not have competitive aspects since they have not yet learned how to be losers. They enjoy group singing games in which everyone has his turn such as "The Farmer in the Dell," "Here We Go 'Round the Mulberry Bush," "Looby Lou," and "Ring Around the Rosie." They are especially interested in games in which words and movements are repeated.

Sources of Musical Experience

The Home and Community

Children have observed parents, siblings, peers and members of the community sing and perform with instruments. They may have examined and experimented with sound producers of many sorts. Some have already experimented with and produced sounds from their own small instruments such as drum, tambourine, and bells. The sound producer most accessible in all homes is the human voice. If children are sung to, encouraged to sing, and brought to listen to a variety of types of music emanating from recordings, tapes, radio, and television, they will be more likely to participate in the music activities of the classroom. Likewise, if they have been encouraged at home to observe and imitate movements seen in nature and to listen to and imitate sounds heard in the home and community environment, they will come to school better equipped to react to such stimuli in the classroom. Some children have been deprived of these types of experiences. In such cases, it is the task of the teacher to influence this type of home to provide an environment more conducive to learning music. One of the most effective ways to initiate this is to invite mothers and fathers to observe their child in the classroom music activities. They may observe the teacher accompanying the child's movements, or singing with or for the child the song he has created. Or perhaps they will observe the teacher encouraging the child to try to make his body do what the instrument tells him to do with it. They may further notice that the teacher capitalizes on every feasible opportunity to assist the child develop his concepts of rhythm, tempo, dynamics, and pitch.

Parent groups should be encouraged to learn how to play simple instruments and to share their musical knowledge with the children and other parents. Parents can be assisted in constructing or selecting simple instruments for the child's use in the home. Among the most important helps are: teaching parents how to relate to their children in positive and stimulating ways; how much guidance to give; how to select and use the many available materials and situations in their everyday environment in creative ways; how to learn to appreciate and to understand the music of the child, and to comprehend the music skills and concepts expected of children of this age. Most parents will need to learn how to encourage children to explore independently by asking questions that will stimulate them to pursue the answers; and to learn to give the children sufficient uninterrupted time to discover aspects of music on their own. Time is also required for child and parent to discuss the child's encounter with music. (Refer to chapter 6 for more information about the relationship of parents to the school.)

Children who come from communities where music is an integral part of the social environment will tend to acquire and reflect similar musical interests.

The Classroom

A second source of information and subject matter children need for a musical environment results from arranging the facilities of the classroom to include concrete and manipulative objects, props, and space. By means of these children can reenact their experiences through creative play, rhythm, chant, rhyme, song, and story. The classroom is made attractive and contains materials, space, and media for developing the child's sensory and perceptual acuity and for the enhancement of his self-image. This planned environment includes various materials which are easily accessible to children; it also contains learning stations: a house-keeping station, a woodworking station, a play station, a dress-up station with props to reenact the roles of various workers—the store-keeper, farmer, baker, minister, doctor, nurse, dentist, policeman, postman, truck driver, and the filling station operator. It may include a block-building station with wheeled toys for hauling blocks, duplicating the activities observed in the community and for learning weights, space, sizes, and counting; a science station containing live and inanimate things that stimulate children's interest in movement and sound as well as creating words, phrases, sentences, chants, rhythms, poems, and stories about them; a mathematics station in which there are objects to count, classify, arrange in sets, compare in weight, and experiment with in space; an art station that contains opportunities for pounding on clay in rhythmic ways, chanting, and creating songs and simple dances associated with clay figures, finger painting, or painting. There should be ample space in which to move about and to use the muscles to imitate roles and rhythms.

Although this type of organization appears unstructured to the casual observer, it involves a high degree of organization by which the teacher diagnoses the levels of competency and interest of each child. The teacher then prescribes performance objectives, learning experiences, and methods which often involve the child. She selects and supplies appropriate material resources and media for the realization of these objectives. In order to move each child to a higher level of accomplishment based on prior learnings, appropriate and varied records must be kept and used in correlating sequentially each child's learning experiences.

If children are to develop consistently and sequentially in all areas of growth, the teacher and other adults in their lives must design environments possessing precision. Everything placed in this physical, intellectual and social environment should serve to develop the cognitive, affective, and psychomotor potential of the child. Overly-cluttered and overly-supplied classrooms create overstimulation and confusion.

During these impressionable years young children should have an aesthetically arranged environment. As they become actively involved in this environment they acquire appreciations, values, and aesthetic tastes from what they experience. "A most important part of the physical environment is its sense of order and beauty. The establishment of bays and the organization of materials help bring about a needed sense of classroom order, but this is enhanced by a conscious effort to make the environment as pleasant and beautiful as possible. Bulletin boards are functional but attractive. Children's work is displayed with dignity and taste. . . A drab wall is covered with bright colored paper; a piece of used velvet transforms an empty table top into a lovely exhibition area for dolls." (Carswell and Roubinek, 1974)

Children require time to freely explore, experiment, to learn at the various stations to use the materials and media necessary to solve problems in unique ways. But they should also have the experience of reordering the objects in their environment. The knowledgeable teacher usually understands that children can realize various learning objectives as they clean and organize the room and materials after they have finished their work. As they return the building blocks to appropriate shelves, they learn to perceive length, width, thickness, and color. They discriminate, compare, interpret, group, categorize, and form concepts. Thus they learn the major cognitive steps which they will use throughout their lives:

1. to perceive—observe, gather data
2. to analyze and interpret—relate common attributes
3. to conceptualize
4. to apply knowledge to solutions of similar and related problems

After the teacher introduces each musical instrument, she uses questions and comments in guiding the children to explore what they can do with these to create different sounds—loud, soft, high, low—to find out what causes these sounds, and to determine of what material the instrument is made. The children can then experiment repeatedly with the instrument, exploring all its attributes. Other instruments are to be introduced singly in like manner. After the children have become familiar with the first instrument, the teacher guides them in comparing and contrasting each newly-introduced instrument with the one or ones they already know. Is it made of the same material? Does it sound the same? Why or why not? After the children have had experience with the attributes of each instrument and are able to compare them, then they are capable of relating, grouping, and categorizing them as they return them to their appropriate containers when they have finished using them.

When the teacher explores the musical instruments with the kindergarten children, such exploration should lead to the learning of concepts and skills in other curricular areas. The children can learn about the materials to make the instrument, the cost of such instruments, how taking good care of them preserves resources and saves money (economics). They may learn how the instruments are made and who does this kind of work (career education). The use of maps may be introduced when the question of where the instruments are produced arises (geography). How the instruments were transported to the classroom may involve a discussion of trains, trucks, ship, or airplanes (transportation). When instruments of other cultures are compared with those of our own in order to find similarities and differences, simple anthropology is involved. Loud and soft sounds, indeed, sound itself involves science. Assuming responsibility for care and storage of instruments so that others may use them, and the sharing of instruments involve citizenship. Also, young children gradually form their own music performance groups, establishing roles and sanctions necessary to enable musical performance to take place. Here they become involved in simple encounters with sociological concepts.

Regardless of how a school environment may be judged from a functional standpoint, it is unusual to find one that is a place of beauty. (Stafford 1978) "Most schools give their students a powerful and effective negative esthetic education: they teach them that interest in the arts is effeminate or effete, that study of the arts is a frill, and that music, art, beauty, and sensitivity are specialized phenomena that bear no relationship to life. The schools teach these lessons in a variety of ways. The most important, perhaps, is the lesson that is taught by the ugliness of the buildings, the absence of flowers, paintings, sculpture, and music; in short, the esthetic sterility of the entire environment." (Silberman, 1970). Beauty is important to the development of all children. With regard to the handicapped, in most situations primary emphasis is given to their particular disabilities, and opportunities for aesthetic enrichment and growth are negligible. This, obviously, should not happen.

Environmental Principles for the Classroom

The teacher should observe the following principles in setting up a classroom environment. They are adapted from Glenn Nimnicht (1969).

1. Attention should be given to neatness and attractiveness. There should be ample light and pleasant colors.
2. Noise should be reduced by using carpeting, separating areas of noisy activities from areas involving quiet activities.
3. Make the concept-formation area the most active and colorful place in the room.
4. Use flexible and adjustable alcoves for small-group activities, and reserve the open space for activities of larger groups.
5. Limit the amount of material at any one time and change such materials as instruments, toys, and puzzles frequently. However, do not risk a child's feeling of security and mastery by removing those the child, having learned the skills involved in their use, finds intriguing and can use creatively in other activities. The drum and tambourine are possible examples of such materials.
6. Store materials intended for use by the children within their reach.
7. Provide observation spaces for visitors so that they do not disturb the children.
8. Vary the situations and ways in which materials and equipment are used in order to offer a new challenge and to expand the understanding of concepts.

Playground Learning Encounters

Playground space, equipment, and activities provide natural stimuli and occasions for teaching music and language. As the child uses his senses of hearing, seeing, smelling, tasting, and feeling, he learns to perceive textures, shapes, sizes, colors, movement, rhythm, sounds, and relationships. "For a child, watching clouds in the sky or patterns of light and shadow through trees or discovering some of the many objects to be found outdoors are experiences of wonder. They feed the eager curiosity of childhood, which is the basis for learning" (Baker, 1968).

Children need outdoor play to release tensions and to extend their knowledge of the natural environment. Outdoor play should, when appropriate, be an extension of the classroom. Outside facilities vary more extensively than those found inside the classroom. The outdoor environment should contain live plants, trees, and animals, as well as some machines to observe and explore. As children observe these they listen to and imitate the sounds of animals, thunder, running water, rain, wind, and machines. The various movements found outside are observed and reenacted in creative ways.

Certain moving things in nature and play seem to compel the child to move to the rhythm observed, and at the same time to create chants and songs for accompaniment. Music appreciation, concepts, skills, and language development are learned as a child runs, walks, crawls, jumps, or hops at different tempos in relatively large areas of space. The teacher can accompany these movements with voice, hand clapping, tambourine, or drum. The child learns to identify music and tempos for such movements. "The beginning of dance exists in the child's response to:

Space
A hill
Muscles which crave action
An ocean with waves rolling on the beach
A balloon
The joy of anything

The sensitive teacher knows when a struck cymbal will add something to the climax of a running jump, or when a drum beat will give courage to the inhibited child waiting for his turn on the bouncing board." (Pitcher, 1974)

When designing classroom and playground environments for young children, the teacher is reminded that the individual differences and abilities that exist among children should be considered as a starting point. Materials and equipment should be varied in type, appeal, and difficulty to accommodate the learning of *all* children. At times several levels of skills and concepts are taught by varying the objectives for the different activities engaged in when all of the children use the same equipment.

"The teacher should vary the way she sets up the equipment. When balance boards on the ground no longer present a challenge to (a child or) children, they can be placed on boxes so that they can learn to walk a foot or so above ground." (Nimnicht, 1969) Likewise, after children have emphasized the "high" and "low" concept as they swing, and create chants or songs to match the positions and rhythm of the swing, the teacher can encourage them to explore concepts of the "fast" and "slow" movements of the swing.

Another source of information comes from children's involvement in planned presentations of songs, rhythms, rhymes, stories, and recordings, and their experimentations with and responses to these presentations, often in such creative ways as dance and pantomime. The teacher, parent, aide, older child, recording, or film enhance these presentations. Afterwards, opportunity is provided for children to ask questions, to discuss their feelings and what they have learned from the experience. Adequate time should be made available for children to interpret the experience and to express their reactions by creating chants, poems, songs, rhythms, dramatic play, and pantomimes.

For additional information regarding planned encounters, refer to "The Music Learning Station" that follows in this chapter.

A Climate for Learning Music

Presentation and Organization of Music

Music teaching for the early years differs from that for older children. The same areas of music content are covered, but the subject matter is taught in different ways. Teachers of young children address the whole group but for very brief periods. The children become involved in discussion: questions and answers are presented at an appropriate level of understanding. These are effective ways to assist children in the clarification of their thinking, to guide the learning of concepts, to strengthen self-image, and to provide opportunities for learning vocabulary and oral communication skills. All of these are basic to an effective music program. Nevertheless, the teacher seldom involves the entire group in discussions, especially at age three or even during the first half of the fourth year, or with the mentally retarded child. She relies heavily on one-to-one or small group encounters and closely observes a child's movement and accompanies his rhythm with clapping, words, or a percussion instrument; she accepts, reinforces and encourages his individual creation and performance. At other times she catches his chant, rhyme, song, or dance and repeats the rhythm or song for him while often sharing his performance with other children. Thus the child receives the positive reinforcement and acceptance needed to stimulate his continued exploration, experimentation, and creation of music. When children find themselves in a warm and encouraging environment, they are set free to become involved in music at their own level and at their own pace. Very soon the children approach the teacher, aide, other children, or parent to share a new creation.

Even though the teacher individualizes the teaching of music, the children who are mature enough and interested are also involved in small group musical performance. The goal is to make music so relevant and attractive that others will join the group even though group participation at this age is usually very short-lived. Cooperative and small group musical participation makes it possible for children to learn from one another.

During these early years, the open classroom or laboratory approach is used. Children are not passive listeners; they are active doers. The teacher arranges materials and experiences that overtly involves each child in doing something; hammering, sawing, swinging, rolling, bouncing, jumping, hopping, crawling, creeping, throwing, leaping, pounding, humming, hissing, whistling, laughing, grimacing, pouring, feeling, listening, smelling. In other words, the child is where the action is, and from action rhythm, words, song, and instrumentation evolve.

Individualization and Teacher-Pupil Ratio

Ideally there should be one teacher, one aide, and a mother or older child to work with a group of no more than five to seven nursery school children. There should be one teacher and at least two aides for a kindergarten group of fifteen to eighteen. Individualization and small group instruction are made possible when these quotas are observed. Children can thus receive immediate assistance, feedback, and encouragement. There is an opportunity to carry out the methods used in the integrated day approach whereby the teacher relates and integrates music into the content of the various areas of the curriculum whenever it is relevant and serves to clarify and enhance learning in any area. For example, music concepts, skills, and appreciations are taught not only as a separate music subject, but are also integrated whenever and wherever appropriate, into such areas as the language arts (speech, oral language, drama, poetry, and stories), creative art, health, safety, science, mathematics, and social studies. Therefore, the physical arrangement of the various learning stations in all areas of the curriculum, whether located inside or outside the classroom, provides a natural setting for learning music at this stage of a child's life.

When to Teach Music

Music cannot be taught in isolation from the other activities of the day, since it arises from children's feelings and immediate interests as they play and work. Music enables young children to communicate ideas derived from their participation in the daily activities planned in every area of the curriculum. But even though this spontaneous outpouring of emotion is the source of natural expression, a definite time should still be reserved for recreating, enriching, and expanding children's experiences. Attention should be given to establishing a balance between teacher-planned and pupil creation-and-responses to music. The maturity, musical background and interest of the children will determine the amount of class time and the type of organization which should be devoted to these activities. The average two- and three-year-olds may participate primarily in spontaneous and free musical involvement, while the more mature three- and four-year-olds and most kindergarten children can profit from and will require more time for recreating and learning new musical concepts and skills as they perform together in small groups.

"The job of the teacher is not so much to stimulate musical response as it is to keep open the avenues for responses. Music springs from an innate force deep down within the child, pushing to be released. The observant teacher will tap this natural musical source and channel its use. . ." (Leavitt, 1958). Thus it becomes an aesthetically, emotionally, socially, and intellectually rewarding experience. The appropriateness of the environment which the teacher structures can serve as a setting and an impetus for stimulating and channeling such spontaneity.

Therefore, designing an environment that utilizes the maximum musical capabilities of each child demands of the teacher careful study and analysis of maturity levels, experience background, musical background, level of performance, musical interest, and needs. As emphasized by Leavitt (1958), "The child's musical achievement parallels that of his physical (psychomotor), emotional (affective), and mental (cognitive) growth. A thorough understanding of a child's level of progress is essential. Singing and dancing (and playing instruments) develop just as talking and walking. They cannot be pushed without frustrating the child and implanting a dislike for music rather than a love for it."

The Music Learning Station

The learning station approach is one effective way to individualize the learning of aspects of music in both the creative-exploratory and skills areas, making provision for differences in interest, abilities, speed of learning, and a child's way of learning. The teacher should go through specific steps when planning to use learning stations that emphasize music skills. He must: (Burns and Broman, 1975)

1. identify the content area
2. pretest to diagnose strengths and weaknesses of pupils in the area
3. determine the skills or learnings to be treated at the station
4. establish a sequence of tasks from easiest to most difficult
5. identify different kinds of instructional materials to use and devise varied ways to present these tasks of graduated difficulty
6. posttest to evaluate each major segment of the station.

Learning stations that are designed for creative-exploratory learning are more open-ended or less structured. The child is free to pursue his own interests and concerns in unique ways.

The music exploratory station may occupy a large table or several small ones upon which may be placed music materials of interest to young children. There can be unconventional sound producers such as aluminum pan lids, stainless steel mixing bowls, and other kitchen implements that produce tones of good quality (see p. 55); a music box to be wound up and listened to by the children; a one-string monochord with a movable bridge by which the experimenting child can change the pitch; sand blocks of varying textures; various sound starters such as a mallet, a drumstick, a metal striker for the triangle, drum brushes; small percussion instruments such as drum, maracas, triangle, cymbals, jingle bells (all of good tonal quality); bells and xylophones of several types including diatonic, simple scale, resonator bells, and Orff-type xylophones and metallophones with removable tone bars; and Orff- and Montessori-type instruments for problem solving. There can be equipment including pictures, picture books, a sturdy record player with records for the children to use, a viewer, a cassette recorder with cassettes for children to play and listen to, and a small bulletin board upon which the teacher can place pictures of instruments, both string and brass, and the music of favorite songs or songs the children have composed. Soft mallets for the xylophones and bells and headsets for the record player and tape recorder reduce the possibility of disturbing other children. Plastic versions of the ukulele and guitar with which children can find how to produce sounds are helpful additions.

Extensions of the music station include a box the size of a four-foot cube with crawl holes through which the children can enter and exit and in which the individual child can experiment with sound experiences planned by the teacher. One side should be removable so that the teacher can place the "discoveries" in the box. Another music station extension is an old piano on which children can experiment with sound, particularly when the strings are exposed. Mallets and snare drum brushes are useful in exploring these sounds. The sounds the children discover might be useful for accompanying or inspiring rhythmic responses, or might add to the class's "sound effects bank" upon which children can draw for their many creative classroom activities.

The teacher needs her own record player and recordings of excellent quality, to which the children do not have access. She also needs a tape recorder and tapes of good quality. The piano and all pitched instruments she plays should be in tune to provide the children with examples of accurate pitch to imitate.

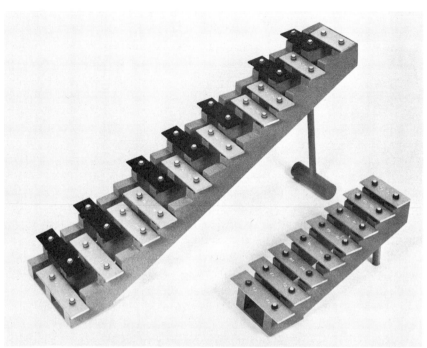

Photo courtesy of Music Education Group
c/o Fretted Industries, 1234 Sherman Ave.,
Evanston, Ill. 60202.

STEP BELLS AND XYLOPHONE

Classroom Instruments and Equipment Described[1]

Classroom equipment is often limited by the financial status of the school. However, the resourceful teachers find ways to obtain sufficient materials to make a good music program possible. This chapter lists materials that some will believe to be essential, while others will consider them to be in the realm of "the ideal." Even though this section presents information on how to make instruments, some instruments must be purchased in order to assure musical sounds of quality. In the final analysis, the environment must have equipment that produces beautiful sounds, since sensitivity to music cannot result from what is unmusical. This means that the instruments, the record player, and the recordings, must be capable of producing musical sounds of quality. Ideally, the children should eventually be able to discriminate between the musical and the unmusical and be able to play instruments and use their voices in ways to produce musical sounds.

Some teachers follow a sequence by first, having the children experiment with the sounds of nonmusical sources such as a hammer, saw (both in use), egg beater, aluminum pot lids with pleasing sound, and such sounds as corn popping; second, having children make their own shakers by placing seeds, pebbles, beads, or shot in cardboard, plastic, tin, and glass containers and experimenting with those as sound-making sources; then, introducing the standard percussion instruments gradually; finally, introducing melody instruments such as the xylophone and bells. Bear in mind that the planned use of high and low storage shelves can help the teacher to either circulate or withhold instruments.

The following is a commercial set of "rhythm instruments" for individual and small-group experimental and guided use. Notice that it excludes the popular rhythm sticks.

1 bongo drum	1 pair sand blocks
1 hand drum	2 jingle bells mounted on handles
1 triangle	2 wrist bells
1 pair claves	1 bell on handle
1 high-pitched tone block with striker	
1 pair finger cymbals with wood handles	
1 low-pitched tone block with striker	
1 pair castanets on sticks	
1 tambourine	

There follows a more detailed guide to many of the instruments used in the classroom.

Rhythm sticks   Used by the teacher and children to produce a dry click or a scraping sound when one stick is drawn across the notches of another. They are used to keep time when singing or marching, or they reflect skip-

1. Also see "Introducing Instruments," pp. 61-64.

ping and galloping when one stick is tapped by another for *short* and one stick is tapped against the floor for *long*. Sections of dowling can be used as a low-cost substitute for the commercial rhythm stick, but these lack notches, and sometimes pleasing tone quality as well.

Coconut shells   Obtained from ripe coconuts purchased at grocery stores. The outside fibers can be removed by a coarse kitchen scraper, or a steel brush. The coconut is then sawed into two equal pieces and the meat scraped out. The teacher can strike the two halves together to imitate the sound of horse's hooves on pavement, cobblestones, or rocky trail. Four- and five-year-olds can explore sound making with the shells by striking them with sticks or by striking two half-shells together in different ways. An imitation of the shell sounds can be produced (though less audibly) by striking two paper cups together.

Claves   A pair of thick, resonant sticks made of seasoned hardwood. When one is struck against the other a sharp click results.

The woodblock   Commercially produced from small blocks of wood that are hollowed out to form a resonating chamber. The player may wish to strike it lightly with a hard rubber mallet on the hollow side near the edge. This produces the most resonant sound.

The tone block   Also commercially produced. The teacher holds it in the left hand with the cut side toward her, and strikes it with a mallet on top and above the cut opening.

Finger cymbals   A delight to use because of their delicate sound. They are miniature cymbals, obtained commercially. Children can hold one in each hand and strike them lightly together at the edge, or they can use them like large cymbals to obtain a different effect. A finger cymbal can be held in one hand as the other hand is used to strike it with a small object, such as a large or medium-sized nail.

The triangle   One of the most useful instruments (and is commercially produced). It is held by a cord so as to free it for vibration, and is struck with a metal rod. The triangle has a bright, bell-like sound with a natural diminuendo. A different effect can be gained by placing the rod inside the triangle and hitting all three sides with a circular motion. To prevent loss of the striking rod, attach it to the triangle with a nylon thread. An imitation triangle is made by suspending a large spike and striking it with a nail.

Jingle bells   Useful if the tone quality produced is pleasing. Some are mounted on sticks and can be shaken vigorously, while other types are worn on the wrist or ankle to enhance rhythmic activities and dance. By holding them downward and moving them back and forth, a small tinkling sound can be produced.

The tambourine   A favorite instrument that can be played as a drum, or when shaken, produces only the sound of the metal jingles around its edge. Or it can be struck like a drum on the hand knuckles, the knee, or elbow while the jingles produce an automatic counter-effect of sound. The tambourine adds interest and color to dance.

The gong   Can be an expensive instrument mounted on a stand, or it can be a length of metal pipe suspended in the air, or perhaps a fine quality metal pan lid, or even a large metal packing can cover suspended by a string. These metal lids are often found on the barrel-like containers used as wastebaskets in schools and containers in which sweeping compound, ice-cream mix, and fancy china are packed.

Sand blocks   Easily made from soft woodblocks of a size that small hands can grasp. Another type is made from flat pieces of wood on which handles are mounted. Such handles can be made from drawer pulls, spools, leather pieces, or small pieces of wood. Number 1-0 sandpaper or emery cloth is used on the rubbing side of the wood, and is often fastened with thumbtacks.

Shakers   Can be genuine commercial *maracas*, or they can be made from gourds in which seeds, pebbles, beads, or bird shot is placed. Children can make different types of shakers from cans, jars, and small cardboard and plastic containers in which they place the same objects. Many other types of rattle can be invented, using such objects as small ice-cream and cottage-cheese cartons, typewriter ribbon containers, pillboxes, and spice cans with which to make them.

Drums   They are indispensable, and appear in a large variety of shapes and sizes. Every classroom should have several, and each should differ distinctly from the others in pitch. Teachers use hand drums to accompany rhythmic movements; children play small hand drums when marching and in dramatic play. Many different sounds can be produced, depending upon how the drum is struck—with the hand, the knuckles, a felted stick, fingers, or fingernails. They can be played loudly, softly, or in any of the many dynamic gradations in between. The children should experiment with how to hold and how and where to strike the drums to obtain the best or desired sound. Usually they will find that the best striking place is halfway between the middle and edge of the head. How to strike the drum is another matter; it will sound best when struck so that the beater bounces away from the head. Most preschool children will be able to find where to strike the drum to make high and low sounds. Many substitutes for commercial drums have been used for reasons of economic necessity rather than of aesthetic choice. Gallon ice-cream containers and coffee cans with plastic lids are among the many types of substitute drums. Interesting drums made in Africa, the Orient, and Latin America are available in particular import stores; these are worth investigating, all the more so because they enhance the learning of social studies concepts.

Bells   Used to give children the satisfaction of making sounds of accurate pitch and good quality; thus, they should be selected with these criteria in mind. The keyboard they embody can give children concepts of pitch distances, high and low, scalelike sounds, and wide intervals. Simple tunes can be created when teachers confine the children to a limited number of bars—one, two, three, four, or five-scale tones, or two, three, four, or five tones of the common pentatonic scale. The piano or bell black keys form this scale pattern, (see p. 89 for examples of pentatonic scale tones). Step bells aid in expanding the concepts of high and low in pitch and melodic contour, the pitch shape of a melody. Children can experiment at playing the bells with a mallet held in each hand, and they can experience what happens when two play at once on the same instrument. Furthermore, they can discover that short bars make high sounds and long bars make lower sounds. Resonator bells can be taken apart and the separate pitches used for many purposes, including composing.

Orff-type instruments of the keyboard variety are: the *metallophone*— alto and bass— which are the lowest-pitched metal instruments of this type; the *xylophone*—soprano, alto, and bass, which are wooden instruments; and the *glockenspiel*—soprano and alto, which are the highest-pitched metal instruments. The latter is the most difficult for young children to play because its small size requires greater use of muscle control. All of these instruments are played with hard and soft mallets and together allow many different contrasts of tone qualities. For example, the alto metallophone can represent a mother's voice and the bass xylophone the voice of a father. Few nursery schools are now equipped with these relatively expensive high-quality instruments, which were originally designed by Carl Orff, the German composer who devoted much thought to the music education of young children.

The psaltery   An ancient stringed instrument. The children can pluck its strings to make the sounds of the C-major scale.

The Autoharp   A larger instrument which can be played by stroking its many strings with a rubber spatula or almost anything the child can handle with facility. However, the felt pick produces the most pleasing tone. The teacher must press the chord bars while the child strokes the strings. This instrument introduces the child to the making of harmonic accompaniments. The plastic carrying cases for the Autoharp are lightweight and convenient when carrying the instrument on home visitations.

The voice An instrument everyone carries with him. Children can learn that the voice can be high, low, soft, loud, short, long, gradually loud, gradually soft, able to go lower or higher in steps or in wide leaps or by sliding (glissando). They can sing words or make sounds like "ah," "ee," and "oh" or nonsense words like "tra-la" and "ee-i-ee-i-o," and they can whistle and hum. Children should discover that each person's voice is distinctive.

Other accessories—Costumes for Dramatization and Dance Crotch and seam hems can be removed to permit children to put costumes over clothing easily. Scarves can be made of sheer drapery scraps and utilized for movement, dance, and dramatization. Skirts can be made from cut-off lengths of sheer curtains, obtained from drapery shops. Side seams can be French-seamed to prevent fraying. A taped sequence of appropriate music is helpful when teachers want to be free to work with children, when a large record collection is not available, and when the teacher prefers not to play the piano. A flannel board is useful as a visual teaching aid. Flannel boards have felt or flannel surfaces to which adhere illustrative materials backed with a substance or texture that clings to such surfaces.

The piano Is used by the teacher to play music from books and to improvise music for special activities. The black keys provide a natural pentatonic (5-note) scale upon which the teacher who lacks piano skills can nevertheless play many kinds of music improvised for the occasion. (McCall, 1966). Because the common pentatonic scale contains no half-steps, practically anything sounded with these black keys, either singly or in massive combination is acceptable. The teacher plays with the right hand to sound a definite rhythmic pattern such as a steady quarter note for walking or marching, a rapid 6/8 pattern  for galloping or skipping, a slow 6/8 pattern for swinging and swaying, and sixteenth notes for running. The left hand should sometimes play single tones or open fifths to provide an underlying beat for the right-hand pattern or melody; at other times it might play slower patterns in the same way the right hand does. For example, "Giant Steps" could begin:

Remember to play staccato eighth notes for "tiptoe music."

Marie Winn (1967) makes different suggestions.[2] Use a common scale for a walking rhythm. Bass chords can be papa bear walking, a lion roaring, and a tiger stalking. When a scale is played so that each note is played twice with the second note played short, it makes good skipping music. Chords played at jumping tempo produce "jumping music." A succession of three adjacent notes played repeatedly can become music for running. Sliding the thumb down a scale can produce music for sliding. A C-chord an octave above middle C, when alternated with the C-chord at middle C, can produce seesaw or swinging music. Rain can be imitated by a chord played in a detached manner, softly and repeatedly, while a black key and the white key immediately above it can be played in fast alternation to imitate a pouring spring shower.

The children can learn much about the piano from playing it; high, low, loud, soft. They can use the black keys creatively as they make up one-note, one-sentence songs, and as they can use the group of two black keys just above middle C to make two-note songs about themselves, their names, animals, events, and people. After this experience, three-note songs are in order and they can use the group of three black keys for this. Songs like "Hot Cross Buns" can be played on these three black keys also, or on three keys of resonator bells (perhaps F-sharp E, and D above middle C), or on whatever pitches the teacher finds appropriate for them. Tone clusters (miscellaneous adjacent notes) can be played on the piano to communicate the idea of large animals walking, or when played softly to relate something mysterious and strange. Children can find scale lines going higher and lower in pitch (up and down the keyboard). They can seek sounds to imitate many things, whether they be an elephant walking, birds chirping, the wind, raindrops, or clocks. Bells can be imitated by holding the pedal down while playing descending patterns such as CBAG with the right hand and FEDC with the left hand. A train whistle sound can be made with F-sharp and the C above played simultaneously.

Types of electric keyboard instruments that have earphones children can use are assets to classrooms. The earphone attachment makes possible free, individual exploration of the instrument without intruding upon other activities in the room. Children can be helped to play simple pieces by marking the appropriate keys with tape or a substance that does not injure the plastic keys.

The music textbooks for nursery school and kindergarten contain piano selections for the teachers to play. These are for rhythmic movement; to learn music concepts such as beat, accent, melodic direction, tem-

2. For other ideas see Mary T. Jaye, *Making Music Your Own*, Kindergarten Book. (Morristown, N.J.: Silver Burdett Co., 1971), pp. 168-77, and Bonnie Mack Flemming, et al., *Resources for Creative Teaching in Early Childhood Education*. (New York: Harcourt Brace Jovanovich, Inc., 1977), pp. 38-44 includes steps in learning to improvise.

po, pitch, mood, dynamics, and articulation (smooth or detached); and for rest and relaxation.

Summary

This chapter has been concerned with aspects of music learning. The relation of music experiences to the hemispheres of the brain, to the stages of development advanced by Piaget, and to "mainstreaming" were discussed. The values and limitations of knowledge of children's developmental characteristics were outlined. The various sources of musical experiences for young children were discussed in detail, and a music learning environment was proposed and described.

Since the content of this chapter relates directly to the chapters to follow, the reader is advised to refer to this chapter from time to time to clarify problems and questions that may come to mind as this book continues.

Suggested Activities

1. Observe groups of three-, four-, and five-year-olds. How do their interests differ? What are the implications of the differences in planning music for these different age groups?
2. Observe a group of children of the same age and take note of how their interests vary. How should this knowledge influence a teacher in planning music activities?
3. Observe a school for young children and describe how the physical environment provides for musical learnings. Be sure to take note of equipment, activities, and space indoors as well as outdoors.
4. Make a list of music materials, equipment, and instruments essential to the development of a balanced music program for three-, four- and five-year-olds. Describe how these might be provided.
5. Draw a diagram of a classroom and a playground for young children. Show in detail the contents and location of the music station and space available for music activities in the classroom.
6. Discuss and contrast structured and unstructured music programs. What do these terms mean to children and parents? What are the pros and cons of each type of program? Should only one of these be used—or both? Justify your answer.
7. What is required of the classroom teacher to formulate an individualized music education plan for special children to be implemented within the regular classroom setting? What data and/or support may he/she need, and how can this information be collected?
8. How can the teacher design environments and learning activities that provide for the educational needs of both the "regular" and the "special" children? How can they be implemented and evaluated?

9. As a teacher of young children, what effect may you have on the attitudes of others toward the "special" children you teach?
10. Specify the requirements for physical design and environmental provisions of public schools to accommodate children with special learning problems.
11. Discuss the strategies you would use in designing and using learning centers in your classroom to meet the "special" needs of the children you teach.
12. What musical responsibilities should be given to a five-year-old that should not be given to a four-year-old? Why?
13. In what ways are music success and a child's self-concept related? Explain your answer.
14. Why is an understanding of "normal" development essential to understanding special intellectual and emotional needs and difficulties in social adaptation and intellectual development?

References

Berson, M. P. and W. W. Chase. "Planning Preschool Facilities." In *Early Childhood Education Rediscovered: Readings*, J. L. Frost, ed. New York: Holt Rinehart and Winston, Inc., 1968.

Blatt, Burton. "Mainstreaming: Does It Matter?", *Exceptional Parent* 6; No. 1 (February 1976): pp. 11-12.

Braun, Samuel J. and Miriam G. Lasher. *Are You Ready to Mainstream?* Columbus, Ohio: Charles E. Merrill Publishing Company, 1978. Helping preschoolers with learning and behavior problems.

Choksy, Lois. *The Kodály Method: Comprehensive Music Education from Infant to Adult*. Englewood Cliffs, N.J.: Prentice-Hall, Inc., 1974.

Dunn, Lloyd, ed. *Exceptional Children in the Schools*, 2nd ed. New York: Holt, Rinehart and Winston, 1973.

Fraiberg, Selma. *The Magic Years*. New York: Charles Scribner's Sons, 1959.

Frost, Joe L. and Glenn R. Hawkes, eds. *The Disadvantaged Child*. Boston: Houghton Mifflin Company, 1970.

Furth, Hans G. *Piaget and Knowledge*. Englewood Cliffs, N.J.: Prentice-Hall, Inc., 1969.

Ginsberg, Herbert, and Sylvia Opper. *Piaget's Theory of Intellectual Development, An Introduction*. Englewood Cliffs, N.J.: Prentice-Hall, Inc., 1969.

Gross, Dorothy. "Equipping a Classroom." *Young Children*, December, 1968.

Hildebrand, Verna. "Getting to Know Children." In *Introduction to Early Childhood Education*, 2nd ed. New York: Macmillan Co., 1978.

Home Play and Equipment. Children's Bureau Publication No. 238. Washington, D.C.: U.S. Department of Health, Education, and Welfare.

Hymes, James L. "A Child-Centered Program." In *Teaching the Child Under Six*, 2nd ed. Columbus, Ohio: Charles E. Merrill Publishing Company, 1974.

Kritchevsky, Sybil, and Elizabeth Prescott. *Planning Environments for Young Children: Physical Space.* Washington, D.C.: National Association for the Education of Young Children, 1969.

Leeper, Sarah H. et. al. *Good Schools for Young Children,* 3rd ed. New York: Macmillan Co., 1974. Presents a developmental sequence chart for singing, listening, rhythms, playing instruments, and creating music, with suggestions to the teacher on how and what to teach in each area.

———. "Providing Physical Facilities, Equipment and Materials." In *Good Schools for Young Children,* 3rd ed. New York: Macmillan Co., 1974.

Moran, Joan M. and Leonard H. Kalakian. *Movement Experiences for the Mentally Retarded or Emotionally Disturbed Child.* Minneapolis: Burgess, 1974.

Orem, R. C. *Montessori and the Special Child.* New York: Capricorn Books, 1970.

Osmon, Fred Linn. *Patterns for Designing Children's Centers.* New York: Educational Facilities Laboratories, 1971.

Pluger, L. A. and J. M. Zola. "A Room Planned by Children." *Young Children,* September, 1969.

National Association of Great Britain and Northern Ireland. *Bulletins: Infant School Playgrounds,* 1964; *The Nursery School.* 89 Stamford St., London SEI 9ND: Association of Great Britain and Northern Ireland.

Rasmussen, Margaret, ed. *Individualizing Education.* Washington, D.C.: Association for Childhood Education International, 1964.

Safford, Philip L. *Teaching Young Children with Special Needs.* Saint Louis: The C. V. Mosby Company, 1978. Excellent.

Smith, Sister Cecilia. "The Thought-Life of the Young Child: Jean Piaget and the Teaching of Music." *Music Educators Journal* 58 (December 1971): 22-26.

Todd, Vivian C. and Helen Heffernan. Chapter Two, "Understanding Preschool Children," in *The Years Before School,* 3rd ed. New York, The Macmillan Publishing Co., Inc., 1977.

Wynne, Susan. *Mainstreaming and Early Childhood Education for Handicapped Children: Review and Implications for Research.* Washington, D.C.: Wynne Associates, 1975.

Zimmerman, Marilyn P. *Musical Characteristics of Children.* Washington, D.C.: Music Educators National Conference, 1971. 32 pages.

3 Theoretical Approaches, Structure, Goals, and Objectives

Theoretical Approaches

Several approaches to music learning have been popular in recent years, and aspects of these have been used successfully by teachers of young children. Three of them are the methods of Madeline Carabo-Cone and Zoltán Kodály, and the approach of Carl Orff. These theoretical approaches are described below.

The Carabo-Cone Method

A method of music teaching that is based on a sensory-motor approach to learning is that of Madeline Carabo-Cone, a New York music teacher, who structured an environment in which elementary-school children learn music through movement, guided games, and play. She worked with a Harlem Day Care Center in 1969 to apply the method to 3-, 4-, and 5-year-olds in a pilot project having as its goal "the intellectual stimulation of preschoolers through sensory-motor experience." The weekly classes in music were approximately one hour long. It was claimed that general perception development and concept formation were emphasized throughout the project.

The structured environment included a piano and large drawings of the grand staff on the floor, on a large table top, and on plastic wall charts. The children were guided to act out certain musical concepts on these. Carabo-Cone claims that her method follows principles of Piaget—that the learning of young children should be by way of objects that can be seen, touched, felt, and responded to by body movement. To this end, the Carabo-Cone Method, unlike other methods, stresses the learning of notation through the unique means mentioned above, with the giant staff on the floor becoming a music gymnasium. She quotes Piaget, "Even infants can discriminate between sticks and circles," and applies this by conceiving of the lines of the staff as "sticks" and the notes as "circles." The notes the children moved on the table staff were cookies—solid round ones for quarter notes and circle-type for half and whole notes, with straight pretzel sticks for note stems. To relate the five lines of the staff to body movement, the children touched toes for the lowest staff line, knees for the next, and waist, shoulders, and head to act out all five. Even the concept of interval was introduced by these techniques.

Further information about the Carabo-Cone Method may be obtained by contacting the Carabo-Cone Method Center, Carnegie Hall Bldg., Suite 862, 881-7th Avenue, New York, N.Y. 10019.

The Kodály Method

The method of music teaching espoused by the composer-educator Zoltán Kodály and adopted officially by the Hungarian government has attracted wide attention. It is not wholly applicable to the United States because in the majority of Hungarian nursery schools music is taught by specialists and the integration of music with other aspects of daily living—discussed in a later chapter—is not stressed.

Three-year-olds are expected to chant nursery rhymes, step and clap the beat (pulse), use simple percussion instruments (drums, cymbals, triangle), respond to loud and soft, recognize familiar melodies, and sing from eighteen to twenty songs and singing games. Four-year-olds will, in addition to the above, develop concepts of high and low pitch, fast and slow, and learn approximately twenty-five more songs. They are expected to recognize familiar songs by their clapped melody-rhythms. Five-year-olds develop further the concepts introduced in the earlier years. "Inner hearing" is stressed, and the children are to clap the rhythm of familiar melodies while hearing them silently "in their heads." They learn to echo-clap simple rhythm patterns.

Songs for all of these children are taught by rote and there is much individualization of instruction. By the end of this three-year period the children are expected to be able to demonstrate their understanding of the concepts of high, low, fast, slow, loud, and soft and to be able to clap and step the beat correctly for familiar songs. The program for the first grade contains quite different content although it is built on these prior experiences. The first-grade children are to sing, identify, write (in simplified notation), and read the tones of the common pentatonic scale, and to use the Curwen hand signs for these pitches. They also will learn to take rhythmic and melodic dictation and to read simple pentatonic melodies.

The Orff Approach

The German composer Carl Orff has many followers among music educators. There are only a few points of similarity between his approach and the Kodály method. These include the utilization of the pentatonic idiom for beginning experiences in melody, and the use of nursery rhymes and singing games. Orff begins with speech and movement, uses children's games and dances, and implies that speech, movement, and music form a unified whole. He recommends a physical, nonintellectual approach to rhythm and melody that includes clapping and thigh-slapping. There is a progression from the spoken rhythm of one word to that of two words and on to encompass a phrase. Singing is begun as in the Kodály method with the natural children's chant (s m, s m l s m). There is considerable use of speech patterns, proverbs, children's rhymes and jingles to work toward an eventual understanding of note values, meter, phrase, and more complex rhythm patterns in later years. Percussion and keyboard instruments of Orff's design are employed to give children immediate access to the opportunity of making aesthetically-pleasing music, and creativity is stressed within planned tonal limits.

The Orff approach has been described in terms of speech, movement, instruments, and creativity, while the Kodály method is based primarily upon singing.

The Structure of Music

One of the major trends in education today consists of identifying the content of a discipline, which is also known as the *structure* of a subject. This structure is composed of the basic generalizations of any subject, contructed from supporting concepts which are formed from data and/or percepts. The teacher assists children toward their comprehension of these, and toward higher-level thinking processes primarily through inquiry based on skillful questioning to draw pertinent information from the child. The primary function of schools for young children is to aid the child in his transition from the sensory-motor perceptual stage of intelligence, where information is assimilated through the several senses, to conceptual intelligence, where symbolization and mastery of simple types of relationships are learned.

"A concept is an abstraction, and an abstraction enables one to *interpret* the environment rather than be forced to react to each stimulus each time as a new event. When concepts are formed, one differentiates among things, draws together what is common, and then abstracts this commonness." (Crosby, 1972)

This author believes that children ages two through five who are at the pre-operational stage are able to form simple concepts which result from percepts that are derived from the manipulation and experimentation with concrete objects whose similarities and differences they can see. She agrees that the structure of the child's concepts are formulated primarily at the representational stage and therefore are less complicated than those formulated at the concrete and formal (abstract) stages of development. She also agrees with Piaget that major emphasis should be focused upon building the child's general cognitive structure.

Jerome Bruner (1960) contends that the extent of a young child's ability to learn has been underestimated. Even though he and Piaget agree on some matters, they disagree regarding the emphasis that should be placed on structuring the curriculum to include specific concepts from the various disciplines. They disagree also regarding the amount of attention that should be given to the establishment of an appropriate environment in which learning at the child's own pace is possible through free exploration, yet under the teacher's guidance. Piaget believes that when given the proper environment the child will structure the learning of his own concepts. Bruner states in his *The Process of Education* that "any subject can be taught effectively in some intellectually honest way to any child at any stage of his development." In so writing, he was stressing not that the child learn concepts at his own pace but rather the importance of recognition and identification by the teacher of those major concepts and generalizations inherent in each discipline, in order to teach them to the child. In other words, his major emphasis was on the curriculum and the inner structure of its disciplines.

When the theories of these two educators are joined, it is reasonable to expect that an improved program for young children will result. For example, the English infant schools were based on the theories of Piaget, the Isaaces and others. But after these schools had been in operation for a number of years, there was a general concern as to the quality of experiences and concepts presented. Therefore, when Bruner stated his ideas about the importance of the structure of the disciplines and the importance of the quality of the curriculum, the teachers in those schools began to combine the two basic theories.

As a teacher designs and implements a program based on the stages of intellectual development as outlined by Piaget, the steps necessary for thinking to occur are utilized. The child must first be able to perceive, then to associate, relate, or interpret, in order to be able to conceptualize. To conceptualize, one must have the ability to compare and contrast, to classify, to sequence, and to generalize.

A generalization is a conclusive statement that is mentally organized from facts about things, people, and events. It contains two or more related concepts. In order to generalize, young children must have time, space, and materials to explore, examine, experiment, and experience the detailed facts necessary to formulate a generalization; much concrete data will be needed. Data should be so organized that relationships are easily observed. Teachers should use formulated and sequenced questions to guide children in learning how to generalize. As young children grow in their ability to perceive, associate, and to conceptualize, they become more efficient in interpreting and relating to their environment and to their world of music. For example, a child may experiment with various sound producers that give out high and low pitches, and as a result of this fact finding and concept forming he may be able to generalize about pitch. He can do the same with other musical elements.

A list of elements of music, adjusted to the young child ages 2-5 is found on page 46.

Children should be helped to assess the similarities and differences in the way objects, people, and animals move, such as comparing the ways a cat moves with the movements of a horse or a rabbit. They need to be helped to compare the sounds of instruments with sounds from the environment, learning about high, low, soft, loud, same, different, fast, and slow in the process of making such comparisons. Reality and make-believe can also be compared. Through all of this, children grow in their understanding and formulation of concepts in music as well as in language. As the teacher relates many concrete experiences to music, many of which involve such concepts as fast/slow, high/low, loud/soft, types of instruments and sounds, and ways to move, the children will learn to categorize and generalize. They should have the opportunity to explore physically and to group objects and ideas in many ways.

Through music young children learn to sequence a series of events—learn which verse comes first, second, and so on. They learn to sequence water glasses in order of pitches from low to high. More mature children will also learn to sequence in reverse order. The assistance of music in developing an understanding of sequencing in reverse is demonstrated by the following example, sung to the tune of "Ten Little Indians" (which can be acted out to further clarify by sight the matter of counting and accumulating, and reversing and subtracting amounts):

One little, two little, three little ponies,
Four little, five little, six little ponies,
Seven little, eight little, nine little ponies,
Ten little trotting ponies.

Ten little, nine little, eight little ponies,
Seven little, six little, five little ponies,
Four little, three little, two little ponies,
One little pony, trotting.

Sequencing can be utilized in pantomiming certain songs and appropriate Mother Goose rhymes. Flannelgraph figures can be used to sequence events of a song; then they can be used backwards to learn reversibility. Songs that assist children to acquire an understanding of the reversal of quantities are important in their development.

Characteristics of young children relative to music, and the sequential progression and development of these characteristics, were enumerated in chapter 2. Research concerning vocal and rhythmic development implies that maturation is a primary influence in this development. However, the opportunity to listen to music and to actively participate in it assists this development; in fact, a great deal of the development could never take place without these musical experiences. Thus, teachers need to know the characteristics of children, the sequential progression of their development, and the experiences in music needed by children to foster this development.

Zimmerman (1971) concludes that: "Findings on perceptual development indicate that perception of loudness develops first, followed by pitch and rhythm, with perception of harmony developing last. The ages of six to eight are marked by a rapid advance in melodic perception."

Conceptual development also follows a sequential pattern. Young children commonly confuse high in pitch, loud, and fast. They likewise confuse low in pitch, soft, and slow. Some of this confusion stems from lack of vocabulary with which to describe and discuss what they hear. Thus the learning of vocabulary by means of the teacher's questioning is of high importance. Affective learning is entwined with perceptual and cognitive, as well as with psychomotor development. Experiences with many types of music in which all appropriate senses are used assist in affective development.

Continuing research has revealed the effect of children's early experiences on their mental growth. Although inheritance plays a part, intellectual development is greatly influenced by what children assimilate from their environment. Studies have shown the importance of nonverbal means for reacting and communicating. Unstructured experience with music is not enough; children should have specific direction and encouragement from teachers who will assist them with both recognition of musical phenomena and the response to such phenomena through movement and in other ways.

The teacher of young children should have a fundamental understanding of music in order to plan and organize music experiences based on reliable theories of how children think and learn. A knowledge of the developmental characteristics of children suggested for each age level will not suffice as the *only* criteria upon which to design instructional programs. The teacher must continue to do viable research and *action* experimentation to arrive at the best means of developing both cognitive and affective learning in young children. She must first diagnose to determine each child's interests and level of performance, then formulate specific objectives and methods (strategies) and provide resource materials and media for the child to use to realize his identified and accepted objectives. Frances Aronoff (1971) says, "it is not enough to know that young children can be taught to move, sing, and play instruments and that they thrive on these activities and accomplishments; we must identify the conditions for transfer of preverbal understandings, provide for the acquisition of needed skills and musical repertoire, and devise teaching strategies to help children develop heuristic techniques for further cognitive and affective growth in music."

Children learn best in an atmosphere of inquiry where there is a balance between the "teacher-structured" and the "child-structured" activities and situations. Choate states that:

"Children need and respect routines but provisions for inquiry may undergird either situation. How the teacher deals with the child's question will determine the kind of inquiry or discovery he develops. If the answer is supplied at once, rather than explored further, closure occurs in the child and generally he turns to something else. The effective approach then is: don't tell! ask! The teacher should strive to generate continuous thought. By doing so, the child's attention is focused and concentrated. His inquiry is given direction." (Choate, 1970)

This kind of guidance leads the child to describe, compare, demonstrate, and possibly draw conclusions. The teacher might ask, "Can we sing the song in another way?" "Is this song as fast as the other one?" "How are they different?" "Show us how the song makes you feel?" "What do you like (or not like) about the song?"

Children should have experiences in looking at, examining, and experimenting with different percussion instruments. They need to discuss the *similarities* of two instruments—what things do they do that are alike? How are they alike in appearance? They need to discuss the *differences* in color, shape, composition, and function.

Children learn through active participation, through experimenting with and manipulating things and through situations found both in their firsthand experiences in the near environment, and those in distant places, as they experience things, people, and situations through travel and via television. They interact with the environment and learn to perceive their world through sound, smell, taste, and sight. As an outgrowth of sensory perception, words and other symbols are associated with objects, situations, and people. Through rich and stimulating home and school environments wherein young children perceive various objects, people, and problems on a day-to-day basis, they learn knowledges, skills, and attitudes, and sensitivities; in other words, they develop cognitively and affectively simultaneously. One type of learning is dependent upon the other. A child relates learning in these two areas as he expresses himself musically by combining his past experiences with present ones and he uses his body freely and creatively to interpret and to express these experiences and his feelings about them and music.

As a child becomes concerned and enamoured with his own movement, interpretations, and musical creations, he becomes deeply involved in the affective aspects of learning in its truest form. Fundamentally, music is involved with the cognitive, the affective, and the psychomotor, being well-suited to serve all three areas. It follows that the teacher should be able to organize objectives in a music program that will lead toward acquisition of music concepts, the skills of listening, moving, singing, playing, and the love of music through self-expression and participation with others.

Goals and Objectives

For a teacher to be able to plan music learning successfully, she should be able to differentiate between two groups of music activities: the first involved with listening, moving, singing, playing instruments, and creating; the second involving activities through which certain specific objectives of musical accomplishment can be achieved. The concept of music as a group of activities has often meant that children are engaged in activities as ends within themselves. The results may be pleasant, sometimes time-consuming, and perhaps of minor importance. However, music competencies and appreciations are not innate. If a teacher begins planning with specific musical goals, instructional and performance objectives in mind, she will find it much easier to select activities that lead to accomplishing these objectives. Such distinctions need not adversely effect children's creativity, spontaneity, or pleasure in music.

Identification of goals is the first important step in music program design. From each goal the teacher identifies three or more instructional objectives, as indicated below with the A, B, C statements under the Roman numeral goals. In turn, each instructional objective becomes an organizational base for identifying appropriate performance objectives that can be measured. Then the performance objectives become the theme of each music lesson or activity. In order to realize these specific objectives in music lessons, the teacher must select appropriate materials and activities, providing adequate time and space so that the objectives can be implemented.

Goals and Instructional Objectives

The teacher organizes the music program in a manner that includes the following goals and general instructional objectives:

I. Development of Nonverbal and Limited Verbal Expression
    A. To express what he sees, feels, thinks, and talks about
    B. To explore and experiment with sounds, instruments, words, sentences, and song creation
    C. To express ideas and feelings about himself, his immediate environment, and the world as he understands it
    D. To strengthen his ability to imagine, create, and observe
    E. To learn the use of judgment and control through movement and rhythmic exploration and involvement
    F. To gain experience in order to enhance or build a more positive self-concept
II. Emotional Development
    A. To express feelings that are otherwise unacceptable
    B. To express strong feelings through psychomotor activity
    C. To handle feelings of happiness and joy but also negative feelings through positive action
III. Social Development
    A. To learn to work as an individual and as a member of an interacting and cooperative small group
    B. To learn to take turns and to share musical instruments
    C. To develop awareness of the cultural heritage through music
    D. To learn to respect others' rights, opinions, and feelings
    E. To begin to develop group leadership and followership qualities

IV. Intellectual Development
   A. To use varied materials to solve music problems
   B. To develop a need for a more mature vocabulary to use in discussing, exploring, and inquiring about different experiences of life
   C. To gain confidence in ability to express himself both verbally and in nonverbal ways
   D. To learn to define problems and to seek solutions
   E. To learn to make decisions (how to move to communicate the music; how to play an instrument; which instrument to use to make a certain sound; how to make the sound of the wind, of an elephant walking, etc.)
 V. Physical Development
   A. To develop control of body—eyes, ears, touch, as well as control of the mind
   B. To learn what parts of the body can and cannot do
VI. Perceptual Development
   A. To increase awareness and use of kinesthetic experiences in growing response to visual stimuli
   B. To develop his auditory awareness and change it to musical and artistic expression
VII. Musical Development
   A. To learn music data, concepts, and generalizations at his maturity level (music content)
   B. To learn music skills (listening, moving, singing, playing, and creating)
   C. To learn to value music, to choose it, and to act accordingly and finally,
   D. To acquire an appropriate music repertoire

Performance Objectives

When teachers formulate performance objectives in specific behavioral terms for the cognitive, affective, and psychomotor areas of learning, each child's progress in understanding music content, in acquiring positive attitudes and values toward music, and in learning performance skills in music can be clearly measured and evaluated by both the teacher and the child. This immediate feedback is used to assist each child to function at his optimum level of performance, and aids the teacher in identifying and sequencing musical experiences in a way that challenges each child. The child is helped to evaluate and notice his achievement in his musical responses. Knowledge of accomplishment serves to motivate the learner to strive to continue to further progress in his musical growth.

When children are guided to recognize and explore component elements of music such as rhythm, melody, harmony, tone qualities, and simple form, their abilities to perceive these elements are strengthened. Four-year-olds can understand that music is a nonverbal means of communication, that music is a result of someone's idea which he communicated in sound, that the composer sees, thinks, and feels something that he expresses in music, and that there are a great many ways in which people can create music. This leads children to communicate their feelings by musical composition of various types.

Music Content Objectives for Young Children

What young children learn in music is essentially the same as what is learned by adults except that the content is adjusted to the child's level of intellectual, social, and physical development. This content is divided here into two sections, the *expressive* elements of music that deal with how music is expressed in terms of tone quality, tempo, and dynamics, and the *constituent* elements of music that deal with those basic elements of which music is comprised.

Expressive Elements of Music	*Constituent Elements of Music*
Sound and Tone	*Rhythm (duration)*
Vocal Sounds	Beat
Unconventional Sounds	Even Divisions of the Beat
Body Sounds	Accent
Glass Sounds	Meter
Paper Sounds	Pattern
Metal Sounds	Rest
Plastic Sounds	Word-rhythm
Wood Sounds	*Melody (pitch relationships)*
Rubber Sounds	High, Low, Same
Sounds of Outdoor	Contour (shape)
Materials	Up, Down (direction)
Traditional Instrument	Chant (kindergarten)
Sounds	*Texture*
Percussion	Monophonic (single line of
nonpitched	melody)
pitched	Homophonic (single line of
Stringed	melody, accompanied)
plucked	Combined Lines or More Than
bowed	One Melody
stroked	Chord (kindergarten)
struck	*Form*
Wind	Same (repetition)
woodwind	Different (contrast)
brass	Phrase (kindergarten)
Electronic Sounds	
Tempo	
Slow and Fast	
Changing	
Dynamics	
Loud and Soft	
Changing	
Accent	

When the teacher plans a music program for children the above musical elements are used to identify the musical learnings that are to take place. These are expressed in general behavioral (performance) terms as follows:

The child will:

Sound and Tone

- Identify various sound sources—vocal, instrumental, electronic, and unconventional.
- Explore and utilize sounds of classroom percussion instruments.
- Utilize various sounds of classroom percussion instruments.
- Utilize various appropriate sound sources in dramatizations and accompaniments. (Specific string, brass and woodwind instruments in grade 1)
- Discriminate between pleasant and unpleasant sounds.

Tempo

- Experiment with slow, fast, and changing tempos, and use these concepts in his musical-rhythmic interpretations and creations.

Dynamics

- Experiment with loud, soft, changing dynamics, and with accent, and use these concepts in his musical-rhythmic interpretations and creations.

Rhythm

- Move, clap, and play percussion instruments in time with the beat.
- Create short percussion instrument compositions.
- Create rhythm patterns with vocal, traditional, and unconventional sounds.
- Chant in time with a group.
- Imitate rhythm patterns with the body and with percussion instruments.
- Recognize rhythm in the environment as well as in music.
- Sense the accents that define meter.
- Identify and use walking, running, and skipping rhythm patterns. (Kg-1)
- Perform simple singing games. (Kg)
- Utilize movement to describe music or to tell stories.

Melody

- Demonstrate understanding of high, low, and same in pitch.
- Match pitch with the singing voice, singing short songs accurately.
- Create short songs.
- Recognize familiar melodies.
- Depict the contour of melodies with whole body movements and hand levels.

- Improvise short patterns with voice and pitched instruments.
- Respond with appropriate movements to melodies heard on recordings.
- Recognize same and different phrases. (Kg-1)
- Sing and gesture patterns formed with s-m, s-l, s-d, m-r-d, d-l, l-s-m-r-d. (Kg-1)

Texture
- Differentiate between accompanied and unaccompanied melodies.
- Differentiate between single-voiced and combined-voiced sounds and melodies.
- Experiment with grouping tones into chords (kindergarten).

Form
- Recognize same and different (repetition and contrast) in selected songs and in selected recorded instrumental compositions.
- Recognize the phrase as an identifiable musical segment (kindergarten).
- Recognize same and different phrases in music (kindergarten).

Summary

In this chapter several theoretical approaches to music learning were discussed. The structure of music as a discipline was outlined, and described as concepts and generalizations constructed from data and percepts gained from experiences with music. General goals of music instruction were stated, along with instructional objectives derived from them. Performance (behavioral) objectives were described as music content objectives and listed under music element headings: sound and tone, tempo, dynamics, rhythm, melody, texture, and form. Appendix A illustrates how performance objectives are used in lesson plans.

Suggested Activities

1. At a parent-teacher meeting you stated that when one teaches music as a worthy school subject, he is helping children learn about music's *structure*. Explain to the parents exactly what is meant by "the structure of music."
2. Explain the difference between the goals of music instruction, instructional objectives, and performance objectives. Also explain how they are related.
3. After studying the lesson plans in Appendix A, write a plan of your own that incorporates the items in question two, adding activities and evaluation to your plan.

4. Now select a goal compatible with your educational philosophy and show how, using this general goal, a teacher forms instructional objectives; then, under each instructional objective she lists three or four related performance objectives. Also enumerate the activities and materials needed in realizing each of the performance objectives. Add techniques for evaluating the plan.

4 Realizing Music Goals and Instructional Objectives

This chapter will treat music as a subject field of its own. That it is often taught in relation to other areas of the curriculum will be emphasized in chapter 5, thus the reader should study both chapters before deciding for himself the position of music in early childhood education.

The concluding section of chapter 3, "Goals and Objectives," can be used as a basis for developing a music curriculum; it described both the instructional objectives that music shares with other areas and music content objectives that are suitable for young children. These were followed by music performance (behavioral) objectives that assist the teacher in establishing goals and measures of accomplishment in music. This chapter will devote attention to presenting some ways to achieve those performance objectives. It will deal with present-day practices and theories, despite the author's acknowledgment that research in early childhood music has not as yet been sufficient to permit an all-out commitment to any one of the theories advanced.

The primary music areas organized by the teacher for the young child are those concerned with body movement, listening, playing instruments, and singing, with creative approaches and individualized instruction throughout all of these. Listening has been called the most basic music activity since without it the others could not take place.

Listening to Sounds and Tones

When a baby hears a raucus sound, it will cry. When it hears a beautiful tone it is likely to be very still, concentrating its attention on the agreeable and non-threatening sound. The ability to make such discrimination is due to the fact that the sense of hearing is fully developed in the normal newborn child. There are those who believe that the unborn child can benefit from hearing good music, and it is obvious that the newborn child is capable of hearing it. While understanding music will come later, the purely sensual response to sound is present. This may indicate that one of the logical places to begin the young child's musical experience is with sound exploration. Those who developed the Manhattanville Music Curriculum Program (MMCP) will agree with this, and composer and music educationalist Carl Orff said that every child needs to pound on something, indicating that these instinctive and rudimentary experiences should lead to the discovery of beauty of tone, no matter how crude the beginning experience might be. Orff practitioners state that the use of instruments should be preceded by body sound accompaniments, each of which is then transferred to a specific percussion instrument.

At the beginning of his conscious development in listening skills, the child becomes aware of different sounds he can make with his body and by striking objects. He also becomes aware of voices and what is sung or played. The two-year-old, at his level of maturity, can be encouraged to explore and identify the sources of many types of sounds—human, mechanical, and those in nature. The teacher provides opportunities for experimenting with sound-producing objects, one at a time. When using music, the teacher employs types having a distinct beat and melody.

The typical three-year-old is capable of enjoying short listening experiences such as listening to a song with content about his world, to an appropriate recording, or to the sound of a musical instrument, and this he can do alone, and with a small group. He can be encouraged to explore, identify, and listen to sounds of his environment—human, mechanical, and those in nature. In addition, the sounds of percussion instruments can be studied, one at a time. Small group listening can be done, with the child having the option of leaving the group whenever he wishes. Bells, recorder, piano, and psaltery, as well as singing, can be listened to. The teacher should try to develop the idea of listening attentively and quietly, but these periods should seldom continue for more than ten minutes.

A typical four-year-old is sometimes capable of enjoying a listening experience with a large group. The teacher can arrange to have the children listen to some songs with accompaniments by guitar, Autoharp, and piano. The teacher selects and plays a few recordings of songs and instrumental music that are excellent examples of beautiful sound and are on a four-year-old's level. Children of this age can be guided to explore sounds of classroom percussion instruments and improvised sound sources and encouraged to use those that enhance songs and dancing. Listening experiences involving bells, recorder, psaltery, piano, flute, violin, and cello can be arranged, as well as those involving songs. These should seldom be continued for more than fifteen minutes. Older children and adults from the community can perform for these children, also. The children should demonstrate their musical learning by becoming able to use and apply concepts as loud and soft, heavy and light, fast and slow, happy and sad. The teacher should ask questions and encourage the children to discuss and ask questions to assist the learning of these concepts.

The typical five-year-old is able to hear and match pitches vocally and on the bells or psaltery, and to make pitch adjustments to correct his errors. He becomes able to listen to a song, a piano selection or a recording, and to play a simple percussion instrument to accompany it. The teacher provides experiences in listening to songs and music of all common orchestral instruments as well as the usual classroom instruments. High quality recording of many types including contemporary can be used if they are on the child's level of understanding. Real or pictured instruments can be shown as they relate to what is heard on recordings. Older children or adults from the community may be asked to perform short programs for the children and to demonstrate the instruments played. Children should have experiences in listening to accompanied songs that employ the guitar, Autoharp, or piano. They should have opportunities to use, discuss, and apply concepts stated above for the four-year-old, and the teacher should ask questions to assist children's learning of these concepts. Most five-year-olds are capable of listening as members of a larger group since they are becoming socially concerned with peers.

Among commercial items available today are the *Sound Kits* obtained from World of Peripole, Inc., designed for use "at all grade levels." These are appropriate for nursery school purposes. The manufacturer's catalog states that the teacher "will get clues for using these materials from the children," explaining that children are curious about things they see, can handle, and the sounds they produce. They ask questions about their experiences with them, and seek answers by experimenting, conjecturing, asking adults and peers. They will unconsciously use elements of the scientific method, form hypotheses and gather data as they seek answers. Pitch, tone quality, dynamics, and duration of sound are explored in a controlled situation. Activity guides accompany each kit.

Contemporary Approaches to Sounds and Tones

The publication MMCP Interaction (Biasini et. al., n.d.) describes an exploratory approach for children in kindergarten and primary grades. However, the first two phases of the method can apply to the nursery school level. They begin with *free exploration* of sounds by individual children, leading to *guided exploration* with the assistance of the teacher. After a sufficient background of experience has been acquired in these two early phases, there follow more organized musical experiences with individuals, small and sometimes large groups in kindergarten and primary grades. These later phases are called, in order, *exploratory improvisation*, *planned improvisation*, and *reapplication*. The experiences are described in small lesson plans called *encounters* through which it is projected that music concepts will be acquired, skills will be developed, and constructive attitudes formed.

The preface of *MMCP Interaction* states, "It is not simply that the child's musical explorations and discoveries can be guided by the classroom teacher; it is that in most cases they should be. As discussed later, with the classroom teacher guiding and initiating musical activities, the children can be offered a much broader range of musical involvement. Musical experiences can be more thoroughly integrated with the many activities which make up the child's school day." (Biasini et. al., n.d.)

The sounds the child makes in the first phase is the starting point, and he repeats them over and over in order to gain more understanding of the sound-producing process, more control of the sound being produced, and more personal satisfaction. Thus he explores a variety of sound sources and discovers a variety of ways of making sounds with them. The teacher is to provide materials, encourage involvement, and eventually encourage the child to identify sound sources, to identify differences and similarities in sounds, and to share his discoveries with others. Next, the teacher encourages the child to investigate sound sources in greater depth, and the classification of them begins. Such classification can be done in categories such as type of tone quality, degrees of loud and soft, high and low in pitch, and the duration of sound. The teacher is to identify individual needs and to design encounters that will serve the needs of each child.

Stimuli to learning can come from tape loops the teacher has made of interesting sounds and sound patterns, and from the child's being asked to find sounds that imitate those produced by the teacher or by another child. Examples of the latter might be tapping a pencil, stamping a foot, dropping a book, walking with heavy or light footsteps, and closing a door. Such questions as "Can you make a sound like Susie's?" or "Can you find a sound that is different from Jimmy's?" can be very helpful. To assist the child in developing aural memory, the teacher arranges encounters in which the child classifies sounds by the ways they are produced. Eventually, the child is able to describe verbally the sounds he produces and hears in the classroom.

In the *exploratory improvisation* phase, the kindergarten children and older children are assumed to have extensive creative interaction in which they learn in small and large groups as well as individually such concepts as "a sound may vary considerably when it is preceded or followed by other sounds," and that "the nature of a sound may change considerably when produced simultaneously with other sounds."

MMCP recommends a classroom arranged as a learning laboratory with materials readily available and arranged to serve the child. A sound materials station is the most important physical concern, and this should be easily accessible. The floor of the station should be carpeted to absorb sound, and the ceiling and walls should be sound absorbent. Carrels (semi-enclosed booths or small areas) are "ideal for individual and small group sound exploration and improvisation because they offer a feeling of privacy." A listening station should contain at least one quality tape recorder and record player with multiple headsets, with a collection of representative tapes and records on hand.

MMCP Interaction contains suggestions for encounters with sounds. These are arranged in series, beginning with one on the sound of paper. Experimentation with paper can contribute to learning about contrasting sounds; moods; judgments; concepts such as slow-fast, loud-soft, gradually louder, gradually softer; and how the various qualities of paper sound. Other series, one of metal and another of vocal sounds, advance these same concepts with the addition of high and low in pitch. The book's expanded list of classified unconventional sound sources is reproduced here; an annotated list of unconventional recordings appears in *MMCP Interaction* on pages 117-19.

Additional encounters concerning sound play with instruments are found in *Music in Early Childhood.* (Andress, et. al., 1973) (This pamphlet is concerned with children ages three to five.) Used in most of these encounters is a "feel me, hear me" box into which children can crawl to feel and play the sound producer selected for the encounter. It is simply constructed with a hole to crawl through and a removable lid. Descriptions of this box and other classroom objects and sound sources are found on pages 26-34 of the pamphlet. On pages 36-40 are eight encounters dealing with

---

Unconventional Sound Sources

Paper
construction paper
wax paper
tissue paper
newspaper
lightweight cardboard
brown bag paper
white stationery paper
sandpaper
cardboard strips
napkins
magazines
cardboard dividers
foils
cardboard boxes
paper balls
old books
egg crates
cardboard cylinders
toilet tissue cylinder
paper towel cylinders
carpet cylinders
material cylinders
corrugated cardboard
fruit crates
straws
milk containers
papier-mâché
toys
paint buckets
ice cream containers
cigar boxes
cups

Rubber
bands
balloons
hose horn
balls
innertubes
tires
toys

Glass
soda bottles
jugs
toys

Plastic
funnel (horns)
ruler
straws
food containers
bottles
sprayers
toys
brushes
buttons
combs
old records
plastic strips
boxes
tools
cups

Wood
ruler
spatula

Unconventional Sound Sources

Wood
yard stick
bowls
bamboo sticks
tongue depressors
pencils
blocks
whistles
toys
tables
chairs
clothespins
poles
Popsicle sticks
broom handles
kitchen utensils
containers
strips

Food
condiments
seeds
kernels
rice
coffee
sugar
cornflakes
bread crumbs
grains
macaroni
coconut shells

Metal
sheet metal
saws
tools
cap tops
pie plates
oven shelves
wire
cans
pails
baking pans
cookie sheets

Metal
pipes
strips
whistles
toys
tables
chairs
washtub
nails
broom handles
screws
washers
bottle caps
paper clips
funnels
scissors
bolts
foils
kitchen utensils
wastebasket
springs
machines

Outdoor Materials
dirt
pebbles
stones
leaves
grass
snow
rain
twigs
branches
pine cones
eucalyptus pods
water

Other
string
rope
twine
flowerpots
calfskin
chamois

sound plays that relate to movement. The sounds are made with percussion instruments, piano strings, a recording, and the teacher's voice. A teacher plays a rattle and asks a small group of children how it makes them want to move. Their reply is "wiggle," and this is followed by directions from the teacher to wiggle different parts of their bodies when the rattle sounds. When it stops sounding, the children are to freeze into statues. They begin to comprehend the concept of the phrase by saying with the teacher while they move, "wiggle, wiggle, wiggle, wiggle, wiggle, wiggle, BOOM!" A stamp or clap evolves when they say BOOM! A drum is used by the teacher, and the children are directed to move only one part of their bodies to the sound until the teacher says, "Freeze!" Half-note and slow quarter-note beats are played on the drum by the teacher while the children beat the air and bounce to the beat, trying to keep the same rhythm. Children take turns playing the drum experimentally while the others move to the drum beats. Soft and loud are learned from the teacher's playing the drum in the usual way, then by tapping the edge; the children walk in a manner indicated by the loud and soft sounds of the drum. In another sound play the concept of *legato* is studied. Sounds on piano strings are used to convey the feeling of a honeylike substance such as glue or syrup. The children "glue" their feet to the floor and sway, twist and move up and down like a syrupy substance. Eventually, the feet are "unglued" and the children develop a form of legato dance to a recording of Saint-Saëns' "Aquarium" from *Carnival of the Animals*. These planned experiences produce clear transitions from sound to movement.

Learning Music by Listening—More Examples

sound exploration and vocabulary	Arrange experiences in the classroom and on field trips so that children can listen to and describe sounds they hear. The teacher helps by asking questions such as, "Are the sounds loud, soft, high, low, steady, or roaring?" in order to call attention to the sound and to build an adequate vocabulary to describe it.
body sounds	Lead children to explore the many sounds they can make with their bodies. Can they discover some of these? (Clapping hands, slapping thighs, rubbing palms, stamping feet, pounding on floor or table with fists, clicking tongues, hissing, "ssh," and others.) "Can we describe these sounds?" It may be possible to organize such sounds into a single *sound composition* and to tape and play it for another listening experience.

loud-soft	When listening to music that is at times clearly loud and at other times clearly soft, establish the beat or a rhythm pattern and ask children to stamp feet when the music is loud and tiptoe when it is soft, reflecting either the beat or the pattern as desired. Consider taping their performance and asking them to evaluate how well they had listened to loud and soft in the music.
imitating sounds	Children are often better imitators of sounds than are adults. Let them have the thrill of imitating sounds that are interesting to them. Try to avoid adult stereotypes such as "bow wow" and "cock-a-doodle-doo" because children can produce more authentic imitations than these.
identifying sounds	Individuals and small groups can play games in which the teacher asks the children to identify sounds she makes behind a screen. The possibilities are endless, but all should be sounds children can succeed in identifying. Possibilities include crinkling paper, pouring water, or tapping with a pencil. After the children have acquired a set of known sounds, have a child make some sounds for others to identify.
classifying sounds	After children have come to know a number of different percussion instruments, have them classify each in accordance with the type of sound it produces: jingle, rattle, click, boom.
same and different sounds	The teacher prepares numerous pairs of identically-sized containers by placing pebbles, seeds, beads, shot, or marbles in them. However, some will have about the same amount of the substance, while others will have more or less of it. The game is to shake them, listen to the sound, and find the pairs that sound alike.
selecting sound effects	Some stories lend themselves to simple sound effects. Young children can select instruments or other sound sources to illustrate characters in stories such as "Three Little Pigs" and "The Three Bears."
each child's voice is distinctive	Plan a game in which children identify the speaking voices of their classmates without seeing the children who are speaking. Later on,

ask the children to classify some of the voices into high, low, and medium-pitch categories.

analyzing sounds

Take any of the percussion instruments (but only one at a time) and make sounds with it. Ask the children such questions as: "Can it make a short sound?" "Can it make a long sound?" "Can it make a soft sound?" A loud sound?" "Can it sound like a song?" "Can it make a jingling sound?" Children may use their body movements to help answer the question or to more fully describe the sound.

listen to discover principles

After children have explored a bell set, encourage them to make such findings as:

A long bar sounds lower.
A short bar sounds higher.
The bells look like piano keys.
To make gradually higher sounds,
  one plays from left to right.
To make gradually lower sounds,
  one plays from right to left.
Easy tunes can be found on the
  black keys.
Bells sound best when struck
  in the middle of the bar.

high and low

Instruments and other sound producers are grouped according to whether their pitch sounds high or low. The children, one or two at a time, play these as they are grouped and listen to the sounds. After this, the teacher mixes all the sound producers and the task for the children is to listen to each one and rearrange them into their original high- and low-pitch groupings.

tonal memory

After children have learned several songs and know them well, the teacher claps or plays a percussion instrument in the melody-rhythm of one of them. The game is to listen to the rhythm, hear the melody silently, and identify the song by its rhythm.

sound exploration center

A center in which children are free to explore sound should contain simple percussion and tonal instruments, both commercial and home-made. It could contain Sound Kits (mentioned earlier) and objects that produce interesting or attractive sounds. The sound center should be located as far as possible from areas in which quiet activities take place, but away from noisy activities in order that the children can listen with discrimination to the sounds they explore.

The company that produces the Sound Kits (World of Peripole Inc.) also makes the Peripole Rhythm Zoo, a collection of musical instruments that includes many which are in the shape of animals. These instruments make animal sounds like the growl of a bear, the croaking of a frog, the quacking of a duck, and the roar of a lion. While some adults may think of these sound producers as toys, they are musical instruments of educational value.

sound effects

The teacher makes up a story of a day in a child's life. Using percussion instruments and other sound sources, sounds heard around the home in the morning or at other times are illustrated. Gradually, have the children learn to produce these sound effects. Vary the story to encourage careful listening when a child makes his sound.

adult instrument sounds

Contrast the sounds, the pictures, or the actual instruments for each of the following: a woodwind and a brass, or a string and a percussion—to teach that such instruments have different sounds. Use live players if possible.

same and different

To identify like and unlike sections of recorded instrumental music, use a recording such as "Fairies and Giants" by Elgar from *Adventures in Music*, Grade 3, volume 1.

background music

Prepare a tape to play so that children can hear good instrumental music while they work quietly or rest. Place on the tape sections of recorded music for strings (trio, quartet, quintet, sextet, or string orchestra) that are of serene nature, not stimulating, but that are audibly beautiful. Aural standards of beauty can be acquired from such contact with good music. Young children generally like music of the classical period—Haydn and Mozart particularly—because the melodies and rhythms are understandable and the texture is clear and uncomplicated.

responses to sounds	Children can be encouraged to listen to sounds, to describe them, to articulate them vocally, and to label them. They can also respond to the request, "Show me (through physical action) how you hear the sound."
body sounds transferred to percussion instruments	Body sounds can be translated into percussion instrument sounds by the following relationships:

finger snap	triangle, finger cymbals
clap	instruments made of wood
thigh slap	tambourine, shakers
stamping	drums

percussion routine	The teacher claps or plays a rhythm pattern. Children listen, then imitate on signal, with soft sounds such as handles of mallets struck together or the vocal sound "Sh." Then children play the pattern on all of the percussion instruments.

Introducing Instruments in Relation to Listening

When children have learned to respond to the beat and the tempo, they can begin learning to play percussion instruments. It is important that the child is free to manipulate instruments and experiment with them, exploring their sounds and ways to produce them. The teacher should not tell him how to hold the instrument at this exploratory stage. Soon, however, he can be helped to discover how best to hold it and how to play it to produce the best sound. "Without some guidance, structure, and introduction of new ideas at some moment along the way, the child may not move to a more sophisticated stage but be content with banging and rattling for an indefinite period of time. If the teacher's purpose is to help him discover *music* as well as just discover, he must . . . enter the scene. He will not impose his ideas and concepts, but will offer them for consideration. And if they are valid the young child, who loves to imitate and model what he admires, will easily accept them and they will become his own." (Biasini et. al., n.d.)

Although some early experiences with sound and tone may be derived from sound sources that are of little musical value, as the musical sensitivity is developing, the teacher must lead the child into experiences with instruments of genuine quality such as the maracas, tone block, xylophone, metallophone, and resonator bells. When the child is mature enough to respect the instruments and care for them, he should have as an initial experience the opportunity of listening to someone play one of them, explain it, and produce a beautiful sound on it. Then it can be passed around to be handled by the child, who enters his exploratory phase with it.

Questions the teacher will ask could include "Can it sing a song?" "What kinds of sounds can you make on it?" "Can it play softly?" "Can it play loudly?" "Does it make jingling sounds?" "Short sounds?" "Long sounds?" or any other question suitable to the particular instrument or for comparison with another instrument. It should be placed where the child can study it and experiment with it on his own. Songs describing the instrument, or songs in which the instrument is used for sound effects or for an accompaniment, might be made up or found. The instrument and references to it may be useful in relation to stories, poems, rhymes, and finger plays.

This type of thoughtful introduction to each instrument should give the children time to know each one individually and be more understanding of the uses for each. It should help to minimize unaesthetic noise and help advance musical sensitivity. The child who *needs* to make noise should be guided into other activities or out-of-doors, where strong feelings can be expressed without interfering with other children.

The teacher should establish situations in which the child can select the instrument he believes to be most appropriate for certain music or to accompany certain songs, poems, and stories. The formalities of the rhythm band of past years, with its required conformity, have resulted in its virtual absence from the modern school: This dictatorial type of instrumental performance is in opposition to sound theories of learning and to the creative approach wherein children are involved in exploring, questioning, designing, and performing music. However, a great deal of musical value can come from the use of these instruments in exploring sound, discovering interesting tone qualities, and the revealing of concepts such as loud-soft (dynamics), high-low (pitch) and rhythm (duration). The immediate response of a percussion instrument is important psychologically, and the better the tone quality, the more satisfying it can be. Combinations of the instruments introduce the concept of texure. Improvising and accompanying are important activities that can be done with instruments. When they are to be used to accompany a song, only those required to make the most musically sensitive contribution are made available. Remember that instruments should be used selectively.

In the learning sequence, the child should be assisted in evaluating the sound in relation to how the instrument is held and played. He will come to recognize the sound of some of the instruments and will use them to accompany his movements, but not always in time with them. Later on he will be able to play in time with another instrument and with recorded music. He will then be able to perform with a small group and can be helped to experiment with the sound of combinations of instruments. His interest may expand to a few adult instruments and he can learn to recognize them by sight and sound. The teacher can bring adult instruments to school and permit children to touch them when this is appropriate. Some-

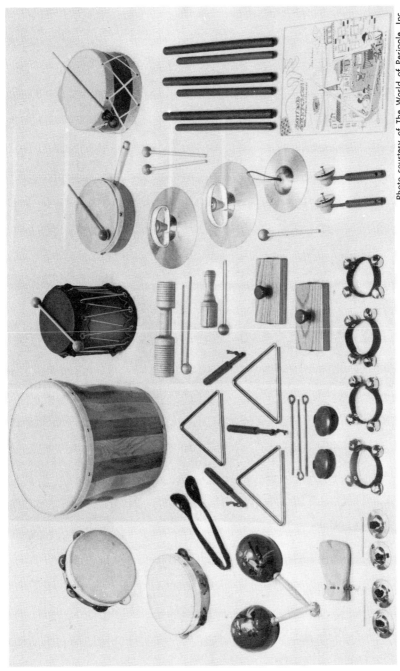

Photo courtesy of The World of Peripole, Inc., Manufacturers and Distributors. Browns Mills, N.J. 08015.

ENRICHED RHYTHM SET P2516

times plastic replicas of adult instruments can be obtained so the children can be perfectly free to handle them and learn about instruments in this way.

The Instruments

tune: The Old Brass Wagon

1. The drum is going to play ...

The drum is going to play, boom, boom, boom, boom.

The drum is going to play, boom, boom, boom, boom.

The drum is going to play, boom, boom, boom, boom.

Lis - ten to the drum. BOOM!

2. The sticks are going to play, click, click, click, click, etc.
3. The blocks are going to play (then make "tok" sound by clicking tongue).
4. The bells are going to play, ting, ting, ting, ting.

Directions: Those children who hold the instrument named will sound it at those times when the words call for a vocal description of the instrument's sound. This song should be repeated until every child has played an instrument.

Children Learn to Listen

In summary, here are some of the ways nursery school children learn to listen meaningfully:

1. by listening to sounds from nature and to those man makes.
2. by listening to the sound effects added to dramatize a story.
3. by listening for the purposes of adding percussion accompaniments to movement, songs, poems, stories, and recordings.

4. by listening to others singing a beautiful song.
5. by listening in order to learn to sing a new song.
6. by listening to older brothers or sisters or to parents playing instruments and singing songs.
7. by listening to the teacher or a visitor play the piano, violin, and other instruments, or to their singing.
8. by listening to radio and television musical programs.
9. by listening to recordings and tapes of music for children.

Use of Recordings for Listening

Recorded music is obviously an important part of everyday living. Children learn to sing songs they hear repeated on recordings or on radio and television, and teachers use them in the classroom. Many parents provide young children with durable, simple record players, and an important part of play for these children is to place their favorite records on their machines, listen to them repeatedly and dance and sing with them.

There are many recordings made specifically for young children. Some of these recordings are listed at the end of this section. An example of one favorite is Ella Jenkins' *You'll Sing a Song and I'll Sing a Song*, Folkways Records FC 7664. However, many companies offer recordings for children. These include:

Bowmar Records, Inc., 622 Rodier Drive, Glendale, Calif. 91201.
Franson Corporation, 225 Park Avenue South, New York, N.Y. (Children's Record Guild and Young People's Records).
Stanley Bowmar Company, Inc., Valhalla, N.Y.
Classroom Materials Company, 93 Myrtle Drive, Great Neck, N.Y. 11020.
Children's Music Center, 5373 West Pico Blvd., Los Angeles, Calif. 90019.
Lyons, 530 Riverview Avenue, Elkhart, Ind. 46514.

All of these companies publish catalogs, some of them concerned directly with early childhood education.

Suggested recordings are listed at the end of this section.

Appreciating music of quality depends in large part upon hearing such music repeatedly. Some of this music is liked at once by the children but they will literally walk away from other selections. However, if they have the opportunity to listen repeatedly to the music they did not like at the first hearing, they often learn to enjoy it and from this unlikely beginning can develop a genuine love of it.

The school record collection need not be large because children of this age enjoy repetition. However, it should encompass a variety of music that will lead the child to know at an early age that there are many different kinds of music in the world—from preclassical and ethnic to carefully selected rock.

Exemplary Recordings for Listening

Bowmar, 622 Rodier Drive, Glendale, Calif. 91201
  Bowmar Orchestral Library (BOL)
  Masters in Music   BOL 62
  Classroom Concert   BOL 68
  The Small Listener   BOL 393

Disneyland Records, 119 Fifth Avenue, New York, N.Y. 10003
  Papa Haydn's Surprise and Toy Symphonies

Educational Activities, Inc., Freeport, N.Y. 11520
  Homemade Band. Record or cassette. A Hap Palmer production.

Franson Corporation, 225 Park Avenue South, New York, N.Y.
  Young People's Records (YPR)
  Sound Records, Ages 2-5
  Music Listening Game   YPR 720
  Muffin in the City   YPR 601
  Muffin in the Country   YPR 603

  Instrument Series, Ages 2-5
  Little Brass Band   YPR 703

  Children's Record Guild, Ages 5-8 (CRG)
  Strike Up the Band   CRG 5027

  Children can learn to identify the instruments in order of their sound on the record: drum, cymbal, woodblock, jingle bells, sticks, triangle, tambourine.

Folkways Records, 701-7th Avenue, New York, N.Y. 10036
  Play Your Instruments and Make a Pretty Sound (Ella Jenkins)

Prentice-Hall Media, 150 White Plains Rd., Tarrytown, N.Y. 10591.
  Once Upon a Sound. A series of 5 filmstrips, the first four of which introduce brass, woodwind, string, and percussion instruments respectively. K-3.

RCA Music Service, Educational Department, 1133 Avenue of the Americas, New York, N.Y. 10036
  Adventures in Music. An extensive educational record collection much of which can be used at all age levels N-6. See the teacher's guide for the detailed instructions for all possible ways to use the recordings.

RCA Records, Educational Sales, P.O. Box RCA 1000, Indianapolis, Ind. 46291. For pre-K-4.
  Music That Paints a Picture, Vols 1, 2 (cassettes).

Scott, Foresman and Company, 2000 East Lake Ave., Glenview, Ill. 60025.
  Sounds I Can Hear. Recordings, stories, pictures, dramatization, with sounds for discrimination and identification.

References

Bailey, Eunice, *Discovering Music With Young Children.* New York: Philosophical Library, 1958, pp. 39-42.
Baldwin, Lillian. *Tiny Masterpieces for Very Young Listeners.* Bryn Mawr, Pa.: Theodore Presser Company, 1958. To be used with *Music Sound Books* recordings, Music Sound Book Press, Box 444, Scarsdale, N.Y.

Biasini, Americole; Thomas, Ronald; and Pogonowski, Lenore. *MMCP Interaction: Early Childhood Music Curriculum.* Bardonia, N.Y.: Media Materials, 1972. K-3.

Mandell, M., and Wood, R. *Making Your Own Musical Instruments.* New York: Sterling Publishing Co., 1959.

Nash, Grace. *Today With Music.* Port Washington, N. Y.: Alfred Publ. Co., 1973. For rhythm and melody instruments and voices. K-3.

Richardson, Allen L. *Tooters, Tweeters, Strings and Beaters.* New York: Grosset and Dunlap Publishers, 1964. An instrument identification book for young children with poems and pictures. Includes six puzzles in pictures.

Weidemann, Charles C. *Music in Sticks and Stones: How to Construct Simple Instruments.* New York Exposition Press, 1967.

Movement

Anthropologists theorize that primitive man enjoyed producing sounds by using things from his environment: striking hollow logs, making sounds by using sticks, stones, and by blowing through hollow reeds. He learned to cause objects to vibrate and thus produce sound. Such sound-making stimulated singing and dancing ceremonies associated with activities and events such as war, hunting, birth, marriage, death, and seasonal festivities. Rhythm developed from body motions and became a foundation upon which music and dance were created. The body was man's first musical instrument; the sounds from vocal cords and from such body movements as clapping hands and stamping feet resulted in the creation of music. Children discover music in this same way. The child's basic music thinking is organized by his body movements; it is through movement that he gains concepts of dynamics, rhythm, and melody, particularly when his rhythmic movements are accompanied by the teacher's voice or playing of percussion instruments.

Gerhardt (1973) writes, "As the child develops control of his movement, he can express such musical concepts as melody. The movement of his body through space can express the shape, length, and direction of melody as well as the changing intensities of the beat. Spatial ideas can be explored through experiences with rhythm, melody, and tempo as music embodies points of reference, balance (rhythm, meter, tempo), direction, distance/length, and volume."

A strong case can be made in support of those who believe movement to be the core of early childhood education because of the great amount of essential learning that takes place through psychomotor activities. Young children *must* move in order to grow and learn, and they constantly move, even in their sleep. They must use all of their senses—hearing, seeing, touching, tasting, and smelling—in order to understand, and then they must express through physical movements their feelings about these things. This becomes a basis for musical expression, becaue the child who experience rhythmic movement will have the urge to express himself in song.

To the young child, moving is an outgrowth of the way he feels and thinks. He often thinks of music and movement as one and the same, and when he hears music he may find it difficult not to move. The manner in which he moves will be influenced by his individual body structure, temperament, and background of experience. Perhaps the only times natural body movements are confusing to the child is when adults attempt to pattern them or to dictate conformity. His movements may be uncoordinated and even incomprehensible to the uninitiated adult, yet they are original, improvised, varied, flexible, and imaginative. His spontaneous rhythmic activities are assumed to form a logical beginning for more formal experiences later. Rhythm is an integral part of his nature, beginning with the heartbeat, and his body is his own sensitive musical instrument with rhythm to be developed from increasing muscular coordination. He is stimulated by a steady beat, rhythmic rhyme, or simple tune even though he may not be able to synchronize his body responses with the steady beat.

In the beginning the child should be free to explore his own movements in response to rhythmic stimuli. Later the teacher can help by making some motions that the child can choose to imitate in certain classroom experiences. The task, then, is to find what rhythmic activities are appropriate for the age group and to understand their importance in rhythmic, vocal, and personality development.

Many specialists in movement assist children by fostering their imagination and ingenuity to move in spontaneous ways in their own identified space. They reason that the child needs and wants to explore space with the body and that there are a number of planes of action in which he must learn to function. Many children enjoy the security of the floor, which makes it a logical place to begin. The floor is the lowest plane—and there the child lies flat on his back—arms and legs extended to the sides. Starting from that position, what can he do? He can discover that he can rock from side to side; lift one arm, both arms, one leg, both legs; place arms in various positions; and lift his head. Then, the child could turn over and lie on his stomach and react to the same challenge to move in various ways from that position. Obviously, the next plane is a sitting position. Rooted to one spot on the floor, the child is to discover what movements he can make in space. On the floor on the knees is another position from which to maneuver. Eventually, there will be moving across the floor from these positions. The teacher can accompany some of the movements, and music concepts such as fast and slow, high and low, staccato (short and detached), and legato (smooth and connected) can be related to them. The teacher's accompaniment is truly an accompaniment at this stage; she takes the tempo from the child performer—she does not dictate it to him, but she builds from his tempo to enable him to eventually follow hers and to change tempo. Through the freedom given to the child for experimenting, he can discover a great many body movements. The teacher assists by helping him relate familiar physical responses to the music and by asking him such questions as, "Is this fast or slow music? Listen to the music and make your body move like the music." There is a sequence that leads from mimetics (common actions such as sweeping and sawing), to impersonation (pretending to be: machines, butterflies, elephants, people, and so on), to dramatization (acting out poetry, songs, and stories), to singing games (organized group games). To further the creative approach, children are encouraged to express through movement the feelings they derive from music. Such responses will be a reflection of the child's past experiences; the teacher suggests no movements in this type of activity.

When planning rhythm activities, Sinclair (1973) asks, "Is the child ready? Is the equipment suitable? Is the situation safe? What help will be needed? What motivation is needed? How can the task be adjusted to differing abilities?" Eliason and Jenkins (1977) warn that creative movement requires limitation and rules. When and if a rule is broken, children "need to be reminded that if they choose to participate, they must abide by the rules; if they cannot abide by the rules, they must be watchers. One of the basic rules with any movement experience is that children must move in their own space; thus they must be alert to avoid bumping into others. . . . Another basic rule must be to stop when the signal is given (music stops, hands clap, whistle blows)."

Suitable space is needed for freedom of movement. But in situations where space is limited and where physically handicapped children are involved, certain substitute motions can be employed, such as "walking" with the hands in the air and marching in place or with only the heels moving. However, oversized rooms can destroy the intimate feeling necessary for group work. Children can learn different ways to clap, such as striking the tips of the fingers of both hands together lightly (tipping), and striking the tips of the fingers of one hand into the palm of the other. To sustain interest, variety is essential. There should be variety of types of movement and variety in the use of music—the teacher's voice, percussion instruments, the piano, the chanting of children's voices, and recordings. Materials to sustain interest include jumping ropes, scarves, bouncing balls, and balloons. Scarves are enjoyed by children; they are made of very lightweight material that permits great flexibility and variety of movement. To achieve the best results with scarves, they should be long—more than double the height of the child. Such scarves are used by children in many rhythmic movements and in dramatization as well.

Remember that the child is never "wrong" in his attempts to move. When one child performs a movement differently than the others of the group, the teacher should, whenever possible, call attention to his action and invite the others to imitate his movement. When working with individuals, the teacher should make a sound that relates to the child's movement and conversely make a movement that relates to the child's sound. Movement and sound should be closely associated.

Rhythm in Movement

Coordinated rhythmic response develops from free rhythmic play. Children use their own individual rhythms first, and few adults can understand these. The very young seldom "keep time" but they are moving in their own mysterious and creative ways to develop foundations for later controlled rhythmic responses. They are naturally rhythmic, however, as testified by the heartbeat, breathing, and walking and running. The teacher's role is to encourage and sustain the creative powers of the child while helping him to learn controlled responses, which imply limitations and conformity.

As previously mentioned, movement begins as exploration in space. At this level, when movements are repeated, rhythm results, and when mood is added to this, dance emerges. (Leavitt, 1958) As simple a movement as the walk or the run can be called to a child's attention as a rhythm when the teacher chants "walk, walk, walk, walk," or "run, run, run, run," in time with the child's motion. As far as possible, these and many other motions should be accompanied by the teacher's voice or by the sound and rhythm of her playing on a drum, tambourine, triangle, jingle bells, tone block, piano, or any other instruments appropriate to the motion. Stamping feet can provide exciting accents. The teacher can call attention to a child's walk, "See how Jay is walking; he has a different way of walking. Can we all walk the way he walks? Can we clap hands with his walk? Can we find an instrument that sounds like his walk?"

As explained above, music can be an aid in the first stage of rhythmic development in that music with definite rhythm and somewhat rapid beat stimulates the child to move, using his large muscles. Music applied this way does not restrict the child to any particular movement nor does it demand that he move in time with it. It should be noted, however, that music does become somewhat restrictive for as the child is able to control his muscles better, he is expected to keep in time with it or to reflect its dynamics, tempo, accents, and durations in other ways. However, the music should never be interpreted as a demand for complete uniformity of response; each child should be able to express what he feels in his own way.

When responding to rhythm it is important to first listen and get the "feel" of it, and then respond. When young children listen, their listening attitude is usually of an active nature; they respond with their entire bodies —they *move* in their effort to learn. When most young children begin their school experience, they are not able to match tones (i.e., sing in tune). It appears logically that there be a sequence of listening to music, responding to it physically, and through this process, gradually becoming oriented to rhythm, pitch, and mood. All of this should result in good singing later. Other values of rhythmic responses include developing body control, imagination, creativity, willingness to experiment, emotional responsiveness, as well as such concepts relating to music as slow-fast, high-low, long-short, same-different, heavy-light. (While the foregoing pertains to the relationship of hearing and movement, the teacher should not forget that seeing is another and an important aid to understanding these concepts.) Children learn about their world through movement; it is unnatural for them to sit still for extended periods of time.

Clare Cherry (1971) lists the major types of movements of young children, with specific suggestions for their initiation in the classroom. These suggestions involve music in several ways. For example, singing "Rock-a-bye Baby" not only helps teach the rocking movement, but in addition, because it lends itself to pantomiming, gets children involved who might otherwise not participate. Cherry further suggests using songs in such a way as to move from one activity to another, and so encourage maximum participation. She advocates the use of familiar tunes, but with the invention of new words for them by the teacher, to describe the movement or pantomime; music adds greatly in encouraging children to respond. Such familiar melodies include "Oats, Peas, Beans and Barley," "Farmer in the Dell," "Three Blind Mice," "Twinkle, Twinkle, Little Star," "My Darling Clementine," "Mary Had a Little Lamb," "Frere Jacques," "Row Your Boat," "Ten Little Indians," "La Cucaracha," "Pawpaw Patch," "Old MacDonald," "I'm a Little Teapot," "Jimmy Crack Corn," "Skip to My Lou," "This Old Man," "The Bear Went Over the Mountain," "My Bonnie," "Mary Wore a Red Dress," "Little Brown Jug," "John Brown's Body," and "Are You Sleeping?" Some of these songs can of course, be used with their traditional words; spoken chants and improvised melodies can also be used. Percussion instruments are commonly employed to assist rhythmic development. Music is a natural companion to rhythmic movement in early childhood education.

Animal movements are interesting to children and can be musically and rhythmically described, or when imitated by the children, can be accompanied by known songs or, more often, by songs the teacher improvises or encourages children to create. The animals could be the cat, mouse, turtle, snail, mole, spider, and bear (all for creeping); elephant (for one type of walking) with chicken suggesting other walks for other animals; grasshopper, kangaroo (for jumping and leaping); horses (for galloping and trotting); many others are possible. The point is that music is commonly employed to assist learning of rhythmic movement and to make the experience more interesting, enjoyable, and satisfying.

It is only after many experiences in rhythmic movement that the child can handle free dancing to recorded music. This should be introduced in story form so that the child's imagination is stimulated and he knows what is expected of him in terms of the music. The teacher improvises stories about such things as a toy shop in which the different toys dance after the storekeeper has gone home, or a circus in which many things appear such as a parade, clowns, and big animals.

Percussion instruments can be used by the children as an extension of their movements when they are able to play them. Random beating of itself has little or no value; the teacher leads the child to higher levels of understanding and performance after his initial explorations. Ordinarily, instruction with them begins with rhythm sticks, and the teacher encourages the child to "make" the sticks walk, run, or gallop, and "sound" like clocks ticking, a typewriter, raindrops, and so on. Next the children learn about other wooden instruments, perhaps the tone blocks, maracas, and claves. After this, they will learn to play simple drum-type instruments. They can begin to classify in terms of how they are played; whether they are shaken, or struck—some with mallets, others with the hand, and some struck one against the other. There are songs in most books that deal with the playing of different instruments and of course the teacher and children can improvise songs for themselves. The tambourine can be especially useful because it is so versatile; many different sounds can be made on it and it is easy to play. Therefore, the teacher should have at least one good quality tambourine on hand. A pair of paper cups can make sounds imitating horses' hooves and heavy corrugated cardboard stroked with a spoon can make a washboard-sound effect.

The piano can be useful for encouraging many rhythmic movements. Should the teacher lack skill in playing and be unable to perform the materials found in many of the series books, she can improvise on the black keys to stimulate many rhythmic responses. With a little practice, any teacher can accomplish such simple improvisations (see pp. 31-32).

To encourage a variety of responses, the teacher asks questions such as:

(with the child in place)

- Can you find another part of your body to do that with?
- Can you do that sitting down? Standing up? Higher? Lower? At the side?

(while the child is moving)

- Can you do that like a little gnome? (a specified animal?) You are in deep water? In soft sand? On a hot sidewalk in summer? In an airplane? In a motor boat? (a given workman or woman?)
- Can you do it more jerkily? smoother? heavier? lighter? bigger? smaller? louder? softer?

Some teachers have discovered that certain motions are highly conducive to learning concepts of the beat (pulse) and note values (duration). For example, using the two hands with palms down to slap the thighs is a very easy and satisfying motion for young children to make. Because it is one of the easiest motions to perform, it is used when working with the beat and quarter- and half-note durations. Slapping harder on certain beats can indicate either the beginning of a note value or the beginning of a measure of a certain meter. When beginning to work with meter, 2/4 and 4/4 are stressed. Fast 6/8, which means two beats per measure, is also relatively easy. However, 3/4 is more difficult for some children and should be used sparingly until kindergarten. Whether or not the teacher wishes to use the terms quarter note and half note is a matter for discussion. One faction believes that the adult terms and pictures of the notes should be used, while another believes that these terms and notes should not be used until the child needs them. However, activities involving the body movements for the beat, meter, and note durations should be planned and initiated.

Games can be invented. For example, a teacher can make two contrasting sounds on percussion instruments or two contrasting sounds or melodies on the piano; the children will be told as they hear them, to do something different for each; this is a listening rhythmic game. Another game can be invented around the doing of a movement to an accompaniment, and when the music stops either to change what they are doing and do something else, or freeze like a statue at that moment. Another game, the humor of which the children enjoy, can be played by asking them to do a planned opposite of what the music says; for example, walk like a giant with slow steps when the music has a light, fairylike quality, with "running" eighth notes and vice versa. Then too, children can invent many variations of follow-the-leader. This can involve moving the body or playing an instrument. Taking turns is another one, in which a child dictates a movement by his clapping, then the others must clap the same rhythm while he takes his turn on the movement. Remember that young children should not be asked to join hands in a circle in these games because the lack of maturity and position of the body when the circle moves clockwise or counterclockwise is such as to hamper the movements of this age group.

When nursery school children move to music, that music collectively should:

1. Suggest movements such as walking, running, hopping, jumping, and crawling.
2. Suggest dramatizations or singing games.
3. Encourage free and individual interpretive response.
4. Suggest movements such as clapping, slapping thighs, or stamping.
5. Permit the child to respond at his own tempo.
6. Suggest animal movements—the lumbering of an elephant, the slithering of a snake.
7. Suggest moods such as happiness, loneliness, or dreaminess.
8. Suggest abstractions such as water, a wheel, or a balloon.
9. Encourage original dance patterns.

Two concepts concerning dance can be considered in early childhood education. One is that *movement* relates to ballet because the dancer is free to communicate or portray feelings and thoughts. The other is *folk dancing* in which the dancer executes prescribed steps. Singing games are in the latter category. Children learn to follow rules in a social situation, learn left and right, the use of the body, and to improve their gross motor coordination. They should choose whether or not they wish to participate in singing games; children should not be compelled to join the group in this activity.

Examples of Learning Music Through Movement

soft-loud	Simple activities are planned with clapping, stamping, and pounding to exemplify degrees of sound volume (soft and loud). Begin with those that are unmistakable and progress to lesser degrees of these two extremes. There are infinite possibilities such as soft and loud walking, soft and loud clapping, soft and loud stamping.
slow-fast	Imitations of animals help to teach these concepts. As the teacher plays a percussion instrument in the tempo and rhythm of a slow rabbit hop, the children are to hop in time with the sound if they can. When this is mastered, the instrument is played faster to describe the rabbit running away, and the children imitate this. There could be a slow elephant walk, a bird walking, and many other kinds of animals, suggesting degrees of fast and slow and heavy and light. Children may select animals such as snails and slugs as the slowest of the animals to be imitated.
beat (pulse)	The teacher first claps, plays a percussion instrument, or improvises on the piano to the natural rhythm of the child's walk. After the child has learned the feeling of synchronizing his walk and the teacher's playing, he is asked to dramatize an activity that can be done with a steady beat, such as rowing, sawing, hammering, chopping wood, and shoveling snow.
heartbeat	Find, feel, and imitate the heartbeat. Fingers on the neck can find it. Children can discover when the heart beats faster and slower.
beat (quarter note)	Children need extensive and steadily repeated experience with the regular beat and its extensions into slow, fast, soft, loud, and accent. The

concept of beat (pulse) is formed from body movements, hearing, and seeing. The child feels the beat in his body responses and by playing percussion instruments (as extensions of the body). He feels the beat as he walks, marches, sways, hops, claps, slaps thighs, and by making other movements. He can also see the beat in repetitions of objects and pictures and in simple notation.

The beat can be described by walking. "How many different ways can people walk?" (slowly, quickly, lightly, heavily, tiredly, happily, like a rag doll, like a toy soldier). Chanting words and appropriate old sayings and poetry can reflect the beat and its divisions. Rhythmic rhymes like "Peas Porridge Hot," "Hickory Dickory Dock," and "Sing a Song of Sixpence" can be used; children can walk and clap the beat on the word syllable accents.

beat

The teacher can strum the Autoharp to the pulse of well-known songs that lend themselves to this activity, such as "This Old Man." The instrument can also be strummed by a child while the teacher presses the chord bars. The child can use rubber or plastic spatulas, certain paintbrushes, and whatever he can handle best to stroke the strings.

dividing the beat (eighth notes)

Running can be dramatized. "How many ways can people run?" (slowly, swiftly, racing-like, jogging-like).

(quarter and eighth) notes combined)

From children's names, select those that can be spoken in one and two syllables. Have children speak the names along with the clapping and drumming done on the first syllables:

name

Su - sy	Jim - my	Bob - by
Tom	Mae	Hope

After the children know how to keep the beat with each type of name, try having them experience the two types at one time by combining two groups of children, one speaking a one-syllable name, and the other speaking a two-syllable name. They can also experiment with combining names horizontally and repeating the pattern through the use of speech and percussion instruments.

Ab - ra - ham   Ma - ry   Ed

drum talk

Various speech-chants can relate to "drum talk" in which the rhythm pattern of the chant is played on the drum. The teacher does this activity first. It could be done in response to a chant such as "I *want* to eat *lunch.*"

This type of activity can be extended into many other rhythms of commonly-known words or instructions. More drum talk can be done with children's names in which the entire rhythm pattern is played. When two drums are used, one of high pitch and one of low pitch, the experience is heightened.

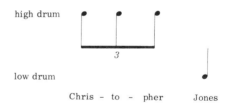

Chris - to - pher   Jones

rhythm pattern

Rhythm patterns that can be clapped, stamped, and later transferred to percussion instruments can be derived from nursery rhymes and sounds from the environment that are regular and uncomplicated. Chants that arise from play or from children's commentaries may also provide rhythm patterns to be imitated and developed with body and percussion sounds. Activities such as sawing, hammering, sweeping, chair-rocking, and knocking at a door can stimulate the recognition of rhythm patterns. Other sources of possible rhythmic development can come from body sounds such as thigh slapping, finger snapping, tongue clicking, humming, hissing, laughing, buzzing, gasping, whistling, and sh-h-h. Recognition of the concept *accent* can come from using rhythm patterns, particularly by changing the accent in the pattern.

ABA form improvising a dance

A well-known example of children experiencing a three-part form by dancing is that using clear examples of the form as illustrated by the song "Shoo Fly." A dance can be improvised, based on the same-different-same arrangement of the melody:

A   Shoo, fly, don't bother me,
      Shoo, fly, don't bother me,
      Shoo, fly, don't bother me,
      For I belong to nobody.

B   I feel, I feel, I feel,
      I feel like a morning star,
      I feel, I feel, I feel,
      I feel like a morning star,

A   Shoo, fly, don't bother me,
      Shoo, fly, don't bother me,
      Shoo, fly, don't bother me,
      For I belong to nobody.

exploratory center

This center requires space in which children can move freely in their responses to music, where they can reflect mood, tempo, rhythm, and melody with their movements. If classrooms cannot supply space for this, gymnasiums and auditoriums may suffice. Dramatic play may also take place in such areas.

singing and moving

The teacher sings:

           s   s   m   l   s   s   m
        "Can you do what I can do?"

and makes a motion. The children sing "I can do what you can do," and imitate the movement.

Representative Action Songs and Singing Games

Jack and Jill
Did You Ever See a Lassie?
Mulberry Bush
Clap Your Hands
Put Your Finger in the Air
Muffin Man
If You're Happy (clap,
  tap, stamp, nod, etc.)
Rig-a-jig-jig (walk, skip,
  gallop)
Farmer in the Dell
A-Tisket, A-Tasket

Can You Dance Santy Maloney?
Jim-Along Josie (walk, jump)
Rabbit in the Wood
A Little Pig
Train Is A-Coming (dramatize)
  This Is Music, Book I, Allyn
  and Bacon
Looby Lou
My Hat
Simon Says
Finger, Nose, and Toes
Pop! Goes the Weasel
Hokey-Pokey

Most of the songs in the *Hap Palmer Songbooks* induce action while at the same time they teach specific concepts found in the other areas of the curriculum. (Published by Educational Activities, Inc., these are contemporary-styled songs.) Other books that have been helpful for many years include *The Fireside Book of Children's Songs* edited by Winn and published by Simon and Schuster, Inc., New York, 1966, and *Growth Through Play* by Farina, Furth and Smith, published by Prentice-Hall, Inc., Englewood Cliffs, N.J., 1959. These books contain instructions for singing games. A typical music textbook, American Book Company's *New Dimensions in Music-K*, includes the following songs for movement:

Put Your Finger in the Air
Hokey Pokey
Jingle at the Window
Bow Belinda
Old Brass Wagon
London Bridge
Pawpaw Patch
Skip to My Lou
Eency Weency Spider
Knock at the Door
Where Is Thumkin?

Old MacDonald
Pony Song
One Elephant
This Old Man
Farmer in the Dell
Yankee Doodle (march)
  —and a section on
  piano pieces for
  rhythmic responses,
  pp. 156-86

Exemplary Recordings for Movement

Bowmar, 622 Rodier Drive, Glendale, Calif. 91201
  The Small Dancer and The Small Player recordings. Creative movement and percussion instruments.
  Rainy Day Records
  Rhythm Time, Albums 1, 2
  Holiday Rhythms
  Bowmar Orchestral Library (BOL)
  Animals and Circus BOL 51
  Marches BOL 54
  Nature and Make-believe BOL 52
  Pictures and Patterns BOL 53

Capitol Records Distributing Corp., Capitol Tower, Hollywood, Calif.
Listen, Move and Dance, Vol. 1. Exciting electronic and instrument sounds with no narrative; a creative approach. 90028.

Educational Activities, Inc., Freeport, N.Y. 11520
Movin'. Record or cassette (Hap Palmer), rock, classical, pop.
Mod Marches. Record or cassette (Hap Palmer).

Franson Corporation, 225 Park Avenue South, New York, N.Y.
Young People's Records (YPR)

Music for Movement, Ages 2-5

Little Indian Drum	YPR 619
Trains and Planes	YPR 706
Building a City	YPR 711
Rainy Day	YPR 712
Circus Comes to Town	YPR 713
Whoa, Little Horses	YPR 714
Jingle Bells and Other Songs for Winter Fun	YPR 718
Another Sing Along	YPR 723
Out of Doors	YPR 724
Look at Mitchie Banjo	YPR 729
Man Who Came to Our House	YPR 737
Who Wants a Ride	YPR 806
My Playmate the Wind	YPR 4501
Let's Play Together	YPR 4503

Dramatic Play, Ages 2-5

The Little Cowboy	YPR 716
The Little Fireman	YPR 615
Groucho Marx—Funniest Song	YPR 719
When I Grow Up	YPR 715
Chugging Freight Engine	YPR 718
Little Grey Ponies	YPR 735
Little Cowgirl	YPR 801
I'm Dressing Myself	YPR 803
Walk in the Forest	YPR 805
3 Little Trains	YPR 809
Let's Be Policemen	YPR 3401
Peter the Pusher	YPR 3405

Children's Record Guild (CRG)

Rhythmic Activity, Ages 2-4

Train to the Zoo	CRG 1001
Skittery Skattery	CRG 1005
Me, Myself, and I	CRG 1007
Castles in the Sand	CRG 1008
Sunday in the Park	CRG 1010
Train to the Farm	CRG 1011
Nothing to Do	CRG 1012
A Visit to My Little Friend	CRG 1017
Daddy Comes Home	CRG 1018
My Playful Scarf	CRG 1019
The Merry Toy Shop	CRG 1022
Sugar Lump Town	CRG 1023

I Am a Circus	CRG 1028
Let's Help Mommy	CRG 1032
Train to the Ranch	CRG 1038
Do This, Do That!	CRG 1040
Jump Back, Little Toad	CRG 1041

Rhythmic Activity, Ages 5-8

Ride 'Em Cowboy	CRG-5001
Strike Up the Band	CRG 5027

Dramatic Play, Ages 2-4

I Wish I Were	CRG 1006
Indoors When It Rains	CRG 1021
Let's Be Firemen	CRG 1024
Rhyme Me a Riddle	CRG 1025
Fog Boat Story	CRG 1027
When I Was Very Young	CRG 1031

Dramatic Play, Ages 5-8

Ship Ahoy	CRG 5003
Riddle Me This	CRG 5015
Silly Wil	CRG 5017
Build Me a House	CRG 5018
The Milk's Journey	CRG 5029

Folkways Records, 701 7th Avenue, New York, N.Y. 10036
This Is Rhythm (Ella Jenkins). Book of same name also available.
Dance Along. Rhythm improvisations.
Skip Rope Games.
Rhythm and Game Songs for the Little Ones (Ella Jenkins).

For Ella Jenkins recordings, see Lyons catalog for handy listing. 530 Riverview Ave., Elkhart, Ind. 46514.

RCA Music Service, Educational Department, 1133 Avenue of the Americas, New York, N.Y. 10036.
Dance-A-Story records and cassettes:
Little Duck
Noah's Ark
Balloons
Flappy and Floppy
The Toy Tree
At the Beach

RCA Records, Educational Sales, P.O. Box RCA 1000, Indianapolis, Ind. 46291. For pre-K-4.
Music to Have Fun By, Vols. 1, 2 (cassettes)

Kimbo Educational, P.O. Box 477, Long Branch, N.J. 07740. Catalog A, *Early Childhood—Special Education.*

Exemplary Recordings for Use with Specific Movement Activities

Note: The symbol AM refers to the RCA *Adventures in Music* albums. The symbol BOL refers to the Bowmar Orchestral Library.

Walking

Thomson: "Walking Song" from *Acadian Songs and Dances* (changes of tempo), AM 1 v 1.

Kabalevsky: "Pantomime" from *The Comedians* (large steps), AM 1 v 1.

Moussorgsky: "Bydlo" from *Pictures at an Exhibition* (lumbering steps), AM 2 v 1.

Prokofiev: "Departure" from *Winter Holiday* (fast steps), AM 2 v 1.

Tschaikovsky: "Dance of the Little Swans" from *Swan Lake* (on tiptoe), AM 1 v 1.

Marching

Herbert: "March of the Toys" from *Babes in Toyland*, AM 2 v 1.

Vaughan Williams: "March Past of the Kitchen Utensils" from *The Wasps*, AM 3 v 1.

Lully: "March" from *Ballet Suite*, AM 3 v 2.

Grieg: "Norwegian Rustic March" from *Lyric Suite*, AM 4 v 2.

Gould: *American Salute*, AM 5 v 1.

Running

Gluck: "Air Gai" from *Iphigenie in Aulis*, AM 1 v 1.

Bizet: "The Ball" from *Children's Games*, AM 1 v 1.

Hopping

Moussorgsky: "Ballet of the Unhatched Chicks" from *Pictures at an Exhibition*, AM 1 v 1.

Bach: "Gigue" from *Suite No. 3*, AM 1 v 1.

Gretry: "Tambourin" from *Cephale et Procris*, AM 2 v 1.

Jumping

Bizet: "Leap Frog" from *Children's Games*, AM 1 v 1.

Massenet: "Aragonaise" from *Le Cid*, AM 1 v 1.

Skipping or Galloping

Gretry: "Gigue" from *Cephale et Procris*, AM 1 v 1.

Bach: "Gigue" from *Suite No. 3*, AM 1 v 1.

Whirling

Rossini-Respighi: "Tarantella" from *The Fantastic Toy Shop*, AM 3 v 2.

Massenet: "Aragonaise" from *Le Cid*, AM 1.

Swaying, Rocking

Bizet: "Cradle Song" from *Children's Games*, AM 1 v 1.

Offenbach: "Barcarolle" from *Tales of Hoffman*, AM 3 v 1.

Saint-Saëns: "The Swan" from *Carnival of the Animals*, AM 3 v 2.

Delibes: "Waltz of the Doll" from *Copelia*, AM 1 v 1.

Sliding, Gliding

Khachaturian: "Waltz" from *Masquerade Suite*, AM 4 v 2.

Prokofiev: "Waltz on Ice" from *Children's Suite*, AM 3 v 2.

Tschaikovsky: "Waltz" from *The Sleeping Beauty*, AM 4 v 2.

Mixed Movements

A Visit to My Little Friend, Children's Record Guild, Franson Corporation 1017 (ages 2-4)

Animals and Circus, BOL 51.

Nature and Make-believe, BOL 52.

Rhythmic Movements
Bartok: "Bear Dance" from *Hungarian Sketches,* AM 3 v 2.

Dramatization (also Mood)
Debussy: "Golliwog's Cakewalk" from *Children's Corner Suite,* BOL 63.
Grieg: "Ase's Death" from *Peer Gynt Suite No. 1,* BOL 59.
Ibert: *The Little White Donkey,* AM 2 v 1.
Kabalevsky: "March and Comedian's Gallop" from *The Comedians,* AM 3 v l.

Tempo and Dynamics
Debussy: *Fêtes* (Festival), BOL 70.

Beat (pulse)
Dvorak: *Slavonic Dance No. 7,* AM 4 v 2.
Herbert: "Dagger Dance" from *Natoma,* AM 3 v 1.
Offenbach: "Barcarolle" from *Tales of Hoffman,* AM 3 to 1.
   —and many marches.

Animals
Griffes: *The White Peacock,* AM 5 v 1.
Liadov: *Dance of the Mosquito,* BOL 52.
Rimsky-Korsakoff: *Flight of the Bumble-Bee,* BOL 52.
Saint-Saëns: "The Swan" from *Carnival of the Animals,* AM 3 v 2.
Saint-Saëns: "The Elephant" from *Carnival of the Animals,* AM 1 v 2.

Machines
Mossolov: Iron Foundry on *Sounds of New Music,* Folkways, FX 6160.
Villa-Lobos: "Little Train of the Caipira" from *Bachianas Brasileiras No. 2,* AM 6 v 2.

Accelerando
Grieg: "In the Hall of the Mountain King" from *Peer Gynt Suite,* AM 3 v 2; BOL 59.

Accent
Herbert: "Dagger Dance" from *Natoma,* AM 3 v 1.
Rossini-Respighi: "Can Can" from *The Fantastic Toy Shop,* AM 3.
Shostakovitch: "Petite Ballerina" from *Ballet Suite No. 1,* AM 2 v 1.

Legato (for resting also)
Bizet: "Cradle Song" from *Children's Games,* AM 1 v 1.
Faure: "Berceuse" from *Dolly,* AM 2 v 1.
Stravinsky: "Berceuse" from *Firebird Suite,* AM 1 v 1.

Staccato
Anderson: *The Syncopated Clock,* Keyboard Junior Records.
Prokofiev: "March" from *Summer Day Suite,* Am 1 v 1.
Vaughan Williams: "March Past of the Kitchen Utensils" from *The Wasps,* AM 3 v 1.

Two-Part Form

Bach: "Badinerie" from *Suite No. 2 in B Minor,* AM 3 v 1.

Handel: "Bourrée" and "Menuetto" from *Royal Fireworks Music,* AM 3 v 2; BOL 62.

Three-Part Form

Stravinsky: "Berceuse" from *Firebird Suite,* AM 1 v 1.

Brahms: *Hungarian Dance No. 1 in C Minor,* AM 5 v 2.

Offenbach: "Barcarolle" from *Tales of Hoffman,* AM 3 v 1.

References

Cherry, Clare. *Creative Movement for the Developing Child.* Belmont, Calif.: Fearon Publishers, 1968. For nursery school.

Gerhardt, Lydia A. *Moving and Knowing: The Young Child Orients Himself in Space.* Englewood Cliffs, N.J.: Prentice-Hall, Inc., 1973.

Groetzinger, Isabelle, and Gode, Marguerite. *Play and Sing: Hayes Action Song Book for Kindergarten and Primary.* Wilkinsburg, Pa.: Hayes School Publishing Co., 1958.

Miller, Mary, and Zajan, Paula. *Finger Play.* New York: G. Schirmer, 1955.

Richardson, Allen L. *Tooters, Tweeters, Strings and Beaters.* New York: Grosset and Dunlap Publishers, 1964. An instrument identification book for young children with poems and pictures. Includes six puzzles in pictures.

Salisburg, Helen Wright. *Finger Fun, Songs and Rhythms for the Very Young.* Los Angeles: Cowman Publications, 1955.

Sinclair, Caroline B. *Movement of the Young Child Ages 2-6.* Columbus, Ohio: Charles E. Merrill, 1975.

Winn, Marie; Miller, Allan; and Kushkin, Karla. *What Shall We Do.* New York: Harper & Row, Publishers, 1970. Play songs and singing games.

Singing

When children of preschool age sing, they do not begin singing the songs we see printed in books; they invent their own little songlets or tonal fragments, during their play. Singing comes naturally for the nursery school child. At first, short songs utilizing only two, three, or four tones may be improvised. Answering roll call by singing, imitating bird songs or sighing like the wind will help find singing voices. Even when children are able to sing melodies that are in the teacher's song books, the words they sing to them may or should be quite different from those in the books. The words children need to sing are those that relate to their everyday living or to experiences they can comprehend and have interest in at their stage of development. Thus, teachers and children may create more songs and song texts of their own than of those they derive from books, and this is the way it should be in nursery school and kindergarten. The approach to singing should be extremely flexible. If some part of the melody is not in the vocal range of the child, the teacher must either use it in a lower key or find some appropriate way to alter the melody to better suit the child or group. Songs should be adapted to children, not children to songs.

The development of singing may begin with the child listening to the singing of others. He next sings spontaneously to accompany his rhythmic movements and actions in his play, and eventually responds with body movements to songs he hears others sing. The teacher remembers not to expect the same response from all children because they are at different developmental levels. The teacher sings with the child whenever possible in order to give him the idea that people can sing the same pitches together.

The typical two-year-old engages in spontaneous singing and the teacher encourages this by singing with the child when appropriate. Unaccompanied singing is best because learning melody is for a child sufficiently difficult without his being confused by other pitches. Repetition is very necessary, and the list of teacher-selected formal songs for a year is not extensive. The teacher makes up chants to use with swinging, resting, rocking, jumping, and in whatever other activity the child is involved. Grouping and formal music periods are to be avoided.

The typical three-year-old experiments with singing with another person or with a small group. He may lag behind in the song and may sing other words. The teacher does not ask all children to sing; he provides opportunities but does not insist. Songs from last year are continued. There is much informal singing, sometimes with several children, permitting children to leave or to join the group as they wish. The song repertoire is expanded with new short songs of different types including action, simple imaginative, holiday, seasonal, and humorous songs. A very simple accompaniment can be added to some songs; this often consists of one percussion intrument.

The typical four-year-old sings with another person or a small group; he is able to match some, most, or all of the pitches and becomes able to sing a song alone. The teacher selects songs with content understood by and of interest to the children, and provides an environment in which singing occurs throughout the day. Songs of greater variety that contain more complex and detailed imagination can be used, including some heard on television. Mother Goose songs, songs about animals and work are favorites. Echo-type songs help in tone matching. Children's original songs are often used. More songs can be accompanied in simple ways, played on the Autoharp, guitar, or bells. Piano accompaniments should be of very simple nature, never interfering with the child's need to hear the melody distinctly. The teacher sings comments and questions to children instead of speaking, but takes care not to overdo this. The late four's and the five's enjoy cumulative songs such as "I Bought Me a Cat," "Old MacDonald," and "Over in the Meadow."

The typical five-year-old has favorite songs, recognizes them, and asks for them. The teacher selects songs of easy ranges at first, beginning with 3-, 4-, and 5-note ranges, and pitches them in the child's natural range in order to assist him to match pitches successfully. The "G" above middle "C" is a likely center of the child's voice range, although there are marked individual differences in this. The range of pitches in songs gradually expands from a five-note range to six notes, and to an octave for the more advanced children. The teacher selects songs that vary in range so that the singing ranges are expanded and the tonal memory is increased. Songs with repetitious parts are good to use to help children match pitches. Simple accompaniments can be used. These children are more interested in work songs than are the younger children, and their interests include animals of the farm, circus, zoo, and animal pets in the home. Outer space, cowboys, Indians, family, types of transportation expressed in song can relate to other subject areas. Songs to dramatize, easy singing games, and more involved action songs can be used. Fives enjoy composing songs that contain imagination closely related to reality. The content of children's original songs is usually derived from their reenacting the events of their daily lives. Through such dramatic play, the child pretends to be the person or thing he knows from his environment and to be involved in events as he understands them. Time should be devoted to utilizing songs originating from this source since they are relevant and absorbing to the child. Hand signs for *so* and *mi* can be used with appropriate singing-listening-moving games.

so   mi

These motions can be introduced to children by a clapping hands position for *so* and a slapping thighs position for *mi*.

Children who are musically advanced may want to learn more hand signs, first that for *la*, then *do* and *re*.

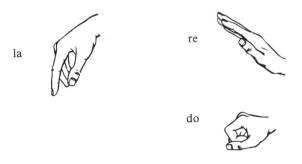

la

re

do

The Beginnings of Singing

In the first year of life, infants engage their speech mechanisms in repetitive sounds such as cooing, babbling, and other such experimentations. The latter half of that year they experiment with different pitches and voice inflections as they continue with this, and these result in sounds such as ba-ba, ma-ma, and da-da. This experimenting is continued by two- and three-year-olds with much imitation of sounds observed in their environment such as those of people, animals, nature, machines, and common objects. Their almost constant motion is characteristically accompanied by chanting, a kind of song-speech. Sometimes the chant will have few or no recognizable words. At other times, the word repetition is very clear and may consist of a short melodic motive or even approach a short song. Some form of chant accompanies most of the activities in which they engage, thus it is going on almost continuously. "Chanting, the most obvious link between speech and rhythm, suggests itself immediately as a most natural response. For the child it is as instinctive as it is delightful. For him it is a part of play, a source of interesting images and sounds. Whether he chants nursery rhymes or rhymes he helps create about people and things with which he is intimate . . . he enters into this activity naturally and joyfully. With guidance, his chanting can open the door to all rhythmic and melodic experiences. Words can begin to take on color; the quality of speech begins to reflect the meanings he is trying to portray. Highs and lows—both in pitch and dynamics—can develop. And, throughout, a feeling for the various kinds of meter is acquired." (Wheeler and Raebeck, 1972) From this background, singing will emerge. While it is evident that children have complete interest and fascination in their own vocal productions, they also enjoy being sung to. At this early age, they enjoy the repetition, simplicity, and word-rhythm contained in many nursery rhymes, poems, and simple stories, especially those in which they may participate in some manner, either vocally or physically.

The process of learning to sing begins with the child playing with sounds. He hears and understands them before he can reproduce them. However, he experiments with voice inflection and responds as best he can vocally, although he may still be unable to reproduce with his voice the pitches his ear comprehends. He may observe when others are not singing correctly even though he cannot sing correctly himself. When he begins to try to sing the songs he has heard, these may be performed only partially as he intends; they may be in part improvised variants of those songs. Eventually he creates songs that possess musical attributes such as recognizable form, phrases, and repetition. He finds extra-musical uses for songs, such as labeling, self image, following instructions, enjoying repetition, and general social interaction. He performs one act at a time, either moving or singing, not both at once. The child's singing ability is part of a developmental process, and he should be recognized as the one who knows best which portion of a song he is able to imitate. The teacher should not waste time trying to have young children reproduce pitches and tunes accurately when they are as yet unable to do so. However, the sense of tonality can be encouraged by such means as the teacher's improvising words in song over one repeated chord on guitar or Autoharp, such as the G minor chord, then encouraging children to do the same.

Learning to Sing

While much is yet to be researched regarding ways children learn to sing, there is a sequential development that, when known, is helpful to parents and teachers. For children not yet using their singing voices, there can be speech activities in which the child learns to control flexible pitch levels used in speech. These activities can include those as simple as saying his name and the names of objects in his environment, saying "Hello" and "Good morning," chanting words, proceeding to speaking children's poetry, and adding variations in pitch to these. When children are experimenting with singing, parents and/or teachers should listen, sing their songs with them, and sing them back to the children, thus encouraging their melodic improvisations. There should be one-to-one singing, with parent, teacher, or teacher's aide helping one child at a time so that he learns that it is possible for two people to sing together on the same pitch. The experiencing of such unison pitch is exceedingly important. It may be done in short melodic phrases and songs in whatever range the child is able to use, either the speaking range or higher. This is tone-matching experience in which some children can match only lower pitches at this stage. In trying to help children with both the concept of singing and of matching pitch, teachers often have them imitate environmental sounds such as the wind, sirens, bird calls, and auto horns. Little echo games using simple melodic patterns of one, two, and three pitches in a higher range than the speaking voice are often helpful. At this point, singing the *oo* sound before singing words of songs is advocated by some.[1] Researchers over the years have emphasized two points: that the child needs (1) to learn to hear, judge, and control his own voice, and (2) to experience unison (matching pitch) which means that the child must learn *how it feels* when he matches the pitch of his voice with that of another sound producer. The teacher's task is to help every young child learn to recognize this sensation.

---

1. This developmental sequence is based in part on the work of A. Oren Gould, *Developing Specialized Programs for Singing in the Elementary School,* as reviewed by Dr. Gould in *Bulletin No. 17* of the Council for Research in Music Education. The research was supported by the Cooperative Research Program of the Office of Education, U.S. Department of Health, Education and Welfare.

Tone Matching Games

Change the pitch to suit the child's natural range.

Tell me if you're here to-day.   Ger-al-dine   (echo by child)   I'm   here!

Don - ald   (echo)   Christ-o-fer   (echo)   An - na - bel   (echo)

Sing "la." Object of the game is for the child to echo back.

The   sun is shin-ing bright to-day.   (la)   If your shoes are black sing back.   (la)

The most effective time to help a child begin a successful lifetime of singing experience is during the nursery school years. When the child is learning to sing, work with him without an instrumental accompaniment. He has all he can do to concentrate on the melody; additional pitches in an accompaniment can only add confusion at this stage. Use songs in which the child sings only a short section. Repetitious and echo-type songs are helpful because children must first listen, then answer. The child is introduced to group singing very gradually. One way to attract him into a group is to tape one of his song improvisations and have the group sing it. Songs should be used and created that grow out of the firsthand experiences of the children.

Songs for the Three-, Four-, and Five-year-olds

When children's normal capacities are considered, one finds that many songs have to be composed by teachers, improvised, or brought to school by the children. This section is concerned with a sequence of ranges for such songs as well as ways to initiate the teaching of singing.

Most children of nursery school age begin singing within a naturally restricted range. The Hungarian composer-educator Zoltán Kodály believed the beginning singing range of most of these children to be from D above middle C to middle line B, the interval of a sixth.

In his book *Fifty Nursery Songs* he suggests beginning songs at the low part of this range. (Zoltán Kodály, 1964) The first songs in the book utilize only two notes, D and E, he next employs three notes, D, E, and G, and the pentatonic framework upon which the book is constructed begins to emerge.[2] After this Kodály supplies songs with four notes, D, E, F-sharp, and A, and finally with five notes, adding B to the four. Denise Bacon follows Kodály's concepts in her songbook *Let's Sing Together!* (Denise Bacon, 1973) In it she utilized the same pentatonic framework to set to music words from *Mother Goose* and other sources suited to American boys and girls. However, she began her book with the two pitches E and G used in songs based on the descending minor third interval, the easiest interval to sing.

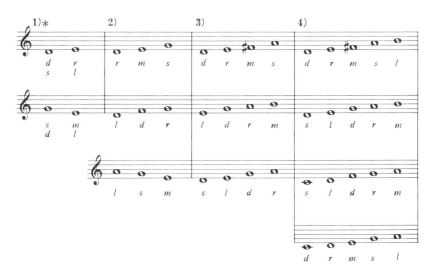

*The *do re* and *so la* songs were found to be difficult for young children. They were abandoned in favor of beginning with the *so mi* and *do la* songs.

2. There are many pentatonic scales in the world, but the one most used by American teachers is compared to the major scale with steps 4 and 7 omitted, thus eliminating half steps, which are difficult for young children to sing.

The Kodály and Bacon songbooks do not use ranges that include middle C; the author has added them. She observed Hungarian children taught by the Kodály method singing middle C and lower pitches. However, she agrees that songs for this age group should not stress the pitch of middle C and lower pitches.

(The following examples are numbered in direct relation to the preceding Kodály song pitches.)

These books exemplify what nursery school teachers can do rather easily: make up their own songs for their own children's needs. Such songs should be brief, easy to sing, with words that are interesting and understandable to the children and which can encourage games and motions. The meter is largely 2/4, and the note symbols are mainly

Denise Bacon includes a few songs in fast 6/8 meter. The nursery school teacher may wish to follow the pitch and range sequence found in the two above-mentioned books.

All of the above examples imply major tonality. It is easily possible to utilize the pentatonic scale in a way that implies minor tonality.

The Kodály method discourages piano accompaniment for such songs and also frowns on the use of the Autoharp. This disapproval is something with which most American teachers disagree, as the Autoharp has become standard equipment in the schools. Those who follow the Kodály method believe that the use of these instruments tends to produce out-of-tune singing. There is reason to believe that young children need to hear a great deal of unaccompanied melody, as stated earlier. However, no one objects to clapping, the use of the percussion instruments, especially the small hand drum, small cymbals, woodblock, and triangles, or the simple uses of the xylophone, bells, and recorder. Many teachers use simple piano accompaniments and many use a well-tuned Autoharp in order to place the songs in a harmonic context. The xylophone, bells or metallophone can sound simple fifths (bourdons) to accompany the pentatonic songs. They are frequently sounded throughout the song:

By using this sequence of song ranges children will be helped to learn to sing well, and after they can sing the five-note songs they will be able to progress to the more difficult songs having larger ranges as ordinarily used in kindergarten. However, some younger children will surprise us by their ability to sing the more difficult songs. We should never lose sight of individual differences in singing (or in any other skill).

The children's chant approach is another view of learning to sing. It begins with the descending minor third interval of G to E. Because this interval is assumed to be the easiest one to sing, it is a natural starting point. Using this interval, the teacher sings names and short sentences that encourage singing responses of the same type from the children.

Example:

5 3 5   5 3 5 3 3 5 5 3

teacher: Hel-lo, what's your name? child: My name is Jo-seph-ine! After the ability to do this echoing has been mastered, C scale-tone 6 is added to these small (but important) improvisations:

5 5 5 6 5 3   5 5 5 6 5 3
Who just had a hair-cut?   I just had a hair-cut.

5 3 5 6 5   5 3 5 6 5
Who can shut the door?   I can shut the door.

5 5 6 5 3 6 5   5 5 6 5 3 6 5
Who is go-ing to the zoo? We are go-ing to the zoo.

The above examples illustrate the tendency of young children to prefer scale tone 5 (*so*) as their concept of the home tone—a different idea than that of many adults who have been conditioned to accept only 1 or *do* as the home tone. They also illustrate the well-known *children's chant* that children use to communicate with each other in many ways and manners ranging from singing lullabys to taunts such as "John-ny has a girl friend." It follows that songs based upon or which include this combination of pitches will be easier to sing than songs organized differently. This method next adds scale tones 2 and 1, which complete the pentatonic scale. After this, octave doublings can be utilized: 1^1, 2^1, 3^1, and 6_1.

Some teachers encourage children to make up short songs about "Susy One-Note," in which only one pitch is used. After this has been done successfully, songs are made up about "Susy Two-Note." The two notes can be the two black keys of the piano or bell set immediately above middle C. "Susy Three-Note" may be the group of three black keys just above the "two-note" pitches. When these are put together, the common pentatonic scale results, and songs are sung within that scale. Other teachers begin with one pitch such as middle C, then add D, E, and on up to F and G. After this they expand the range upward.

With all these methods, the teacher should remember that by giving a child a limited number of resonator tone bars that reflect any of the tonal groupings mentioned in this section, the child can create tunes and songs within that given range. This is one of the avenues for children's improvisation and composition.

Many improvised songs are not worth saving since their value is greatest at the time of immediate need or in the act of creation. However, good ones should be written down to be used again. Should the teacher not be able to notate a song, the tape recorder can be used to preserve it to play for another teacher or a parent who can notate it. Some songs children create should be tape-recorded in order for the child to hear a good performance of it (be sure it is good enough to bolster his confidence in composing) and to retain a record of it so that it can be notated if this seems desirable. Children like to see their songs in notation whether or not they undersand notation to the extent of reading it.

When the singing range of children has expanded to encompass the octave, an easy way to improvise songs is to move up, or up and down, the C major scale. If each pitch is used only once, a statement with eight syllables is needed to go up or down the scale. Example: "Twelve o'clock is time for our lunch." Scale songs can grow more complex with repeated pitches. An example of a traditional scale song is "Taffy." Some children may be able to play it on the bells.

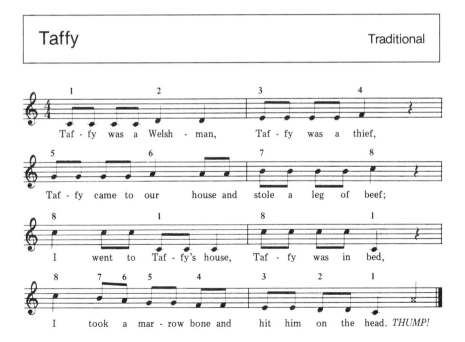

Song or story-in-song dramatization in opera style is an activity that encourages children to use their singing voices. A theme song might be created, such as:

s m l s m
Let's sing a sto-ry;

m m r s m
Sing what we will do.

s m l s m
Let's sing a sto-ry;

m m r s d
We will act it, too!

The story could be from a nursery rhyme such as *Mary Had a Little Lamb, Old King Cole,* and *Little Miss Muffet;* or a plot can be created about shopping, a trip to the zoo, or any subject of interest. The plots are to be changed or extended, with singing conversations. Tonality is not stressed; the singing should be free improvisation, except for the known songs.

Songs and Music Concepts

When he sings, the learner is involved with both the rhythm of the song or chant and with pitch, thus songs are useful in teaching many aspects of rhythm and pitch concepts. High and low in pitch are difficult adult abstractions that must be taught. They are concepts that can be learned through songs that lead children to act out high and low and the degrees of each. Octave and scale songs can be found by using the indexes of the music series books, but teachers often make up their own songs to teach these concepts. Words such as "The sky is up high; the grass is down low" can be sung to high and low pitches, with the children reaching high, then touching the grass (low). Later on, scale-line melodies can be acted out to show descending or ascending pitches, and concepts of melodic contour begin to emerge, with body movement dramatizing the changing pitches. Loud and soft singing is learned when different subject matter is sung; lullabys must be soft to put babies to sleep; fire engines will be loud when sung about, and trains become gradually louder as they approach and gradually softer after they pass by. The teacher should plan to use songs that are contrasting to illustrate staccato and legato, slow and fast, loud and soft, same and different, short and long, up and down, and pitch step and skips. Tone matching, tonal memory, beat, meter, and at least rudimentary concepts of the phrase and song form can also be taught through songs. Tone quality can be studied by seeking the best way to communicate the message of a song in tone. The tone quality needed for a lullaby is different than that needed for a marching song, for example.

Song Sources

Folk songs are often beautiful and easy for children to learn. Many are pentatonic in origin. Since most of them are also adult in origin, the words are frequently changed or abandoned and other verses substituted that are understandable to young children. However, some adult songs have high appeal because they are rhythmically and/or melodically attractive and have subject matter that children understand. The nursery school and kindergarten books of the various music series provide easy access to folk songs and other songs selected for specific teaching purpose. Song collections devoted solely to the needs of nursery school children are very few; this means that the teacher is often compelled to review many pages of elementary-school song collections to find those that are applicable to the nursery school. On the other hand, some appropriate songs are "caught" by young children from radio and television, and can be brought into the classroom from this source. The teacher should feel completely free to change melodies and words to fit the classroom situation. There are elementary school folk song collections by Ruth Crawford Seeger that have been useful sources of melodies and words for many teachers: *American Folk Songs for Children* and *Animal Folk Songs for Children* are those most widely used. Some foreign nations have emphasized the nursery school and supported it for many years, and if one can read the language, their elementary school song collections provide another source of song material. *Gentil Coquelicot* (Pretty Field Poppy) by Henriette Goldenbaum, obtainable from Editions du Scarabee, 3, rue de la Montagne Ste-Genevieve, Paris-V, France, is one such volume. The fifty songs it contains are for children ages 3 to 7. In this country. *Singing With Children,* published by the Wadsworth Publishing Company, Belmont, Calif., is an elementary school collection for teachers that includes songs suited for the nursery school, and Marie Winn's *Fireside Book of Children's Songs,* published by Simon and Schuster, is another. *The Hap Palmer Song Books,* and cassettes published by Educational Activities, Freeport, N.Y., consist of composed songs with a contemporary flavor. The Choksy reference at the end of this chapter also contains useful songs.

A source of songs that must not be overlooked is the children themselves. They bring with them the songs of the home, of their cultural orientation, and those they have absorbed from recordings, radio, and television. This song source can be very helpful to the teacher and should be utilized whenever appropriate to teach music and to develop the self-esteem of the children who contribute the songs. Certain television programs for young children have produced many songs they learn and enjoy singing, and those that come from America's diverse cultural communities can be particularly fascinating and instructive. Parents can assist with this, and teachers should ask their help in bringing the songs of the home and the school together in the child's own naturally integrated world.

Teaching Songs

When children are rested and ready for a new experience they will enjoy hearing the teacher sing a new song for them. The song will have been well learned and memorized so that its performance will be accepted by the children as a sincere communication of something interesting. Such a song will have been selected by the teacher in view of her objectives; she knows why the song is of value in helping children learn music and possibly in helping them understand some other subject area also, as the following chapter will illustrate. She may introduce the song by telling a short related story or by stating background information or arousing interest by questions such as "What?" "Where?" "Who?" "How?" and "Why?" when these are applicable. Some songs need no introduction; they communicate directly. A new song is sung in its entirety once or twice. The teacher may need to explain words of the song not clearly understood by the children. If there are aspects of dramatization or rhythmic response, the children may participate in these ways almost at once. Over a period of several days the teacher will continue to sing the song. Those children most interested will begin to sing parts of it with the teacher, especially if the song calls for answers to questions or contains a dialog between two people, a person and an animal, or two animals. Some children will respond at first only with physical actions; others may sing only a word or a short section, while still others may sing along but not at the same time as the teacher, lagging behind and not always with the same words. Arranging for brief opportunities for children to listen, then sing, will eventually result in successful singing. Be careful about asking children if they want to sing; some may say "No." The final learning of a song is often done by singing the song in sections, possibly in phrases or short verses, before it is sung in its entirety by the children. Children should never be forced to sing. The teacher may hum or sing a song being learned during other work or play as a reinforcement procedure.

When children have learned familiar melodies, new words can be sung to them. These new song texts can be created by children or teacher to refer to events of the day. For example, the new words to the tune of "Mary Had a Little Lamb" might be "Suzy has new shoes today," or any other idea that suits the moment.

Songs can be made more interesting by planning new or different aspects to be added to them as they are sung over days and weeks. For example, various visual aids can assist. Introducing a song by means of a question such as, "I am going to sing a song about a . . . ," and having the children identify or guess which song it will be, is another small change in procedure. Accompanying a known song with different but appropriate percussion instruments will give the song a new feeling. Pantomime is another method. Pitch-level conducting can assist children to sing pitch changes more easily, and it gives them something different to watch. Role playing and dramatization can add further variety. Taking turns is another variant; the teacher sings one verse and the children sing another, or the teacher sings a question in a song and the class answers, or vice versa. If the teacher gives this some thought, a song can be presented somewhat differently almost every time it is sung, and interest in singing can be heightened measurably. However, children also like the security of repetition, so that a sensible balance between repetition and change should be the rule.

Criteria for Selecting Songs

Young children like songs that are simple, direct, and repetitious, and having subject matter with which they are familiar. They enjoy songs about themselves, animals and what they do, nature, machines, holidays, playthings, and seasons. Nonsense and humorous songs hold high appeal. A good song will possess some of the following criteria:

appropriate range
usually short
a clear pulse and
    distinct rhythm
a simple, easy-to-sing
    melody

repetition and/or echo parts
dialog (question and answer)
understandable content
elements that help children
    learn music concepts

Other attributes include the text being worthy and easy to sing, the text and music agreeing in mood, and the fact that other children and the teacher have liked the song.

A song such as "John the Rabbit" is good because children enjoy the story of the rabbit eating the garden to the distress of the gardener, and because all they need to do at first is to sing the part of the rabbit—one pitch repeated at intervals throughout the song while the teacher sings the part of the gardener. The venerable "Are You Sleeping?" and "Three Blind Mice" are useful after children gain control of an octave range because the echo parts are built into the melody. When using these the teacher needs to have a sign for when she sings and when the children sing; this sign is usually simply pointing toward herself when she sings and pointing to the children when they are to echo the part she just sang. Another useful song of the echo-and-answer type is "The Sparrow's School" or "Chichi-papa," a song from Japan that appears in several of the music series.

There are always exceptions to any criteria, and one is that if interest in a song is sufficiently high, four-year-olds will learn comparatively long and complex songs. No teacher should hold a child back if he is able to accomplish skills above the norm; he should be put in contact with songs of interest to him through which he can grow musically at his own rate.

Examples of Songs of Limited Range Found in Many Books

Three-note Range

Hot Cross Buns	This can be played on bell and piano black keys
Merrily We Roll Along	Teacher change the word "roll" to an action such as walk, clap, etc.
Good News (refrain)	
Trampin' (refrain)	

Four-note Range

Hokey Pokey	This song is found in many places including *Music for Early Childhood* in the New Dimensions Series, American Book Company, and in *Fireside Book of Children's Songs,* Simon and Schuster
Sally Go Round	The version referred to here is found in *Basic Music* by Nye and Bergethon, Prentice-Hall, Inc.
A-Hunting We Will Go	The version with this range is also found in *Basic Music*

Five-note Range

Mary Had a Little Lamb	In *Singing With Children* (SWC) and many books
Go Tell Aunt Rhody	SWC and *Basic Music*
Lightly Row	*Basic Music*
Jingle Bells (refrain)	SWC
Grandma Grunts	*Basic Music*
Oats, Peas, Beans and Barley	*Basic Music* and *Fireside Book of Children's Songs.* Sing "la" rather than the words
Sleep, Baby, Sleep	*Basic Music*
Elephants or the Elephant	SWC, New Dimensions Series *Music for Early Childhood*
Ring Around a Rosey	*Songs for the Nursery School,* Willis Music Co.
My Dreydl	
Jim-Along Josie	

Six-note Range

Hush, Little Baby	SWC
The Ducklings	SWC
Down by the Station	SWC
This Old Man	SWC
Old MacDonald	Traditional
Baa Baa Black Sheep	Traditional
London Bridge	Traditional
Skip To My Lou	SWC
Hickory Dickory Dock	SWC
Looby Lou	SWC
Queen Caroline	*This Is Music For Today*: Book One, Allyn and Bacon, Inc., 1967.

Recent Music Textbooks

Music textbooks have long included the kindergarten; now they are beginning to include the nursery school as well. Nursery school teachers have used kindergarten books because much of the material in them is adaptable to the nursery school. However, they are often written with the large group in mind rather than the small group or individual child.

An advantage in using music textbooks is that the songs are grouped and classified for specific purposes. Helpful suggestions for the teacher accompany each song, and the indexes make finding songs about the family, holidays, people and their work, animals, nature, etc., an easy matter. Thus the author suggests that the reader examine these and subsequently published textbooks to find the songs that will assist the teacher in planning her music program. A careful study of their indexes will be rewarding.

> *Comprehensive Musicianship Through Classroom Music.* Reading, Mass.: Addison-Wesley Publishing Co., 1972.
>
> *Discovering Music Together: Early Childhood.* Chicago, Ill.: Follett Educational Corp., 1968.
>
> *Exploring Music: Kindergarten.* New York, N.Y.: Holt, Rinehart and Winston, 1975.
>
> *Silver Burdett Music: Early Childhood.* Morristown, N.J.: Silver Burdett Co., 1978.
>
> *New Dimensions: Music for Early Childhood.* New York, N.Y.: American Book Company, 1976.
>
> *Spectrum of Music: Teacher's Resource Book K.* Riverside, N.J.: Macmillan Publishing Co., 1974. (Lacks classified index)
>
> *This Is Music for Kindergarten and Nursery School.* Boston, Mass.: Allyn and Bacon, Inc., 1965.

Exemplary Recordings for Singing

Bowmar, 622 Rodier Drive, Glendale, Calif. 91201
> *The Small Singer,* Vols. 1, 2. Songbooks and recordings.

Educational Activities, Inc., Freeport, N.Y. 11520
> *Folk Song Carnival.* Record or cassette (Hap Palmer).

Folkways Records, 701-7th Avenue, New York, N.Y. 10036
> *Early-Early Childhood Songs* (Ella Jenkins).
> *You'll Sing a Song and I'll Sing a Song* (Ella Jenkins).

Franson Corporation, 225 Park Avenue South, New York, N.Y.
> Children's Record Guild, Ages 5-8 (CRG)

Bring a Song, Johnny	CRG 5010
Come to the Party	CRG 5032

> Young People's Records, Ages 2-5 (YPR)

Sing Along	YPR 722
Singing in the Kitchen	YPR 730
Mary Martin Sings	YPR 731

Golden Records Educational Division, Michael Brent Publications, Inc., Port Chester, N.Y. 10573.
> *Ding-Dong School Singing Games*
> *Musical Mother Goose*

Songbooks

Bailey, Charity, and Holsaert, Eunice. *Sing a Song with Charity Bailey.* New York: Plymouth Music Co., Inc.

Bertail, Inez. *Complete Nursery Songbook.* New York: Lothrop, Lee & Shepard Co.

Fowke, Edith. *Sally Go Round the Sun.* Garden City, N.Y.: Doubleday & Company, Inc., 1969. Three-hundred songs, rhymes, and games for children ages four through ten.

Glazer, Tom. *Eye Winker, Tom Tinker, Chin Chopper.* Garden City, N.Y.: Doubleday & Company, Inc., 1972. Finger-play songs for preschool and kindergarten.

Jenkins, Ella; Krane, Sherman; and Lipschutz, Peggy. *The Ella Jenkins Songbook for Children.* New York: Oak Publications, 1966. Twenty-six songs and chants.

Kersey, Robert E. *Just Five.* Melville, N.Y.: Belwin Mills. A collection of eighty-four pentatonic songs.

Landeck, Beatrice. *Songs to Grow On.* New York: Edward B. Marks Music Corp., 1950. Also *More Songs to Grow On,* 1954. Recorded by Folkways Records.

Landeck, Beatrice, and Crook, Elizabeth. *Wake Up and Sing.* New York: Edward B. Marks Music Corp., 1969. Fifty songs and numerous rhymes.

Marquis, Margaret Hurley. *Songs for All Seasons and Rhymes Without Reasons.* New York: Edward B. Marks Music Corp. Rhythmic speech and movement, singing, simple dance patterns, rhythm and mallet instruments. Preschool and primary.

McCartney, Laura. *Songs for the Nursery School.* Cincinnati: Willis Music Co., 1937.

McLaughlin, Roberta, and Schliestett, Patti. *The Joy of Music: Early Childhood.* Evanston, Ill.: Summy-Birchard Co., 1967. Songs to teach singing, rhythm, instruments, and other activities. Well indexed.

Nye, Robert; Nye, Vernice; Aubin, Neva; and Kyme, George. *Singing With Children.* 2d ed. Belmont, Calif.: Wadsworth Publishing Co., 1970. An elementary school song collection with many useful for nursery school, with suggestions as to how to use them in the classroom.

Richards, Mary Helen. *Pentatonic Songs for Young Children.* Belmont, Calif.: Fearon Publishers, 1967. The voice range is of six tones or less.

———. *Threshold to Music.* Kindergarten Experience Charts with Guide. Belmont, Calif.: Fearon Publishers, 1964.

Seeger, Ruth Crawford. *American Folk Songs for Children: Animal Folk Songs for Children.* New York: Doubleday and Co.

Smith, Robert, and Leonhard, Charles. *Discovering Music Together: Early Childhood.* Chicago: Follett Publishing Co., 1968. Albums of recordings to use with a teacher's book for kindergarten. Songs begin with small range and gradually expand this. Integrates singing, playing, moving, and creating.

Wessells, Katharine Tyler. *The Golden Song Book.* New York: Simon and Schuster, 1945. Sixty favorite children's songs and singing games.

Winn, Marie. *Fireside Book of Children's Songs.* New York: Simon and Schuster, 1966.

Seeing

While listening and feeling have been emphasized, another of the senses, seeing, should not be underestimated when music is to be learned. Pictures, chalkboards, charts, posters, movie boxes, and overhead transparencies are common visual aids that can assist learning, provide variety, and attract interest. Puppets can be fascinating additions to any learning program, and they can assist in learning to sing. Songs that include action words can be illustrated visually by pictures of the actions.

After children have learned the feel of common note values, they can relate to visual concepts of what they have felt with their bodies by walking, running, clapping, thigh-slapping, and other actions. The charts in *Threshold to Music,* 2nd ed. for early childhood and for level one, published by Fearon Publishers, Belmont, California, 1974, include drawings of rudimentary note values that can be well comprehended by children, including those who are retarded. They relate to walking, then to the beat, to phrasing, the quarter note, quarter rest, and eighth notes. Quarter and eighth note notation appear as | | ⊓ | . These are related to children's names and to percussion instruments. The syllables and hand signs are introduced, and all of this leads easily and clearly to note reading of simple music from the large charts.

Rhythm patterns can be related to long and short line notation, and accents can be seen by drawing heavier lines to show them.

Photo courtesy of Scientific Music Industries, 823 S. Wabash Avenue, Chicago, Illinois 60605.

TONE EDUCATOR BELLS 88948

Hot Cross Buns

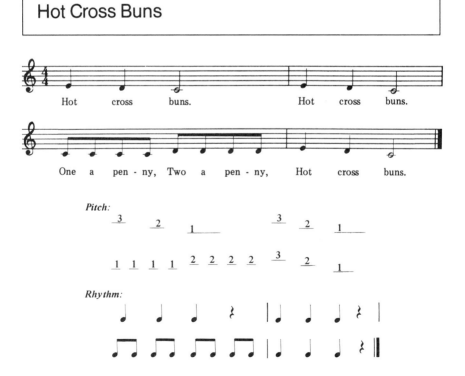

Young children can learn to play simple melodies when they see numbers on a chart, and can associate them with numbers on the bars of a bell set or xylophone. While teachers can make their own notation and can mark bell sets with crayon or taped numbers, a commercial product that has been successfully used is *Songs I Can Play* by Peg Hoenack. Obtainable from World of Peripole, Inc., the Hoenack materials include several types of marked bell sets and a xylophone, child's book that stands up, teacher's guide, and classroom chart. Children can see the pitch differences on the instruments and in the numeral notation. Program No. 1A—P3080 is for nursery school and kindergarten.

1   2   3   1   1   2   3   1
Are you sleep-ing?   Are you sleep-ing?

Another way to approach this reading of simple notation and playing the instruments is with the alphabetical names of the notes.

C   D   E   C   C   D   E   C
Are you sleep-ing?   Are you sleep-ing?

An experience with pitch contour can be provided when the teacher draws a picture of sound in the air and children improvise their imitation of the "picture" with their voices. Later, children can take the place of the teacher and draw the "picture." Melodic direction can be drawn on chart or chalkboard, either by a series of short lines that show pitch intervals clearly or by continuous lines that are not as precise.

Form can be represented by different shapes, either geometrical (triangle, square, circle) or by pictures of objects; and children can create their own drawings showing same and different in phrases or sections of music.

Suggested Activities

1. Tape-record the chants and song-sounds of young children at play. Play them back for your study and try to find ways to utilize some of them in your music teaching.
2. Design a sound encounter for an individual child or for a group. Plan this experience with specific music objectives that encompass cognitive, psychomotor, and affective domains. Design questions and plan any vocabulary development that may grow from the encounter. After the experience, evaluate the results in terms of your objectives.

3. Observe a child's movements and his tempo. Accompany him with a percussion instrument or by clapping hands in time with his tempo.
4. Observe a classroom for young children and take note of how the teacher plans and organizes for music instruction. How does she employ instruments? Record the ways the teacher individualizes the teaching of music; if she groups, explain how the groups are organized and for what purpose.
5. Discuss the values of children working in small or class group when appropriate.
6. Develop a set of criteria for evaluating recordings for young children.
7. Listen to and evaluate three recordings designed for use with young children. What is to be learned from them? How will they be introduced?
8. Develop a set of criteria for evaluating songs for young children.
9. Learn three songs appropriate for young children. Write lesson plans that include performance-stated objectives and use them in teaching the songs to members of the college class.
10. Examine the index section of a music textbook for "nursery school" or "kindergarten." Besides the alphabetized list of songs, find and use indexes such as "Musical Learnings," "Topical Index," and "Classified Index." Look for subsections such as "Songs Classified by Range," "Moving to Music," "Instrument Identification," "Piano Music for Movement," "Musical Concepts," "Pentatonic Songs," "Creative Activities," "Poetry," "Animals," "Occupations," "Dramatization and Pantomime," "Dances," "Travel and Transport," "Rhythm Instruments," "Fun and Nonsense," "Action and Game Songs."
11. Read pp. 142-47 in *The Spectrum of Music: Teacher's Resource Book K* (Macmillan Publishing Co.) for brief descriptions of the Kodály and Orff methods in a kindergarten book. Choose some aspects of these methods to use in your teaching and evaluate their effectiveness.
12. Select a dance song with a definite ABA form and encourage children to create a simple dance for it that emphasizes the form.

References

Bentley, William G. *Learning to Move and Moving to Learn.* New York: Citation Press, 1970.

Burnett, Millie. *Melody, Movement and Language.* San Francisco: R & E Research Associates, 1970. Includes Orff-related procedures.

Choksy, Lois. *The Kodály Method: Comprehensive Music Education from Infant to Adult.* Englewood Cliffs, N.J.: Prentice-Hall, Inc., 1974.

Eliason, Claudia F. and Loa T. Jenkins. *A Practical Guide to Early Childhood Curricula.* St. Louis: The C. V. Mosby Company, 1977. Chapter 18.

Greenberg, Marvin. "Research in Music in Early Childhood Education: A Survey with Recommendations." *Council for Research in Music Education No. 45*, Winter, 1976. pp. 1-20.

Music For Children, Orff Schulwerk American, Edition 1 Pre-School. New York: Schott Music Corp., 1979.

Music Educators Journal, March, 1974. (Contains three articles concerning early childhood education by authors Frances Aronoff, Miriam Gelvin, and Virginia Austin.)

National Association for the Education of Young Children. *The Significance of the Young Child's Motor Development*. Washington, D.C.: The Association, 1971.

Sandor, Frigyes, ed. *Musical Education in Hungary*. London: Barrie and Rockliff, 1966. Contains chapter on music in nursery schools.

Schickedanz, Judith A. et al. "Methods and Activities for Instruction in Music and Movement." In *Strategies for Teaching Young Children*. Englewood Cliffs, N.J.: Prentice-Hall, Inc., 1977.

Simons, Gene M. Early Childhood Musical Development: A Bibliography of Research Abstracts, 1960-1973. Athens, Georgia: University of Georgia, 1976. Supplementary report update for 1973-75 is available.

Stecher, Miriam B., Hugh McElheny, and Marion Greenwood. *Music and Movement Improvisations*. New York: The Macmillan Company, 1972.

Todd, Vivian E. and Helen Heffernan. *The Years Before School*, 3rd ed. New York: The Macmillan Company, Inc., 1971. Chapter 14.

Tossi, Aaron. *Musicbook O For Pre-School and Early Grades*. St. Louis: Magnamusic Baton. Pulse, pitch, rhythm, form, dynamics are dealt with.

5   Music in an Integrated Curriculum

Because of its almost innate appeal to young children, music can be employed to assist and enhance all types of learning in other curricular areas: expansion and enrichment of vocabulary; memorization, speaking and listening skills; the development of motor skills that aid the child in the control and use of his body and to express himself more effectively in nonverbal ways; use of the body in more flexible and appropriate ways in explaining his scientific, social, and aesthetic world. Music further assists the child in concept attainment and reinforcement, in social skills and affective learnings. These are functional uses of music. The functional goals of music should never be so stressed that the natural joy and content of music are forgotten.

Through music children experience pleasure, joy and creative expression. Music provides a meaningful setting in which to release and express feelings and moods. It can soothe or relieve children's frustrations, establish moods for listening, and aid in releasing hurt and disturbed feelings; it can enhance the child's feeling of self-worth.

Children should have the opportunity to become involved in music as an integral and supportive factor in all areas of the curriculum; they should be encouraged to interpret music in unique ways, to create new words, melodies, and movements. Language can be developed and enriched through music, since songs often introduce new words. Furthermore, the child's attention span can be extended through listening to songs that tell a story (ballads) or to those that give directions. Many songs can call attention to clothing the child is wearing or to physical attributes that children possess. Not only should music be planned for every day, but it should also be used spontaneously to support other parts of the curriculum, to create variety, and to provide transitions into activities.

Music is a part of every child's environment whether it be in the song of a bird, clattering of horse hooves, a TV commercial, the rhythm of raindrops, a woodpecker pecking, fast steps in the hall, the crack of lightening, the rumble of thunder, songs sung or music played on instruments. It becomes more meaningful and interesting when integrated into all areas of the curriculum. One way of organizing the classroom for integrated teaching is through the use of the *open education* design. The integrated curriculum, which some authorities equate with open education, is currently attracting many teachers and parents. This approach is of special concern here because the interweaving of subject areas, characteristic of open education, is reflected in this chapter. The object is to integrate dramatic play, body response, and music with the other subjects of the curriculum, and in turn, the other subjects with music.

Open education emphasizes the *process* of learning. Although it in no way neglects subject area content, it deemphasizes specific content in favor of teaching young children *how* to learn. There is a flexible approach to the curriculum that raises no barriers between subject fields but places emphasis on the goal of teaching children where and how to employ their own knowledge. The child is allowed to use the style of learning best suited to him so that he may pursue his interests in a self-paced and independent manner, and to develop his special skills and unique ways of learning. However, teachers who use the integrated or open approach do not rule out the importance of specific subject matter and the types of activities in which they can involve children to learn content. When a child is involved in an activity, in a project, or in an area of experiences designed to accommodate his interests, this, too, does not imply less emphasis on the development of intellectual skills.

The child is not a compartmentalized being in whom there are divisions labeled music, language arts, movement, and social studies. He is a fully integrated person in whom the physical, social, emotional, and intellectual interact upon each other and in whom there is not subject matter per se but total experience instead. Thus it is natural that his educational life, particularly in the early years, consist for the most part of integrated experiences in which (to the child) subjects of study are only arbitrary divisions of little or no importance. While the teacher plans integrated experiences for the child whenever these are feasible, she also plans objectives that provide for achievement goals in the various subject areas as well as for a learning program that balances the cognitive, psychomotor, and affective domains. However, she must never forget learning from the child's point of view; it is one of integrated experience.

Music and Cognitive Development

Music can be used to increase the child's vocabulary, supply him with knowledge of his physical abilities, and expand his knowledge of concepts that relate to all forms of activity and objects in the classroom environment.

Cognitive and affective learnings cannot be separated; thus, through the affective elements of music the child discovers that he can express himself artistically and affectively, and simultaneously think about what he is doing. As children participate in an effectively designed and implemented music program they obtain knowledge of their physical selves and the physical world; they also encounter various concepts in new contexts, an experience which expands their knowledge background. For example, as they examine an instrument they are learning to perceive, observe, ask pertinent questions, analyze, draw conclusions, then possibly use that instrument to create music. Such physical notions as size, shape, property, color, texture of instruments are acquired. They develop such concepts as fast-slow, high-low, loud-soft, angry, sad, under-over, beside-behind, on-over. Goals of a music program can incorporate music content along with the so-called basic content of the curriculum, as music can be used to enhance the learning of many cognitive concepts besides those found in music itself.

Music Throughout the Day

When children experience the singing of lullabies by their mothers at bedtime, they retain pleasant feelings associated with the loving warmth of that experience. Later, when they hear a lullaby, those pleasant feelings return to them. In like fashion, when a teacher uses music in pleasant ways for purposes of classroom routine, music then comes to be associated with pleasant things of life and in return assists children in all areas of learning. A song that is appropriate to the occasion can be found or more often composed by the teacher. Music can be expected at any time during the child's day at home or at school. Parents can use music in similar ways while teaching the child knowledges, skills, attitudes, and values. Whenever teacher or parent feels the urge to make music, he should do so within the context of the situation.

Music and Routine Activities

Classroom routines and home routines are made easier and more pleasant with music. The signal for group activities at school may be a "good morning" song. New music experiences are often introduced at this time when children are rested and ready for learning. The parent can sing a song to signal that breakfast is ready or that it is time to go to bed. The teacher can sing "Juice time, juice time, now we're having juice to drink," when it is time for refreshments. A "thank you" song can be sung whenever this response is appropriate.

Music can be helpful in moving children from one activity to another. By incorporating children's names in a song, the teacher can give them permission to do things in turn in a game or playtime atmosphere. Children who get excited by some musical activity can, by having them take turns, be induced to a lower emotional response; if they are tired they may be helped by playing a familiar recording to which they do a rhythmic response. Another selected recording or a teacher's song may signal a quiet time for resting, and another song or recording may signal the end of the rest period. Using music in these ways can make some verbal instructions unnecessary; music can communicate in pleasing and nonthreatening ways. In brief periods of relaxation between activities, the teacher might sing to an Autoharp accompaniment or do some pleasant strumming on the instrument. Music is helpful in drawing children into group work; when a child enjoys music he becomes more easily adapted to a group. Music can smooth out many rough spots for teachers and parents.

In order to establish routines, children must learn to follow directions. They do this when they listen to and follow directions for action songs and finger plays. Teachers select and compose songs to direct them to do such things as going out to play, hanging up coats, and putting away, cleaning up, and organizing materials. Directions on tapes and records are usually given the listener in musical ways. A current example are those directions given in some of the recordings of Hap Palmer.

Music textbooks for nursery school and kindergarten contain songs that assist routine. One finds "good morning" and "good-bye" songs as well as those that imply that rest time has come. Some examples of books with definite sections devoted to the use of music to teach routine are:

> Saenger, H.; Hardy, Belva; and Peter, Katherine. "The Kindergarten Day." In *Beginning With Music*. San Francisco: Century Schoolbook Press, 1958.
> McCall, Adeline. "Singing Through the Day." In *This Is Music: For Kindergarten and Nursery School*. Boston: Allyn and Bacon, 1967.
> McConathy, Osbourne, et al. *New Music Horizons: Music in Early Childhood*. New York: Silver Burdett Company, 1952, pp. 26-27.
> Grentzer, Rose Marie, and Hood, Marguerite V. "School." In *Birchard Music Series: Kindergarten*. Evanston, Ill.: Summy-Birchard Publishing Co., 1958.

Index sections of other books will normally guide the reader to similar music for classroom routines. However, some of the more recent publications have temporarily overlooked this function of music, apparently due to an almost exclusive emphasis on music learnings. Remember that many of the best songs grow out of the routines themselves, and are composed by the teacher and the children.

Music and Science

Science at the early childhood level includes a large body of subject matter concerned with seasons and weather, the sun, moon, and stars, animal and plant life, health and safety, and the study of machines and sound.

Music and the Changing Seasons   Changing seasons are matters of interest and concern to children because seasons affect their activities. The color of the growing or dying foliage, the blooming of flowers, the sprouting of seeds, the harvesting of crops, the rustle of fallen leaves, the feel of a green leaf as compared to the feel of a dry dead brown one, gathering nuts, seasonal storms, autumn rains, snow, and clouds are all matters of interest. Songs and movement help children learn about seasons and weather. The teacher will phrase questions that guide children in discussion concerning the differences between seasons and the activities associated with them—swimming in summer, sledding in winter, birds flying south in the fall, playing in fallen leaves, playing in the snow—and songs and pantomime should reflect all of these. Dramatization and rhythms, poetry and song creation, and other activities should be used in teaching science concepts. Recordings can prompt children's dramatization of weather phenomena. For example, the storm portrayed in Grofés *Grand Canyon Suite* may be dramatized or danced to depict the wind, clouds gathering, thunder and lightning, rain and sun.

Music and Movement in the Environment   Fast and slow are among the concepts learned from watching and imitating the movement of animals; such imitations are a "natural" for teaching these music concepts. A well-known source of songs related to animals is Ruth Crawford Seeger's *Animal Folk Songs for Children* (Doubleday and Co., 1950). Through the use of songs, and melodic and rhythmic accompaniments to animal poems, books, recordings, and films, children can be guided to become more proficient in knowing the variety of patterns in their scientific world. They learn about animal names, physical characteristics, reproduction, life cycle, habits, food, and adaptations. Thus, songs, rhythms, poems, and stories about animals can provide an interesting and meaningful approach to scientific inquiry. With proper presentation, questions, discussions, and pupil reinforcement and involvement, the teacher encourages interest, curiosity, observation, and exploration. Selected sections of the recording of Saint-Saëns *Carnival of the Animals* have been found useful to encourage the acting-out of various animal movements. A progression from the floor is recommended; the movements can include crawling, walking on all fours, jumping, and flying.

The changes that children can observe in growing plants such as the sprouting of seeds, the growing of leaves, and the bursting of buds can be dramatized. The movement of machines too has a place in such science study; children are often fascinated by vehicles, the sounds and moving parts of machinery, and they naturally want to act them out.

Music and the Sounds of Living Things   Children are attracted by all living things, particularly by those that produce sound. The sounds made by birds and other animals are universally attractive to children. They devote much time listening to these sounds, analyzing them and attempting to imitate them. Teachers can use this natural interest in sound as a foundation for learning various musical concepts. Some animal sounds will be loud, some soft, and others will be high or low. Some make happy, angry, fearful, or sad sounds. Many will be found to be musical while others will not. The song of a bird may encourage creating a song about a bird. Teachers often ask children to make statements about a bird's song; then they sing those words back to the children. In so doing, these statements become a song. Music and movement are vehicles to express what children learn about living things. See also section on "The Classroom" and "Playground Learning Encounters" chapter 2.

The Study of Sound

For young children, the study of sound involves observation of all sounds in their environment, sounds made with paper, stone, metal, wood, and other common materials, sounds made by objects intended to be or which are musical instruments, sounds made by people, and sounds made by machines and by nature. Children learn to identify sounds, learn that vibration produces sounds, and learn to differentiate between music and noise. In so doing they can expand musical and scientific concepts. Because this was discussed in chapter 4, we will proceed directly to some specific activities to use when children study sound, which is, of course, the study of simple acoustics.

vibration	The child can experiment with stretching a rubber band around an open-top box or around the back of his chair. When he plucks it he can
string sounds	discover that it quivers (vibrates) at a rapid rate and that this in turn produces the sound. If he stretches it, he will hear a higher sound when it is plucked. If he pulls the band farther out and lets go, a louder sound will be produced; if he pulls it a short distance, a softer sound will be heard.
wind sounds	The child can learn concepts dealing with sounds produced by both woodwind and brass instruments by blowing simple whistles, and blowing across the open tops of bottles. When he blows across the open end of a bullet shell, the column of air in the shell vibrates and produces a sound. The child can sometimes feel the vibration in his lips when they touch the rim. Older children can change the pitch resulting from blowing across a bottle by adding or reducing the amount of water in the bottle. This lengthens or shortens the vibrating column of air. There are many varieties of whistles to blow, and teachers' questions can assist

metal sounds

body sounds

vibration

the child in having fun and learning science at the same time.

Some metal pot lids with knobs for handles have beautiful tones. When the lid is struck, it vibrates to produce the sound and the child can feel this vibration when he touches the lid and stops its sounding. With lids of different sizes and thicknesses there can be experiences in comparing pitches; some will be higher or lower than others.

Children find all the ways they can make sounds with their bodies. These will include hand clapping, foot stamping, thigh slapping, and various mouth sounds. Children can also hold fingers on their larynx and feel the vibration as they speak and sing.

An Autoharp is placed on an orange crate that is standing on end. As the teacher strokes a chord on the strings, a child experiments in several ways. He can put his head inside the crate to listen; he can touch the side of the crate with his fingertips or with his ear to feel the vibration| He can sing his name, hopefully in tune with the chord being sounded.

The Echo

Old Children's Tune

Kate Forman

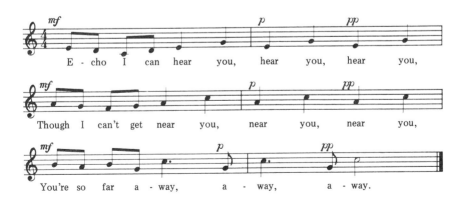

Suggested Musical Activities Related to Science

Children are attracted by all things that move and make sounds. Therefore they enjoy interpreting such movements and sounds by imitating them with their bodies and voices.

Weather   Create songs and accompaniments, then perform them. Learn songs and instrumentation composed about weather. Imitate sounds: create and dance movements of wind, rain dripping, snow falling quietly and softly, sleet and hail bouncing, autumn leaves falling or blowing in the wind. If the children have seen a tornado, dance a tornado.

Sounds   Identify and imitate sounds:

Pets
Seasonal sounds
Playground sounds
Sounds heard at a fair
Sounds heard on a farm
Sounds heard in all parts
  of the home
Country and city sounds

Sounds associated with holidays
  and special days
Animal sounds: zoo animals, circus animals, farm animals, animal babies, desert animals.
Sounds made by people
Insects: bees, crickets, katydids, mosquito

Identify, imitate, and classify sounds of different qualities:

happy
sad
frightening
lonely
angry
excited
light

soft
quiet
noisy
loud
heavy
weary

Invisible sound sources: identify, classify, and imitate through movement:

jet aircraft (sonic boom)
wind

thunder

Moving things we can't hear:

birds flying in the distance
clouds moving
stars twinkling
fly-away seeds

feathers
butterflies
snow falling
fish swimming

Plants   Create songs and instrumental accompaniments about seeds and plants; learn songs and how to accompany them with simple instruments; make seed rattles (seed pods and gourds used as percussion instruments as well as hard seeds in small containers as shakers). Dramatize and dance seeds in the act of

sprouting
bursting
gradually growing
  into a plant

Dramatize: plants following the sun; picking fruit from plants; plants drying up in the fall; leaves falling and blown by the wind; seeds traveling; the care of plants. Perform the musical dramatization of "The Little Red Hen."

Machines　　In creating dance, songs, and instrumental accompaniments, children will enjoy observing, interpreting, analyzing, and reproducing the movement and sounds of machines and those of each part. Chenfeld (1978) states that "A simple way to introduce the idea of machines is to ask one child to start a mechanical movement and so on, until all the children have contributed their special patterns and sounds." When children discover that they can work together and build wonderful machines with their hands, they extend this talent to other experiences.

Tape-record familiar sounds and have children identify and imitate: clock ticking, timer buzzing, water boiling, telephone ringing, car starting, and create accompaniments and songs about these sounds and perform them.

Resources for Science-Music Relationships

Songs

In any music textbook series there is a classified index that guides the teacher to songs listed under headings such as animals and birds, nature, health and safety, seasons and weather. Sometimes songs dealing with sound are found under the heading of listening. Listed below are examples of what can be found in such books.

    A. Animal Songs
        Eency Weency Spider
        Little Duck
        Old MacDonald
        Pony Song (My Pony)
        One Elephant (The Elephants)
        Little Bird (has interesting meter changes)
        Riding a Horse
        Bingo (dog)
        I Had a Cat (The Barnyard Song)
        Songs in *Singing with Children* and many other books
        Little Pig
        The Ducklings
        Over in the Meadow
        Songs from *Mother Goose*
        Baa Baa Black Sheep
        Mary Had a Little Lamb
        Hickory Dickory Dock
        Pussycat
    B. Plants (sometimes related to seasons)
    C. Machines
        "Machines" is not a commonly-found category in music textbook indexes. Perhaps it should be, because children are normally attracted by machines and try to imitate their sounds and movements. Under the heading "Transportation" one finds songs about trains, ships, and automobiles, but there is little more than that.

Sometimes a song about a steam shovel will appear under "Community Helpers." This gives the teacher and children more opportunities to compose their own songs about the machines in their environment. Examples are:

Down By the Station	(in many books)
Train Is A-Coming	*This Is Music: K-N*
Monorail	*New Dimensions-K*
Shoosh! The Jet Goes By	*New Dimensions-K*

Little Ducklings
German Folk Song

1. See my lit - tle duck - lings swim - ming ev - 'ry - where,
2. See my lit - tle duck - lings swim - ming 'round and 'round.

Heads down in the wa - ter, Tails up in the air.
Now they're right - side up and now they're up - side down.

Down by the Station
Traditional

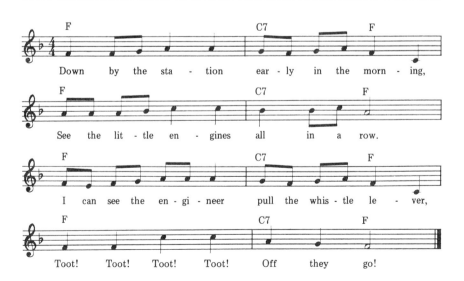

Down by the sta - tion ear - ly in the morn - ing,

See the lit - tle en - gines all in a row.

I can see the en - gi - neer pull the whis - tle le - ver,

Toot! Toot! Toot! Toot! Off they go!

Rain, Rain Go Away   Traditional

Rain, rain go a-way, Come a-gain an-oth-er day.

D. Seasons

Seasons have substantial recognition in most textbooks. The songs are usually not familiar folk songs; the words or music are created to meet a need, thus the titles are seldom well known. Familiar songs such as "Jingle Bells" do have reference to seasons. Again, there are many opportunities for teachers and children to compose their own songs in which they comment on the seasons. "Winter Is Here," in *Discovering Music Together: Early Childhood*, is a traditional German folk song known internationally, while "There Came to My Window," in *New Dimensions-K*, is an English folk song concerning a robin in spring.

E. Weather

Typical of songs in textbooks are:

Slosh, Slosh
How Sweet to Be a
  Cloud
Blow, Ye Winds   all in *New Dimensions-K*
Blow the Winds   *Singing With Children*
  Southerly   *Discovering Music Together:*
Raining Again Today   *Teacher Education Edition*
Snowflakes Softly   *This Is Music: Book One*
  Falling Down   *Together We Sing: Music Round*
Jack Frost   *The Town* (Follett)

F. Sound

This is a category not normally found in textbooks. *Growing With Music: Book One* contains a section with this title; it includes songs about trains and train whistles, sounds of musical instruments, sounds of nature, sounds of a tugboat, of bells, of animals, and refers the teacher to recordings of African and electronic music. This may yield clues for teachers of young children. Refer to "Listening" in textbook indexes. *This Is Music: Book One* suggests experiments with sound (on page 7).

The Echo   *Music in the Elementary School*
                   (Prentice-Hall) and others

I Hear a Sound (long   *The Spectrum of Music-K*
  and short sounds)

G. Changing World

This is a category of importance that has not yet been accepted in the textbooks as a separate song classification, thus songs must be found or created that deal with a world in change. Teachers can use old songs like "Looby Lou" and "Riding in a Buggy" to help children comprehend the mechanical changes from the past with implications for changes in the future. Find or compose songs concerning inventions.

Space Ship	*Exploring Music With Children* (Wadsworth)
Little Satellite	*The Joy of Music* (Summy-Birchard)

Recordings

A. Animals

Animals and Circus	Bowmar Orchestral Library 51
Flight of the Bumblebee	on Bowmar Orchestral Library (BOL) 53
Nature and Make-Believe	BOL 52
The Swan and *Elephants*	from *Carnival of the Animals* BOL 59
Animals, Vol. 1	Folkways FC 7021
More Animals, Vol. 2	Folkways FC 7022
Birds, Beasts, Bugs and *Little Fish*	Folkways FC 7010
Birds, Beasts, Bugs and *Bigger Fish*	Folkways FC 7011
Peter and the Wolf	VOX PL 9280
Winnie the Pooh	Golden Records LP 95

B. Plants and Animals

Nature Songs	Children's Music Center CB139

C. Machines

Iron Foundry	on Folkways FX 6160 *Sounds of New Music*
"Little Train of the Caipira"	from *Bachianas Brasilieras No. 2,* Adventures in Music (AM) 3 v 2
Trains and Planes	Young People's Records 706

D. Seasons

All About Spring	Educational Activities. A record
All About Summer	and a book for each title.
All About Fall	
All About Winter	
Changing Seasons	Children's Music Center CB139

E. Weather
   What Will the Weather   Children's Music Center CB144
   Be?
F. Sounds
   See "Exemplary Recordings for Listening," Chapter V
   Child's Introduction to   Golden Records
   the Orchestra
   Sound Patterns   Odyssey 3216-0156. Mouth
                                 sounds.

   Sounds I Can Hear   Scott, Foresman and Co. Sounds,
   02765   pictures, and stories for identifi-
                                 cation and discrimination in kin-
                                 dergarten.

   Sounds of New Music   Folkways FX 6160
   Strike Up the Band   Children's Record Guild 5027.
                                 Identifying percussion instru-
G. The Changing World   ments.
   Space Songs   Children's Music Center SAR4
   Step Into Space   Children's Music Center CB140
H. Special Source
   Best Records, Books, for Early Childhood catalog, Children's
   Music Center, Los Angeles, Calif. 90019. See sections titled "Na-
   ture and Science," and "Concepts."

Films and Filmstrips

(See sources listed in the Appendix section of this book.)
A. Animals
   Bowmar Nature Series: The Ways of Animals.
   Filmstrips with cassettes. Bowmar, Glendale, Calif.
A set of ten sound filmstrips with the narrated version of the story with
natural sound effects that children enjoy imitating. (Ten books, ten
sound filmstrips, teacher's guide.)
   Animals Friends, FAC. 10 min. c, b & w.
   Animal Stories, filmstrip set NS 8114. Lyons, Elkhart, Ind.
   Cows Don't Say Moo, Coronet, 55 fr, c.
   Frisky the Calf, Coronet, 11 min., c.
   Learning About Zoo Animals. Set of five color captioned film-
       strips, Educational Activities, Freeport, N.Y.
   Mother Duck and Her Friends, EBF, 14 fr., c.
   Spiders, FOM, c. (filmstrip)
   Woodland Friends, EBF, 37 fr., c.
B. Seasons
   Fall, Winter, Spring, Summer, FSR 424, Pre-K-2. Four full color
       filmstrips, two records or cassettes. A child's eye view. Educa-
       tional Activities, Inc., Freeport, N.Y.

Finger Plays

(See finger play references listed at the end of this chapter for finger plays for animals, plants, machines, seasons, weather, sounds, the changing world, and health and safety.)

A. Animals

Anderson, Paul S. *Language Skills in Elementary Education.* 2d ed. New York: Macmillan Co., 1972.

"Five Little Squirrels"
"Two Dickey Birds"
"Two Telephone Poles"
"Little Turtle"
"Itsy Bitsy Spider"
"Caterpillar"

Hildebrand, Verna. *Introduction to Early Childhood Education.* New York: Macmillan Co., 1971.

"Mr. Bullfrog"
"Five Little Rabbits"
"Robin Redbreast"
"I Had a Little Pig"

McAfee, Oralie, et al., *The New Nursery School: Learning Activities Booklet VI.* New York: General Learning Corp.

"Five Little Goslings"

Poems and Rhymes

(See poetry references listed in the general bibliography at the end of this chapter for poems referring to animals, plants, machines, seasons, weather, sound, the changing world.)

A. Animals

"The Frog." In *Cats and Bats and Things With Wings,* by Conrad Aiken. New York: Atheneum House, 1965.

A Gopher in the Garden and Other Animal Poems, by Jack Prelutsky. New York: Macmillan Co., 1967. Tongue-twisting rhymes.

"The House Cat." In *For Days and Days,* by Annette Wynne. Philadelphia: J. B. Lippincott Co., 1919, 1947.

"The Monkeys," by Edith O. Thompson. In *Time for Poetry,* by May Hill Arbuthnot. New York: Scott, Foresman and Co., 1951.

"The Little Duck," by Joso; "Ducks at Dawn," by James Tippett; "The New Baby Calf," by Edith Chase; and "The Pasture," by Robert Frost; all in *The Sound of Poetry* by Mary C. Austin and Queenie B. Mills. Boston: Allyn and Bacon, 1962.

"My Little Birds." In *Favorite Poems Old and New,* by Helen Ferris. Garden City, N.Y.: Doubleday and Co., 1957.

"*Nibble, Nibble, Poems for Children,* by Margaret Wise Brown. New York: Young Scott Books, 1959. An excellent collection about plants, animals, and insects.

"Pitty Patty Polt," "I Have a Little Pony," "Trot, Trot, Horsie," and "Shoe the Pony Shoe." These traditional poems are found in *This Little Pig Went to Market,* edited by Norah Montgomerie. New York: Franklin Watts, 1967.

B. Seasons

"Autumn Woods" in *A World to Know* by James S. Tippett. New York: Harper and Row, 1961.

"Barefoot Days," by Rachel Field. In *Poems to Grown On,* by Jean M. Thompson. Boston: Beacon Press, 1959.

"Rain in the Summer" by Henry W. Longfellow.

"Seasons" by Randall Cadman, 507 Gracie Drive, Eustis, Florida: Etna Crowder.

C. Weather

"Raining Again," by Dorothy Adis. In *All Together,* by Adis. New York: G. P. Putnam's Sons, 1952.

"Wind Is a Cat." In *"White Peaks and Green,* by Ethel F. Miller. New York: Harper & Row Publishers.

"Galoshes," by Rhoda Bacmeister. In *Poems to Grow On,* by Jean M. Thompson. Boston: Beacon Press, 1959.

"Wind and Water" section of *Time for Poetry,* by May Hill Arbuthnot. Chicago: Scott, Foresman and Co., 1961.

D. General Science

Exploring Science Through Poetry K-3 1971. Two color filmstrips, records, cassettes. Includes poetry about weather, the sea, color, machines, living things, the earth, seasons, the universe. Excellent.

Books

A. Animals

The Runaway Bunny, new ed., by Margaret Wise Brown. New York: Harper & Row, Publishers, 1972.

Wheel on the Chimney, by Margaret Wise Brown. Philadelphia: J. B. Lippincott, 1954. This poetic, illustrated book gives an account of the storks on their migratory journey to Africa and back to their nest in a wheel on a chimney.

Once a Mouse, by Marcia Brown. New York: Charles Scribner's Sons, 1961.

The Very Hungry Caterpillar, by Eric Carle. Omaha: World Publishing Co., 1970. Dramatizes the metamorphosis of a butterfly.

The Turtle Book, by Mel Crawford. New York: Western Publishing Co., 1965.

The Cat Book, by Kathleen N. Daly. New York: Golden Press, 1974.

The Baby Animal Book, by Daphne Davis. New York: Western Publishing Co., 1964.

May I Bring a Friend? by Beatrice de Reyiers. New York: Atheneum, 1964.

The Bug Book, by William Dugan. New York: Western Publishing Company, 1965.

Angus and the Ducks, by Marjorie Flack. New York: Viking, 1944. A delightful story about a spirited little dog.

Paddy the Penguin, by Paul Galdone. New York: Thomas Y. Crowell, 1959.

The Animals of Farmer Jones, by Gale Leah. New York: Western Publishing Co., 1963.

The Country Bunny and the Little Gold Shoes, by DuBose Heyward. New York: Houghton Mifflin Co., 1939.

What's Inside, by May Garelick. Omaha: Scholastic Book Services, 1970. The hatching of an egg from the first crack to the little wet gosling.

Be Nice to Spiders, by Margaret Graham. New York: Harper & Row, Publishers, 1967.

The Cow Who Fell in the Canal, by Phyllis Krasilovsky. New York: Doubleday & Co., 1957.

I Can Fly, by Ruth Krauss. The Golden Press.

A Dog Came to School, by Lois Lenski. New York: Oxford University Press, 1955.

Make Way for the Ducklings, by Robert McClosky. New York: Viking Press, 1941.

Listen to the Birds, by Mary B. Miller. New York: Pantheon, 1961.

The First and Last Annual Pet Parade, by Mary Neville. New York: Pantheon, 1968.

Animals Around the Mulberry Bush, by Tony Palazzo. New York: Doubleday and Co., 1958.

The Three Little Kittens, by Tony Palazzo. Garden City, N.Y.: Doubleday and Co., 1961.

The Three Little Pigs, by Tony Palazzo. New York: Doubleday and Co., 1961.

Curious George, 1941; *Curious George Gets a Medal,* 1957; *Curious George Takes a Job,* 1947, by Hans Augusto Rey. Boston: Houghton Mifflin Co.

Great Big Animal Book and *Great Big Wild Animal Book,* by Feodor Rojankovsky. New York: Golden Press.

When Animals Are Babies, by Elizabeth Schwartz and Charles Schwartz. New York: Holiday House, 1964. Realistic drawings; how baby animals eat, sleep, grow and how they are cared for.

All About Eggs, by Millicent Selsam. Reading, Mass.: Addison-Wesley Publishing Co., 1952. About the beginning of life.

When an Animal Grows, by Millicent E. Selsam. New York: Harper & Row Publishers, 1966. Explains the ways newborn animals are cared for and how they grow. Gorilla, lamb, duck, sparrow.

Let's Find Out About Animals, by Martha Shapp and Charles Shapp. New York: Franklin Watts, 1962.

This is the Way Animals Walk, by Louise Woodcock. New York: William Scott.

Farm Animals, by Irma Wilde. New York: Grosset & Dunlap, 1960.

B. Machines

Mike Mulligan and His Steam Shovel, by Virginia Lee Burton. Boston: Houghton Mifflin Co., 1939. Mary Anne is a steam shovel who digs into a deep hole and can't get out.

Hi, Mister Robin! by Alvin R. Tresselt. New York: Lothrop, Lee & Shepard Co., 1950. A robin shows a little boy how to look and listen for signs of spring.

Wake Up Farm, by Alvin R. Tresselt. New York: Lothrop, Lee & Shephard Co.

C. Weather

Who Likes the Sun? by Beatrice de Regniers. New York: Harcourt, Brace and World, 1961.

Gilberto and the Wind, by Marie Hall. New York: Viking Press, 1963.

Going Barefoot, by Aileen Fischer. New York: Thomas Y. Crowell Co., 1960.

The Day We Saw the Sun Come Up, by Alice Goudey. New York: Charles Scribner's Sons, 1961.

Let's Go Outdoors, by Harriet Huntington. Garden City, N.Y.: Doubleday and Co., 1939.

Time of Wonder, by Robert McCloskey. New York: Viking Press, 1957. Children explore seashore and forest.

Hide and Seek Fog, by Alvin R. Tresselt. New York: Lothrop, Lee and Shepard, 1965. Also *White Snow, Bright Snow; Hi, Mr. Robin; Rain Drop, Splash,* by the same author.

Up Above and Down Below, by Irene Webber. Chicago: Scott, Foresman and Co., 1943.

D. Plants

The Flower, by Mary Louise Downer. New York: William R. Scott, 1955.

Seeds and More Seeds, by Millicent E. Selsam. New York: Harper & Row, Publishers, 1959. Includes how to plant beans and produce seeds.

A Tree is Nice, by Janice Udry. New York: Harper & Bros., 1956.

Bits That Grow Big, by Irma E. Webber. Reading, Mass.: Addi-

son-Wesley Co., 1949. An excellent introduction to plant reproduction with easy experiments for young children.

Your Friend, the Tree, by Florence M. White. New York: Alfred
A. Knopf, Inc., 1969. Gives many uses of trees.

E. Sounds

Bow Wow! Meow! A First Book of Sounds, by Melanie Bellah.
New York: Western Publishing Co.

The City Noisy Book, by Margaret Brown. New York: Harper &
Row, Publishers, 1939.

The Seashore Noisy Book, by Margaret Brown. New York: Harper
& Row, Publishers, 1941.

The Summer Noisy Book, by Margaret Brown. New York: Harper
Row, Publishers, 1951.

The Winter Noisy Book, by Margaret Brown. New York: Harper
& Row, Publishers, 1947.

F. Our Changing World

My Five Senses, by Aliki. New York: Thomas Y. Crowell Co., 1962.
Taste, sight, smell, hearing take on new meaning.

All Around You, by Jeanne Bendick. New York: McGraw-Hill
Book Co., 1951. The why and how of the physical world in simple
words and cartoons.

The Shadow Book, by Beatrice de Regniers. New York: Harcourt,
Brace and World, 1960.

Where Does Everyone Go? by Aileen Fisher. New York: Thomas
Y. Crowell Co., 1961.

Space Alphabet, by Irene Zacks. Englewood Cliffs, N.J.: Prentice-
Hall, 1964. A is for Astronaut, G is for Galaxy.

The Giant Book of Things in Space, by George J. Zaffo. Garden
City, N.Y.: Doubleday & Co. An introduction to the aerospace
world.

All Falling Down, by Gene Zion. New York: Harper & Row, 1951.
Teaches the concept of falling down: rain, snow, leaves, apples.

Early Childhood Catalog, Children's Music Center, 5373 W. Pico
Blvd., Los Angeles 90019. Refer to "The Wonder of Things" section for listing of books.

Music and Mathematics

The child learns numerical concepts from selected singing games, finger
plays, rhymes, and counting songs. Many of the concepts learned through
music are basic mathematics. There are the vocabulary words dealing with
measures such as fast-slow, high-low, big-bigger-biggest, and large-larger-
largest. There are shapes such as round, square, and triangle. Body exploration in space is another basic way to measure. Ordinals are learned
through songs and singing games. Songs are sung about days of the week
and months of the year, which are also units of measurement. Eventually

children feel meter in beat groupings of two's and three's and the study and application of meter, beat, and divisions of the beat relate directly to mathematics.

Space

Concepts of space as well as of shapes, time, and number are outgrowths of a teacher-planned and organized learning environment that gives realistic opportunities for exploring space as a first step. The child explores space with his body; he swings high, crawls through tunnels, climbs up and down on the jungle gym, jumps from high places, crawls and runs up, down, over, under, on top of, beside, behind things. These space experiences serve as a natural framework for creating or using songs, recordings, rhythms, and finger plays that serve as a stimulus for learning directionality, *laterality,* and space concepts.

Counting

The three-year-olds begin with simple number concepts of one, two, and both. At age four children can usually count and arrange objects and groups of three, while five-year-olds will generally be able to count by rote in a series to ten and accomplish one-to-one relationships.

Since young children tend to be slow in understanding the counting process, the teacher or parent provides them with interesting and realistic experiences at each sequential step of their development through utilizing those experiences in their learning environment—blocks in the learning centers, materials and props in the housekeeping center, the play store, and through a generous use of number songs, rhymes, stories, and finger plays using digits up to five at nursery age, and to ten for five-year-olds. By the use of the above-mentioned means, children can experience counting and sequencing and learn about the *more* and *less* concepts in mathematics. They can also be aided in their understanding of conservation and reversal of numbers when care is used to present only one dimension at a given time.

The teacher sets the stage by arranging for objects that will be conducive to numerical thinking in all areas of learning throughout the day, since clarification of mathematical concepts takes place through free, spontaneous experiences as well as through directed learning. The teacher sings, "Can we walk with big steps?" (short steps, long steps, high steps) "How many babies did the mother rabbit have?" "John, feed the rabbit one carrot." "Today is Mary's birthday; she is four years old." Some three-year-olds can learn to count up to five and subtract up to three. The teacher, realizing the significance of utilizing concrete and everyday situations to teach numerical concepts to young children, capitalizes on these quantitative situations and utilizes songs, rhythms, instruments, poems, stories, rhymes, and finger plays to involve children in physical, emotional, social, and intellectual ways.

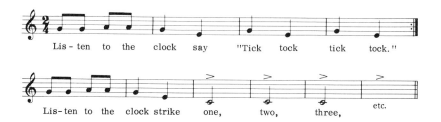

The Clock

V.T.N.

Lis - ten to the clock say "Tick tock tick tock."

Lis - ten to the clock strike one, two, three, etc.

Besides the counting exercise and time concept, this song emphasizes note lengths: one beat for the "tick tock" (quarter) notes and two beats for the clock-striking (half) notes. Divide the children into two groups, one to sing the "tick tock" part and the other to sing the counting part. When the groups sing their parts at the same time, they can hear the two note lengths combining to make interesting music.

A game to play is one in which children march in a circle and stop on a number the teacher designates. Also, the children can be signaled to stop, then asked on what number they stopped. They can clap hands as many times as there are lines or drawings on a chalkboard (these drawings have numbers placed above them). They can count the beats in the beginning pitches of songs having regular quarter-note notation. Example: "Mary Had a Little Lamb" would be 1 2 3 4 5 6 7.

As soon as children have learned to read numbers, they can play tunes by reading numerals drawn on bars of bell sets, possibly with crayon. For example, "Hot Cross Buns" can be played on bars C, D, and E, beginning with middle C, marked 1, 2, and 3 respectively. The notated music for the tune could appear as follows:

	3	2	1	-
1/4	3	2	1	-
	1 1	1 1	2 2	2 2
	3	2	1	-

It could also be written in 4/4 meter: 3 2 1 - | 3 2 1 - |
11112222 | 3 2 1 - |

Some teachers circle numbers to represent groups of eighth notes: 1111 2222. A book that introduces numeral notation is *Timothy's Tunes* by Adeline McCall, Boston Music Co., 1943. McCall further describes this notation in *This Is Music for Kindergarten and Nursery School*, Allyn and Bacon, 1966, pp. 153-56.

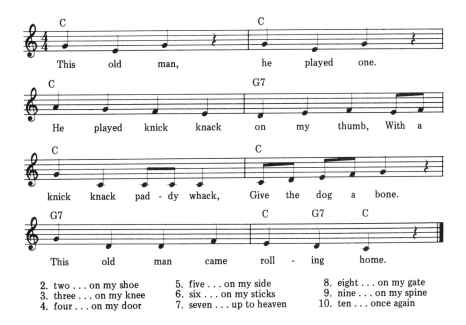

This Old Man

Traditional

This old man, he played one.
He played knick knack on my thumb, With a
knick knack pad - dy whack, Give the dog a bone.
This old man came roll - ing home.

2. two . . . on my shoe
3. three . . . on my knee
4. four . . . on my door

5. five . . . on my side
6. six . . . on my sticks
7. seven . . . up to heaven

8. eight . . . on my gate
9. nine . . . on my spine
10. ten . . . once again

Music, recordings, rhythms, rhymes, finger plays are used to teach young children succession of numbers so that they learn to verbalize them; then they are taught to count. They like counting songs that involve them in some active way.

s   l   s -   d   r   m -
Tap your foot, one, two, three
s   l   s -   m   m   r -
Tap your foot, tap, tap, tee
s   l   s -   d   r   m -
Stamp your foot, one, two, three
s   l   s -   m   r   d -
Stamp your foot, look at me

During water play children observe spatial discrepancies in volume. They should be guided to observe that when a quart of water is taken from a container, *less* water remains in that container than formerly. Then they pour the liquid back into the container and observe that the total amount *increases* again.

Piaget (1952) says young children use single dimensions as a criterion for comparison. When children observe liquid being poured into a tall glass and the same amount poured into a low glass of greater diameter, and are asked if each glass contains the same amount of liquid, they will usually say that the tall slim glass contains more. That is because they use only the single dimension on height and remain oblivious to the difference in diameter. When an equal amount of liquid is poured into several small containers that are emptied into one large container, they observe only the dimension of how many and do not comprehend the volume each container holds. Through this type of behavior it is evident that a young child does not understand conservation of number and reversibility as explained by Jean Piaget. Learning conservation of number and reversibility cannot be hurried. A child's opportunity to internalize mathematical facts and concepts through music and movement at this age is an effective means of assisting the learning of these concepts.

When teaching children to count and to deal with more-less, big-bigger, it is important that teachers be aware of how the child thinks mathematically. Number, sizes, and amounts can be comprehended more effectively if children have a chance to experience them in psychomotor ways. As they use the entire body, including all senses, to manipulate and experience mathematics, understanding and mastery are simplified. Through songs and movement all aspects of mathematics can be made meaningful and interesting because children can be physically, emotionally, socially, and cognitively involved. They count children, age, measure, compare size, measure height, weigh, count blocks, crayons, paints, toys, pets, animals, seed—and songs and dances can always be found or created that involve numerical learnings.

Volume, Size, Length, Weight and Distance

Children never seem to tire of water play. When water is colored it becomes more visible in containers of various sizes and shapes as the children pour it back and forth and into these varied containers. At snacktime they are anxious to pour the milk or orange juice and they enjoy measuring ingredients for cooking. Then, someone must measure the animals' food and feed them. The author observed children in their dramatic play, using a plastic wading pool as a boat. These children discovered volume and space as they experimented with how many children could get into the make-believe boat. When three or four children attempted to pull the "boat" they found that there were too many children in it and they would have to lighten the load. They eliminated one child at a time, checking each time to see if they could move the "boat." This process continued until they were able to move the "boat" with three children in it. They constantly created and sang chants—"Too heavy," "Too many people."

Children experience concepts of length and distance as they compare length of boards used as swing seats, length of tunnels, heights and lengths of balancing boards, lengths of dresses, and as each child is measured and weighed by the teacher. Concepts of length and distance can also be experienced as children take short field trips in the building or near the campus and compare relative distances of buildings in relation to the school, and observe the direction of such buildings from the school.

Concepts of long-short, big-little, wide-narrow, large small, high-low are learned as the children use boxes, jars, and blocks of various sizes and weights. Weight is learned also from their balancing on teeter-totters or seesaws.

Speed is learned by children when they observe how things move. Trains move both fast and slow and so do cars and buses. Animals move with different speeds. Children experiment with speed through imitating the movement of objects, plants, animals, and people and by using swings, rolling objects and wheel toys of varying weights and sizes. They find that music has different speeds (tempos) too. These activities serve as stimuli to developing mathematical vocabulary and concepts and to creating songs, rhythms, instrumentations, and rhymes. They also provide a meaningful context for learning words, rhythms, and instrumental accompaniments to selected songs concerned with size and weight.

Shapes

As children build and haul blocks, set the table, play with wheel toys and use equipment on the playground, they are involved in arranging and naming various shapes such as round (balls, wheels, tables, cookies, plates, bowls, saucers) and square (boxes, cookies), rectangles (tables, books, cookies), and triangles (shapes). In hauling and building blocks they work with blocks that are round, square, triangular, and rectangular. They classify and categorize objects and place them in various shaped containers that may be square, round, or rectangular. They fill cylinders with sand and sing their own songs in their newly-created rhythms as they do it. Many children experience basic shapes as they play with educational toys before they enter nursery school.

After children have used various shapes in their environment the teacher can then provide a series of objects, using only the attribute of shape at first. Next she can add such attributes as size or color or both to that shape. These shapes can be made with felt backing for use on a flannel board. Some teachers provide shapes made of plastic. Through discussions, naming, dramatizing, singing songs, and learning poems and stories involving names and information about shapes, shape concepts are learned by the children. Through action songs, rhythms, and physical interpretation children move in straight lines, in circles, march around in a circle, stand in a square, and form triangles. Songs can be selected that teach shapes and designs or they can be created for and with children. The teacher sings a question and the children hold up the cardboard circle, rectangle, or triangle shapes the teacher makes available.

> 1   1   2   3 -
> T. Who has the square?
> 1   1   2   3 -
> P. I have the square.
> T. Ma-ry put the square in the box, and so on.
> 5   6   5   4   3 - 3   4   5

Of course this type of song can be expanded to include many other attributes:

> 1   1   2   3   1
> T. Who has the big square?
> 1   1   2   3   1
> Who has the blue square?
> 5   4   3   3   3   4   5
> Put the red square in the box.

Time

Concepts of space, time, and number relationships appear to be too abstract for some three-, four-, and five-year-olds. But according to Piaget (1960) this very fact is what make the learning of time, space, and number concepts an important part of their preschool experience. These are the foundation for subsequent study of mathematics.

A child's first experiences with these mathematical concepts need to be correct, realistic, pleasant, and arise from the child's daily activities. The importance of these concrete experiences as a foundation for comprehending relationships of space, shapes, time, and number are presented by Gesell and Ilg (1949). "Time, space, number, form, texture, color, and causality—these are the chief elements in the world of things in which the child must find himself . . . he acquires his command of these elements by slow degrees, first through his muscles of manipulation and locomotion, through eyes, hands, and feet. In this motor experience he lays the foundation for his later judgments and concepts."

When teaching concepts of time teachers observe how children use such concepts in their conversation and dramatic play. They are aware that of all mathematical concepts those of time are the most difficult for children. The three-year-olds deal primarily with the present; four-year-olds begin to use concepts of past events, i.e., yesterday, this morning, last night. The five-year-old begins to add to his concepts of past and present those related to the future such as tomorrow, next Monday, next week, last week, and Christmas. Children at this age often confuse past, present, and future.

A child's concept of time has as its base his knowledge of the movement of objects in space and of changes that have occurred in his own size and growth during his life span. He likes to sing songs about when he was a baby, and when he was little. He contrasts what he did, the clothes he wore, the food he ate, and his ability to run when he was younger and smaller with his present abilities, likes and dislikes. Songs about babyhood size and his present activities are appealing to the three-year-old because he is able to relate time-wise to this period of growth. He enjoys songs, poems, finger plays, and picture stories that relate to this interest. By the age of four a child begins to develop an elementary understanding of time in relation to other people. He begins to comprehend that older people were once children, and he enjoys singing simple folk and created songs about the things his mother, father, grandparents, and other adults did when they were small and young.

Four-and five-year-old children begin to relate to the world of the present, contrasting it in simple and elementary ways with the past. They discuss, sing, and dramatize real and imaginary animals, people, forms of transportation, and work of the past. As the teacher uses appropriate films, recordings, songs, rhythms, poems, rhymes, and stories related to time, children capitalize upon these interesting and meaningful sources of data by discussing the content, expressing feelings and understandings of concepts through listening, creating body interpretations through dance, composing their own songs, accompaniments, dances, or in creative motor responses using dance and dramatization.

Children's birthdays hold personal interest and meaning, especially at age four, but at age five they enjoy including their friends in their birthday celebrations. Birthday songs that can be altered by substituting various children's names are especially popular. Through birthdays they begin to grasp time concepts as they relate to self and others. The time concept of a year can be taught through songs concerning the days of the week, months of the year, and songs and dances about birthdays and holidays that happen only once each year.

The teacher must listen carefully to children's comments and patiently say back to them the proper time concepts. Furthermore she knows that children learn mathematical concepts through psychomotor activities; she therefore selects and formulates objectives for teaching time concepts. Next she plans appropriate activities and materials by which to realize the stated objectives. Books, recordings, films, poems, stories, and finger plays that present similar concepts to those learned in a song can be used as a basis for creating their own dances, songs, and accompaniments.

The teacher can use music to clarify a child's present numerical concepts and to introduce new mathematical concepts. Each new mathematical concept should be closely related to what the child already knows.

Planning musical experiences that enhance the learning of musical and mathematical concepts should be done carefully, concretely and in terms of objectives for both subject areas.

Suggested Musical Activities Related to Mathematics

Think, describe, and dance shapes such as round and square. Following the listing and dancing of these, have children tell what a particular shape makes them think of, and how it makes them feel.

Children can experience the concepts of moving slowly and moving rapidly by physical dramatization to appropriate recorded music.

Children can pretend to be an hour, a minute, or a second hand on a clock, and move accordingly. Some of these activities can be performed to music, and interesting percussion effects can be invented, from ticking to the sounding of chimes.

Concepts in mathematics can be more easily learned if rhythm is experienced. For example, the children can count rhythmically by slapping thighs and clapping hands:

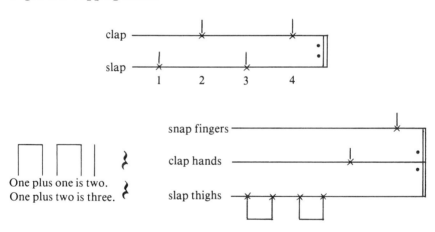

Resources for Mathematics-Music Relationships

Songs

Listed below are some exemplary songs, recordings, films, finger-play sources, poem sources, and stories that can be used in teaching mathematical and music concepts, skills, and appreciations.

New Dimensions in Music: Music for Early Childhood
Bow Belinda (left, right laterality)
Count With Me (counting)
Five Little Chickadees (counting)
One, Two, Buckle My Shoe (counting)

Walking with the New Math (shapes)
Music for Young Americans, Book Two
Department Store Elevator (counting, space, high, low, scale)
Exploring Music: Book One
Five Little Pumpkins (ordinals, Halloween)
Hap Palmer Song Book: Learning Basic Skills in Music Vol. I
Number March (counting, circle)
Growing (time concepts)
Put Your Hands Up in the Air (directionality and space awareness)
Hap Palmer Song Book: Learning Basic Skills in Music Vol. II
Paper Clock (telling time)
One Shape, Three Shapes
Lucky Number March (counting)
Triangle, Circle, and Square (shapes)
Spectrum of Music: Book One
Angel Band (counting)
Songs from *Math Readiness,* a Hap Palmer Record Album
Paper Clocks (telling time)
One Shape, Three Shapes
Lucky Number March
High and Low
Walk Around the Circle
Count Up, Count Down
Show Me the Shape Just Like Yours
Moving By Numeral
Make a Set
Show Me a Card (0 to 9)
Clapping Sets
Can You Catch a Set?
Discovering Music Together: Early Childhood
Roll Over (counting)
Singing With Children and many other books
By'm Bye (counting, high, low)
Old Brass Wagon (left, right, circle)
One Elephant (counting, size)
Over in the Meadow (counting)
This Old Man (counting)
Traditional, in many books
Clocks and Watches (long, short, divisions of the beat)
Hokey-Pokey (left, right, arm, foot, whole self, turn about)
Hot Cross Buns (beginning counting)
Humpty Dumpty (wall, fall, put together)
(See Classified Indexes of music textbooks)

Old Brass Wagon

American Folk Song

Rhythmically

1. Cir - cle to the left, The Old Brass Wag - on,
2. Cir - cle to the right, The Old Brass Wag - on,

Cir - cle to the left, The Old Brass Wag - on,
Cir - cle to the right, The Old Brass Wag - on,

Cir - cle to the left, The Old Brass Wag - on,
Cir - cle to the right, The Old Brass Wag - on,

You're the one, my dar - ling.
You're the one, my dar - ling.

Ask the children to invent other motions.

Recordings

All About Number and Counting 1003 MB. Counting instruments of the orchestra, going up in a department store elevator, adding cars to a freight train. Lorraine Music Co.

Math Readiness: Vocabulary and Concepts, by Hap Palmer. Album AR 540-1 or cassette. Music and action songs that teach concepts and vocabulary needed for basic mathematics. Educational Activities, Inc.

Math Readiness: Addition and Subtraction, by Hap Palmer. Album AR 541-1 or cassette. Games and movement activities for helping children to understand concepts and memorize addition-subtraction facts. Educational Activities, Inc.

Dancing Numerals Pre-K-2. Teaching mathematics concepts through music, games, and chants by Henry Glass, Rosemary Hallum and Charles

Barker. Album AR 537-1 or cassette. Essential concepts in math readiness programs are taught in these original classroom-tested activities. Children understand the ideas because they physically perform them. Educational Activities, Inc.

Counting Games and Rhythms for Little Ones, by Ella Jenkins. Folkways FC 7056.

Filmstrips

Dancing Numerals AR 537 (see same title under Recordings). To be used with record or cassette. Singing and Movement for math readiness. Educational Activities, Inc.

Finger plays

(See the sources for finger plays listed in the general bibliography at the end of this chapter.)

Anderson, Paul S., *Language Skills in the Elementary School,* 2d ed. New York: Macmillan Co.

Five Little Squirrels
Two Dickey Birds
Five Little Pumpkins
Five Little Children

Poulsson, Emily, *Finger Plays for Nursery and Kindergarten.* New York: Lothrop, Lee and Shepard Co.

Here Is a Beehive, Where Are the Bees?

Scott, Louise Binder and J. J. Thompson, *Rhymes for Fingers and Flannelboards.* New York: McGraw-Hill Book Co.

Five Jack-o-Lanterns
Five Little Chickadees
I Have Ten Little Fingers
Bunnies Now Must Go to Bed

Poems

See poetry and nursery rhyme anthologies in the general bibliography at the end of this chapter for poems that contain concepts about mathematics: space, shape, size, weight, time, and counting.

One Wide River to Cross by Barbara Emberley. Englewood Cliffs, N.J.: Prentice-Hall, 1966. This old folk song provides children counting practice as Noah's animals come two by two, three by three, and ten by ten.

One Two Buckle My Shoe, by Gail E. Haley. A great collection of counting rhymes.

The Twelve Days of Christmas, by Ilonka Karasz. New York: Harper & Row, Publishers, 1949. The story begins with the first day of Christmas and a partridge in a pear tree and progresses with the ordinal numbers through twelve. The book contains the music of the song.

Gaily We Parade, by John E. Brewton. New York: Macmillan Co., 1958. Contains:
Counters, by Elizabeth Coats
Penny Problems, by John Farrow

Books about Space, Size, Weight, Time, Shapes, Counting, and Measuring

Allen, Robert. *Numbers.* Bronx, N.Y.: Platt & Munk Publishers, 1968. Colorful pictures of familiar objects for children to count.

Atwood, Ann. *The Little Circle.* New York: Charles Scribner's Sons, 1967. Pictures illustrate a circle used in many different settings.*

Baier, Howard. *Now This, Now That.* New York: Holiday House, 1957. Encourage close observation of objects from different directions and distances as it presents position and comparative vocabulary such as under, on, far, near, up, down, high, low, long, short, big, little.*

Beim, Jerrold. *The Smallest Boy in the Class.* New York: Wm. Morrow, 1949. The concept of smallest boy in the class is used to stimulate comparisons of smallest, small, big, biggest, tall, short, and little.*

Berkeley, Ethel S. *Big and Little, Up and Down.* New York: William R. Scott, Inc., 1960. Assist in developing concepts of directions and space.*

———. *Ups and Downs.* New York: William R. Scott, Inc. Contains questions and presents concepts of up-down, top-bottom, high-low, over-under in clear and concise language.

Black, Irma S. *Busy Water.* New York: Holiday House, 1958. An introduction to concepts of gravity. Water flows down and increases in volume as it joins other springs, rain, brooks, rivers, and the ocean.*

Blair, Mary. *The Up and Down Book.* New York: Golden Press, 1964. A very simple picture book views the world as a child sees it. "The clouds are up; the grass is down."

Borton, Helen. *Do You See What I See?* New York: Abelard Schuman, 1959. A story about lines, shapes, and colors. There are tall, short, curved and slanted lines. As they are placed in different positions they form round circles like a ball, curved lines like a bird, and squares, triangles and rectangles.*

———. *North, South, East and West.* New York: Thomas Y. Crowell, 1966. Develops the concepts of position.

Buckley, Helen E. *The Little Boy and the Birthdays.* New York: Lothrop, Lee and Shepard, Inc., 1965.

*Lydia A. Gerhardt. MOVING AND KNOWING: The Young Child Orients Himself in Space. (©) 1973 Lydia A. Gerhardt, pp. 184-189. By permission of Prentice-Hall.

Budney, Blossom. *A Kiss Is Round.* New York: Lothrop, Lee & Shepard Co. Shows many things in a child's world that are round*

Burton, Virginia Lee. *Mike Mulligan and His Steam Shovel.* New York: Houghton Mifflin, 1939. A hole gets bigger the more you dig and remove (take away).*

Carroll, Ruth. *Where's the Kitty?* New York: Henry Z. Walck, 1962. Develops concepts of under, in, on, beside, etc.*

Chwast, Seymour, and Moskoff, Morton. *Still Another Number Book.* New York: McGraw-Hill Book Co., 1971. The book progresses from one ship to ten jugglers and then reverses. Assists children in learning reversibility of numbers.

Duvoisin, Roger. *Two Lonely Ducks.* New York: Alfred A. Knopf, 1955. Children count the eggs laid by the mother duck, count the days she sits on them, and count the ducklings that hatch out.

Emberly, Edward. *The Wing on a Flea—A Book About Shapes.* New York: Little, Brown & Co., 1961. Illustrations of things in the world that are triangular, circular, and rectangular.*

Falconer, Rebecca. *Tall Enough Tommy.* New York: Children's Press, 1948. Shows advantages in being any height.

Flack, Marjorie. *Tim Tadpole and the Great Bullfrog.* New York: Doubleday, 1954. As time passes Tim grows into a big bullfrog.*

Freeman, Don. *Fly High, Fly Low.* New York: Viking Press, 1958. Pigeons fly high, low, up, down, away from, and toward.*

Fritz, Jean. *Growing Up.* Chicago: Rand McNally & Co., 1956. A child is always bigger or smaller than something.*

Gag, Wanda. *Snippy and Snappy.* New York: Coward-McCann, 1935. Relative size; how does a chair look to a tiny mouse?

Green, Mary McBurney. *Is It Hard? Is It Easy?* Reading, Mass.: Addison-Wesley Publishing Co., 1960. Some tasks take a long time while easy tasks usually take less time.

Hawkinson, John, and Hawkinson, Lucy. *Days I Like.* Chicago: Albert Whitman and Company, 1965. Exciting things to do every month of the year.

Heide, Florence, and Van Clief, Sylvia. *How Big Am I?* Chicago: Follett, 1968. A little boy compares his size to all types of objects about him.*

Hengesbaugh, Jane. *I Live in So Many Places.* Chicago: Children's Press, 1956. Space as it relates to location of home (house), town, state, country, and world.

Hogan, Inez. *Twin Lambs.* New York: E. P. Dutton & Co., 1951. Develops ideas of same size, same shape, together, and distance.*

Horwich, Frances. *My Goldfish.* Chicago: Rand McNally & Co., 1958. Round bowl, rectangular aquarium, large and small goldfish.*

Ipcar, Dahlov. *Brown Cow Farm.* New York: Doubleday & Co., 1959. The farmer counts from one horse to 100 goslings.

Jacobs, L. B. *Is Somewhere Always Far Away?* New York: Holt, Rinehart & Winston, 1967. Time and place simplified.

Jean, Priscilla. *Pattie Round and Wally Square.* New York: Ivan Oblensky, 1965. A square longs to be round like a circle; a new world of squares.*

Kahn, Joan. *Seesaw.* New York: Harper & Row, Publishers, 1964. Two children tell what they see when they are up and down.*

Klein, Leonora. *How Old is Old?* New York: Harvey House, 1967. What is old? What is young?*

Kohn, Bernice. *Everything Has a Size.* Englewood Cliffs, N. J.: Prentice-Hall, 1964. Big cake, big candles, little cake, little candle, etc.

Krasilovsky, Phyllis. *The Very Little Boy.* New York: Doubleday & Co., 1962. Language of comparison as a boy grows bigger.*

———. *The Very Little Girl.* New York: Doubleday & Co., 1953. Language of comparison as a girl grows.*

Krauss, Ruth. *The Big World and the Little House.* New York: Harper & Row, Publishers, 1964. Relative size.*

Langstaff, John. *Over in the Meadow.* New York: Harcourt, Brace and World, Inc., 1956. A Caldecott Award winner. Assists in relating counting to realistic objects.

Lenski, Lois. *On a Summer Day.* New York: Henry Z. Walck, Inc., 1953. Also *Now It's Fall* and *I Like Winter*, 1948 and 1950. Builds concepts about the sequence of seasons.*

Lionni, Leo. *On My Beach There Are Many Pebbles.* New York: Ivan Obolensky, 1961. Sizes and shapes of pebbles.*

Reed, Mary, and Osswald, Edith. *Numbers.* New York: Golden Press, 1955. Child explores surroundings to discover numbers.

Schatz, Litta. *When Will My Birthday Be?* New York: McGraw-Hill Book Co., 1962. Benjy waits for his birthday through a succession of seasons.

Schlein, Miriam. *Fast Is Not a Ladybug.* Reading, Mass.: Addison-Wesley Publishing Co., 1953. A study of fast and slow.*

———. *Heavy is a Hippopotamus.* Reading, Mass.: Addison-Wesley Publishing Co., 1954. Size and weight are not relative.*

Schlein, Miriam. *Shapes.* Reading, Mass.: Addison-Wesley Publishing Co., 1952. Roundness, squareness, and straightness.

Schwartz, Julius. *Uphill and Downhill.* New York: McGraw-Hill Book Co., 1965. Up, down, gravity, bigger, smaller, the hill as an inclined plane for lifting and rolling.*

Seignobosc, Francoise. *Jeanne-Marie Counts Her Sheep.* New York: Charles Scribner's Sons, 1951. Teaches children simple and meaningful counting.

*Lydia A. Gerhardt. MOVING AND KNOWING: The Young Child Orients Himself in Space. (©) 1973 Lydia A. Gerhardt, pp. 184-189. By permission of Prentice-Hall.

————. *What Time Is It, Jeanne-Marie?* New York: Lippencott, 1933. Simple time concepts.

Slobodkin, E. *The Wonderful Feast.* New York: Lothrop, Lee and Shepard Co., 1955. The amount of food for each animal is related to its size.

Stanek, Muriel. *One, Two, Three for Fun.* Chicago: Albert Whitman and Co., 1967. Counting familiar objects in familiar geographical settings from one to five.

Stover, Joann. *Why? Because.* New York: David McKay Co., 1961. Some language of geometry with amusing reasons.*

Sullivan, Joan. *Round is a Pancake.* New York: Holt, Rinehart and Winston, 1963. Round objects in picture and rhyme.*

Tamburine, Jean. *Almost Big Enough.* New York: Abingdon Press, 1963. Eventually one grows to be "big enough."*

Taylor, Paul. *What Is???* Series: *Round, Square, High and Tall, Long and Short, Triangular, Little and Small.* Glendale, Calif.: Bowmar. A set of six books appropriate for preschool and kindergarten to develop concepts of shape, distance, and size.

Tresselt, Alvin. *Follow the Road.* New York: Lothrop, Lee and Shepard, 1956. A study of distance.*

————. *How Far is Far?* New York: Parents Magazine Press, 1964. As far as, as big as, with points of reference.*

Tudor, Tasha. *1 is One.* New York: Henry Z. Walck, Inc., 1956. Delightful counting book and artistically illustrated.

Watson, Nancy Dingman. *When Is Tomorrow?* New York: Macmillan Co., 1951. Enjoying today and planning for tomorrow.

Wildsmith, Brian. *The Hare and the Tortoise.* New York: Franklin Watts, 1967. Fast, slow, and distance.

Windsor, Marie. *Let's Play Store.* Chicago: Follett, 1964. Children buy and sell objects using play money.

Witte, Eve, and Witte, Pat. *Look Look!* New York: Golden Press, 1961. Backward, forward, up, down, taller, shorter, fast, slow, big, and little.*

Wittram, H. R. *Going Up, Going Down.* New York: Holt, Rinehart & Winston, 1963.*

Zion, Gene. *All Falling Down.* New York: Harper & Row, Publishers, 1951. Down go snow, leaves, nuts, sand castles, shadows, and even some stars.*

Zolotow, Charlotte. *Over and Over.* New York: Harper & Row, Publishers, 1957. Young children grasp the understanding that there is a sameness about each year as activities of each season are presented in a repetitive and successive format including holidays and seasons.

Music and Physical Development

There is a close relationship between music and the physical and the health and safety development of children. Many of the activities in physical education are accompanied and enriched by the use of music. Folk dances that are often considered part of the physical education program are derivatives of folk songs, such as "Pawpaw Patch," "Captain Jinks," and "Chiapanecas." Awkward and untrained muscular and skeletal control lead to accidents, thus relate to safety. Through movement, rhythm, and dance children learn to control the muscles and the actions of the body with precision and skill. Since music can involve a physical as well as a cognitive and affective response it is of great assistance to the child in developing the muscles for control and coordination of body movements.

The body is a means of communication that is sometimes underdeveloped in our schools. Physical movement through imitation, dramatic play, rhythmic and expressive gestures or dance should be natural forms of artistic expression for the young child, since expression through movement or action is an integral part of learning, particularly at these ages.

Music assists the physical education program in achieving such objectives as balance and coordination, body image and awareness, *laterality,* directionality, and eye-hand coordination. The development of gross motor skills can be realized by combining marching to the beat, clapping the hands in the rhythm patterns of songs, rhymes, and poems, bending the knees to show the meter and changing body movements in accord to the phrases, and singing the words of a song. Through songs the child may be taught to recognize and name the parts of his body and to imitate body movements. His muscles and his entire body are used as he moves freely in reponse to rhythm and as he dramatizes songs. Frost (1976) writes, "Free movement with music as a stimulus and involving children in a room, helps the child learn how to cope with changes in space, to seek alternatives to problems, and to gain skill and agility in moving safely around obstacle."

As the child plays rhythm sticks, drums, resonator bells and other instruments his eye-hand coordination can be improved. And too, the use of hand puppets by the child while singing develops the fine finger and hand muscles and makes the child aware of his hands and what he can cause them to do.

Laterality is the quality of having distinct sides. Until a child learns *laterality* and *directionality* of parts of the body and objects in space, all forms of learning are hampered. Music is useful in acquiring these concepts. Singing games can teach the child to identify right and left hand, foot, or side of the body, and to sense direction, such as in, on, above, beside, behind, and under. Examples of these games include "Hokey Pokey" and "Looby Loo," the latter song concerning the old-time Saturday night bath in which children danced around a metal tub and dipped their fingers and toes in the water to determine its temperature.

Resources for music-movement relationships can be found in Chapter 4.

If You're Happy   Traditional

Gaily

If you're hap - py and you know it, clap your hands, *(clap   clap)*

If you're hap - py and you know it, clap your hands, *(clap   clap)*

If you're hap - py and you know it, Then your face will sure - ly show it,

If you're hap - py and you know it, clap your hands. *(clap   clap)*

2. . . . tap your toe, *(tap, tap)*
3. . . . nod your head, *(nod nod)*

Have the children invent other motions.

Music and Health and Safety

This area is one in which there are a great many contrived songs. Some critics have termed them "propaganda songs." Be that as it may, this is in the grand tradition of humanity, for music has always been used in this manner. We use it today in television commercials and songs that promote various ideologies from antipollution to political goals. Thus, through dramatization, movement, and singing selected songs the child learns about safety and health concepts, and their vocabulary. He sings songs about safety—safety at home, on the school playground, and in relation to machines and animals. He may also learn songs about food, manners,

Looby Loo

Quickly

Here we go loo - by loo, Here we go loo - by light,

Here we go loo - by loo, All on a Sat - ur - day night.

I put my right hand in,

I take my right hand out, I give my hand a

shake, shake, shake, And turn my - self a - bout. Oh,

clothes, personal appearance, and cleanliness. He creates and participates in music activities that can include the learning of concepts and skills concerned with brushing teeth ("This is the Way We Brush Our Teeth" sung to the tune of "The Mulberry Bush"); proper eating habits: eating balanced meals and various types of food; and the use, functions, and care of clothing. Young children are interested in creating songs and rhythms about the health and safety of pets and animals in general. Music helps to make learning in this important area more pleasant and more effective because of its appeal to feelings and, if properly selected and performed, because of its aesthetic qualities. Despite the fact that teachers and children will and should compose many of their own songs, it would be helpful if composers of stature would become interested in writing songs to serve this area of living. However, while we wait for them, we will continue to create our own. Many teachers create their own verse to be sung to the old familiar tunes such as "Mary Had a Little Lamb," "Twinkle, Twinkle, Little Star," "Mary Wore a Red Dress," and many others. For example, a teacher might sing the tune of "Here We Go 'Round the Mulberry Bush"

Hokey-Pokey

American Folk Song

Fairly Fast

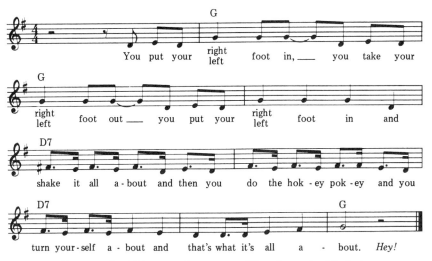

Encourage the children to make up verses adding other parts of the body.

and ask the children to substitute words related to personal grooming such as: This is the way we wash our hands, or brush our teeth, brush our hair, clean our nails, polish our shoes, iron our dress or shirt, take a bath, eat our food, and so on.

For a rhythmic experience, have the children try to step words while chanting them:

Traffic Lights

The teacher can ask the children to echo her singing of the first measure, then the second measure (tone matching). Everyone can sing together during the last two measures after the song has been learned.

Songs. Health and safety songs are commonly found under that heading in the classified indexes of music textbooks. Most are composed songs such as "Safety" in *New Dimensions-K,* but a few folk songs like "Looby Lou," which concerns children taking a bath, are used also. Songs from the Hap Palmer Album *Health and Safety* are contemporary in style and add interest to this area of instruction. Titles in the album include:

Take a Bath	Brush Away (teeth)
Buckle Your Seat Belt	Cover Your Mouth
Posture Exercise	Alice's Restaurant (foods)
Keep Germs Away	Exercise Every Day
Safe Way (crossing streets)	

Resources for Health-Safety-Music Relationships

Recordings

Health Can Be Fun	Lyons NS 6883, Lyons, Elkhart, Indiana
Health and Safety Highlights Kit	Scott, Foresman and Co. Songs, pictures, charts, and a recording done by Ella Jenkins of health songs.
Health and Safety Through Music	Lyons NS 6883
Learning Basic Skills Through Music: Health and Safety by Hap Palmer	Educational Activities, Freeport, N.Y. Catchy lyrics and happy songs teach concepts of cleanliness, balanced diet, exercise, safety rules, and the reasons behind them.

Films and Filmstrips

Caring for Your Toys, McGraw-Hill, 11 min. b & w.

Dental Health Stories by Jean Wood. FSR 423, Grades K-3. Two-color filmstrips, two records or cassettes. Educational Activities, Freeport, N.Y.

Keeping Safe and Healthy, FOM, 30 fr., c.

Safe and Sound at Home SVE, 35 fr., c.

Safety To and From School, McGraw-Hill, b & w, 10 min.

Safe and Sound Along the Way, SVE, 37 fr., c.

Street Safety, EBF, 45 fr., c.

Music and Social Studies

The child's entry into school is possibly one of the biggest leaps into the social world that a child ever makes. Here he finds that his "me first" attitude or egocentric behavior must be quickly expanded to include other "me firsts" in the classroom environment. Children find that there is fun in sharing and doing things with others. Thus they are usually interested in creating chants, songs, rhythms, dance, instrumental accompaniments, poems and stories about the many activities in which they engage. One begins a chant and usually others join him in improvising and expanding the chant. These efforts almost always arise from some individual or physical school activity, and thus are an extension of movement. Nine-tenths of the subject matter of the natural chant of children grows out of the social environment, that is, persons, objects, machines, animals, food, and occupations. Children use chant to establish limits of activities and ownership. Both created and composed songs can serve as vehicles for role playing, discussion, dramatization, creative composition and use of instrumentation as well as for creative interpretation through movement. The teacher formulates questions about this music, which prompt discussion and creative thinking.

Self-Awareness

An individual's sense of identity and awareness of self are developed in the very early years of his life. Positive, wholesome concepts about himself result from the ways other people accept and respond to him, and these concepts usually correspond directly to what he is capable of doing. Music, movement, and literature serve as natural avenues through which the child can discover who he is.

According to McFee (1969), "a child's self-concept is closely associated with his name, and since most children are unable to pronounce their names when they begin nursery school, individual names should be used as frequently as feasible in connection with both planned and spontaneous musical activities. Songs should be created or selected in which the name of each child in the group may be substituted and used, or the name should be used in a finger play, rhyme, poem, or story. Hearing his name sung or repeated in connection with various activities not only helps him to learn it but also helps him to know himself as a unique individual with a special label for the "I" that at this time in life is so extremely important to him.

As a child participates in creative rhythmic movement and dramatization, sings and creates chants and songs, recites and creates finger plays, rhymes, and poems to interpret and communicate his ideas and his proposed solutions to the social problems of man as he presently understands them, he becomes important to himself and others, and they in turn become important to him.

A child learns of his own power and importance only as he becomes actively involved in creative and practical solutions to problems. Music is an avenue through which he can do this. When he plays an instrument it is the power of *his* body and *his* mind that causes sound to be produced. Through his involvement he is able to demonstrate what he can do by playing instruments and by using his body to hop, skip, clap, trot, act out a character in a song, poem, or story, or dramatize the actions and roles of community workers, create or reproduce a rhythm pattern or dance, sing a song, speak a rhyme, or dance to a recording. Thus he develops confidence and self-reliance through music as he can do in no other area of learning. Music performance and creative activity increase the mastery of social studies skills and concepts. Research indicates that through music activities that employ psychomotor skills, pupils can develop their creative and problem-solving potential to a greater degree than through any other area of the curriculum.

The Pillsbury Foundation Studies (1978 5th ed.) were conducted on the basis of child freedom to explore musical sounds with a minimum of adult interference. "It was obvious that music as an individual and social activity could reach its natural form only if individuals and social groups within the school were free to evolve their own forms. Socially the children showed increasing ability to develop patterns of interrelated groupings constantly dissolving and reforming, directed largely by themselves and inspired by their own interests." When children are free to explore sound through musical instruments, they eventually form small groups. These groups often have directors (one who plays a commanding instrument), and the children find ways of starting and stopping together. A strong implication of the Pillsbury studies is that children must be relatively free of adult domination, thus the warning, "Don't structure the child's school life too soon."

As children participate in music they can express and release feelings of acceptance, aggression, anger, joy, and fear. The aggressive four- and five-year-olds who are anxious for attention regardless of how it is obtained have opportunities to express those feelings in acceptable ways through their active involvement. As a child moves and sings he can express positive and negative feelings both verbally and nonverbally. A child's feelings of self-awareness, self-concept, security and acceptance result from activities in which he can succeed at his own level and can learn through physical trial and error to solve relevant problems. The development of competencies in self-expression, acceptance of others, and positive and secure feelings about self results from freedom of expression, experience in music and in creative movement. His positive feelings about self are automatically transferred to the way he accepts and works with teachers, parents, and peers in his immediate world and his world of the future.

Songs for Self-Awareness   A song such as "Hokey Pokey" assists the child in naming and moving body parts, which relates to self-awareness. Action songs referring to head, shoulders, knees, and feet are in this same category. The child's self-concept is strengthened as his name is included in a song. He is usually delighted when he is addressed in this tunefully personal way. The teacher and the children may compose simple, short songs or song fragments that include a child's name and something that he possesses. In many instances the child's name and comments about him are sung to familiar folk tunes or parts of them, such as:

Frere Jacque
Row Your Boat
Li'l 'Liza Jane
Happy Birthday to You
Clap Your Hands
If You're Happy
Mulberry Bush

Mary Had a Little Lamb
Ten Little Indians
Hot Cross Buns
Hey, Betty Martin
Old Joe Clark (same as "Clap Your Hands")

Examples: *Mary Had a Little Lamb*

John-ny has some new red shoes

Old Joe Clark

Kate,   Kate,   walk with me,   We will walk to - geth - er

Mulberry Bush

Mar-sha Scott, here is your juice,   is your juice,   is your juice,

School Activities

Music contributes to the development of a positive attitude toward school and the activities involved therein and it provides an overall motivation for learning. Therefore children will need to learn songs about the various activities in which they will be involved at school. For example, if saluting the flag is one of those activities, they may need to be taught a song that will teach the meaning and the skill of saluting the flag. Many of the songs learned at first may be of this practical type which involves children physically in the learning process.

Children with Special Learning Problems. Music is perhaps the best avenue for helping handicapped children to gain self-awareness, initiative, and confidence. Some children demand or need to sing the same song in exactly the way it was first learned, and want an identical sequence of activities, even to the same key and tempo, because they desire the security of the predictable. Some can identify real instruments but may fail to recognize them in pictures because of the difficulty of relating a concrete object to its symbol. The teacher should know the characteristics of the various types of handicapped children, adapt the activity in accordance with their needs, watch for signs of pressure, and if pressure is indicated, change the activity calmly or otherwise reduce the pressure to avoid explosive reactions.

Three-year-old Stanley can see himself in a portable mirror and beats a drum in response to the teacher's song   s   m   s   m
           "Where is Stanley?" by beating the rhythm of "Here I Am." The teacher will sing Stanley's name very often, and when Stanley swings a scarf to music while watching himself in a large mirror, he will learn about himself and his uniqueness. Handicapped children can play simple instruments along with the piano and learn to start, stop, play fast and slow, loud and soft. They can enjoy moving parts of the body in accordance with directions on a suitable recording. Very young children are encouraged to show initiative by making some effort to reach for the instruments, animal figures, or scarves, because if they do not, they are passed by. (At first, the teacher moves the child in the appropriate response.) Structure and sequence can be learned by singing songs with several verses, especially those like "This Old Man," "Miss Mary Mack," "Hush Little Baby," and "Noah." First responses to pitch are likely to be non-verbal, beginning with beating drums to "answer" in the correct places in songs such as "Mary Had a Baby" and "John the Rabbit," then responding by playing the bells, and eventually by playing kazoos. When confidence is stronger, singing on pitch can become an important goal. Perfect pitch or tone production cannot be expected; an approximation is welcomed. The children can study concepts such as high and low; they can learn whether or not to play up (for high) or down (for low) on step bells, or on smaller or larger bell bars, or strings. The *Threhold to*

Music 2nd ed. *Early Childhood Experience Charts* and the *Level One Experience Charts* have been used successfully with handicapped children to introduce notation. (Fearon Publishers, 6 Davis Drive, Belmont, California 94002) Among the many companies offering recordings designed for special children are Bowmar, Kimbo Educational, Children's Music Center, and Educational Activities.

The activities for the so-called "normal" child can usually be used also with children with special abilities, needs, and interests. However, these activities will possibly need to be presented in a more highly structured format for the learning-disabled or in a less structured format for the child with superior abilities. More time, more teacher guidance, more repetitions, and coverage of less material will be required for the learning-disabled to master musical concepts and skills than for the average "normal" learner. For further discussion see Chapter Two, "Mainstreaming," and Chapter Six.

Home

Children are most comfortable when they are creating and learning chants, songs, dance and dramatization, rhythms, instrumentation and stories about the familiar world they know best; this world is their home and family. The home is the first social group of which the child becomes a participating and usually an accepted member. The experiences the child has in this setting become a point of reference or a base for all other social learnings. He enjoys discussing and reenacting these activities at school. Music in this area, when carefully chosen and created, aids in strengthening the child's appreciations, attitudes toward his family and home, and serves as one avenue through which he can learn to value his home and the members of his family.

Songs pertaining to this source should be carefully selected to reinforce positive attitudes toward home and family. As rhythms, rhymes, songs, and stories are presented, children should be encouraged to discuss them and to interpret them in a number of ways including dramatization. Furthermore, they should be induced to create their own songs about the members of their families and their activities. The teacher stimulates this creative act by asking questions and reinforcing and encouraging the children's efforts.

Community and Music

As the child becomes involved in the activities of the school he soon finds himself expanding into the broader community world. When he becomes interested in the expanding world of the community, he will need to understand how it effects his own and other people's lives. Again, an excellent way to initiate interest in the activities and concepts related to the community is through song, movement, and instrumentation. The creation and

Sleep, Baby, Sleep

Traditional

Slowly

Sleep, ba - by, sleep! Thy fa - ther guards the sheep, Thy
moth - er shakes the dream - land tree, And from it falls sweet
dreams for thee; Sleep, ba - by, sleep! Sleep, ba - by, sleep!

2. Sleep, baby, sleep! The large stars are the sheep.
   The little ones, the lambs, I guess,
   The gentle moon, the shepherdess,
   Sleep, baby, sleep! sleep, baby, sleep!

use of carefully selected songs, instrumental compositions, listening activities, dramatizations, movement, dance, poems and stories comprise an important strategy for teaching.

Information about community workers and consumers has been an important part of the content of the social studies for young children. Every early childhood music textbook provides songs pertaining to the workers and consumers found in communities, but children should also be encouraged to make up songs about these people, dramatize their work, and learn to respect the various occupations and the people who are involved in them. Music, paintings, poetry, and rhythms are employed to help children absorb the concepts concerned with people and their work. There are not only songs about the dentist, farmer, mailman, barber, grocerman, fireman, bus driver, policeman, sailor, fisherman, miner, and virtually every occupational worker, but there are also songs and rhythms about consumers. They enrich this area of social studies and help children learn by providing specific concepts, activities, and an atmosphere of interest, enjoyment, and creativity.

Travel and Peoples of the World

Music serves as children's main source for learning of the values and cultural behaviors of people throughout the world. Through music and dance they are introduced to the fact that mankind the world over is the same or similar in many aspects. Through music they learn about fun and recreation, work, transportation, communication, concerns with health and safety, and the people's love for country, family, and friends. They learn of the holidays and heroes of other peoples, and relate them to their own.

A brochure published by Bowmar in 1973 states, "Through song children learn of the diversity and of the oneness of mankind. Although countries and language differ, children will discover that everywhere man is concerned with his relationship to his environment, with his search for work and love, joy, and laughter, and his need for worship, music and dance, art and language. They will see that man seeks ways to express his humanity through the universal language of song."

Singing Games as a Socializing Experience

As a child's interest in play expands, he usually demonstrates an increasing desire to share his experiences with other children. The singing game is an effective emotional and physical release and provides a vehicle for socialization, learning new words, concepts, and skills. The children should be given freedom to explore unique and creative ways to organize and interpret a singing (folk) game or dance. For instance, they should decide how they will play "Tideo" (Jingle at the Window"), how they will make the "windows," how they will take turns being "it," and so on. Two excellent sources for traditional musical games are:

Katharine Wessels, *The Little Golden Book of Singing Games*. New York: Simon and Schuster, Inc., 1947.

Edna Potter, *This Way and That*: New York: Oxford University Press, 1930. Contains twenty-four favorite, illustrated musical games.

Folk Songs

Much folk music is valuable and relevant to the development of social concepts and values. However, the teacher must present music in ways that make for better understanding of people, their beliefs and customs. She should select music that depicts the experiences, customs, and beliefs of the people and that also contains opportunities for teaching true musical values. To enrich and further extend children's appreciation of folk music and literature, dramatization, dance, and musical accompaniments should be used. Consideration should be given to human likenesses when appropriate, stressing that in all countries people sing for similar purposes; therefore singing is a means of communication used by all humans. One of the teacher's major tasks is to select good folk songs from the various cultures of the world that can be sung and enjoyed by young children or that can be adapted for their use.

Patriotic Songs

Songs, instrumental music selections, movement and dance, role playing and dramatization of songs, poems and stories will be used to introduce young children to their responsibilities as citizens of the community, country and world. This is an effective avenue to teaching principles, concepts, attitudes and values of the history of their country. The teacher will need to explain thoroughly the importance and meaning of each selection and **why it was** produced.

Holidays and Special Days

Special days are of paramount interest to the young child. Through study of holidays and special days the child begins to learn time concepts related to people who have made exceptional contributions to the home, school, nation and world, especially the birthdays of community, state, national, and world figures. They also learn concepts and values in the areas of the social sciences through music, song, dance and dramatization. Related to this topic—holidays and special days—children will learn birthday songs in relation to themselves, their peers, and historical figures, as well as songs relating to special days and holidays such as Valentine's Day, Halloween, Thanksgiving, and Christmas.

Young children not only enjoy special days and holidays related to their immediate environment but they are also interested in those of people in strange and faraway places. Through learning and singing special day and holiday songs children learn of the history and customs of world cultures and how and why other peoples celebrate special days and holidays. But more important, the development of positive and receptive attitudes toward all people has begun. Children's personal values concerning themselves and the peoples and things in the world are established at a very early age. Therefore children should have the opportunity to learn music relating to the important holidays, festivals, and activities of various countries. There are ample recordings, poems, and stories that can be combined with songs to build concepts and appreciations of others. "The arts (music) deal with the real characteristics of the human condition which do not lend themselves to scientific methodology. The human condition is best understood through art (music) processes and art methodologies." (Hanshumaker, n.d.)

The development of specific job-oriented skills is not the solution to changing societal needs brought about by an increasingly technological society. We need the arts through which to express social science concepts, but more significantly we need them as vehicles to express and communicate the feelings, sensitives, and values of the human race.

The teacher of nursery and kindergarten pupils should choose songs, rhythms, rhymes, poems, finger plays, and stories that assist these pupils in learning about

Self-awareness and individual roles
Roles of boys and girls
Roles of family members
Roles of community workers and consumers
Life in the city and in the rural community
Responsibilities and roles involved in going to school

How people in the world are alike

Special days and heroes
Special holidays
Playing together

Resources for Social Studies-Music Relationships

Songs

There are innumerable folk songs and composed songs available for enrichment of social studies. Any music textbook should have a classified index that guides the teacher to songs listed under social studies headings such as holidays and special days, travel and transportation, lullabies, home and family, occupations, patriotic songs, songs around the world, songs of the United States, fun and games, names, clothing, and so on. Thus, the first suggestion is to refer to nursery school and kindergarten music textbooks. Many songs for first grade can be used or adapted as well. Refer also to the collections of appropriate songs from other sources listed at the end of the "singing" section of Chapter 4.

Rather than attempting to list songs from the tens of thousands one might choose from, the author has selected a typical music textbook for use as an example of what the teacher can expect to find when she examines such books, *New Dimensions in Music: Music for Early Childhood,* American Book Company, 1976.

A. *Family, Self-Awareness, and Feelings*
   Helping Mother
   My Family
   My Son John
   Quiet, Quiet
   Rocking with Grandfather
   Thanksgiving
   Wake Up
   With Daddy
   Quiet, Quiet

B. *Community and Work*
   Building With Blocks
   Dentist, The
   Farmer in the Dell, The
   Fire Song
   I Like the Policeman
   Ice Cream Man, The
   It's Fun to Go to the Grocery Store
   Johnny, Get Your Hair Cut
   Mailman, The
   Moving Man
   Old MacDonald

C. *Transportation and Machines*
   Erie Canal
   Four in a Boat
   Le Train (The Train)
   Michael, Row the Boat Ashore
   Monorail, A
   Taxis
   Train Is A-Coming, The
   Whoosh! The Jet Goes By

D. *Holidays and Special Days Categories*
   Christmas
   Easter
   Father's Day
   George Washington's Birthday
   Halloween
   Hanukah
   Lincoln's Birthday
   Mother's Day
   New Years Day
   St. Valentine's Day
   Thanksgiving

E. *Action and Game Songs*
   Farmer in the Dell
   Four in a Boat
   Goin' to School
   Helping Mother
   My Country's Flag
   My Family
   Shoes

F. *Welcome to School*
   My Country's Flag
   Goin' to School
   Riding Bumpity Bump
   Nodding
   From Book One:
   On the Playground
   After School
   Sing Together
   Let's Play
   A Happy Song

G. *Town and Country*
   Going to the Fair
   Stop, Look and Listen
   Fire Song
   Here Comes the Postman
   Stop Go
   Boatman's Song
   Wheels Are Turning
   The Happy Bus

H. *People in Other Countries* This typical textbook contains a lengthy index of songs including some from Africa, Columbia, England, France, Germany, Guatemala, Hungary, Israel, Jamaica, Japan, Mexico, The Netherlands, Scotland, as well as many from the United States. It also includes foreign language songs. Other sources include songs selected from books such as:
   Children's Songs of Mexico. Highland Music Company, Hollywood, Calif.
   Folk Songs of China, Japan, and Korea. New York: John Day Company (K-5).
   Folk Songs of Africa. Highland Music Company, Hollywood, Calif.
   Echoes of Africa in Folk Songs of the Americas. New York: Edward B. Marks Music Corp.
   Children's Songs of Japan. New York: Edward B. Marks Music Corp., 1960. Fifty songs describing life in Japan.

I. *Special Holidays*

This typical textbook lists songs concerning Christmas, Easter, Father's Day, Washington's Birthday, Hallowe'en, Hanukkah, Lincoln's Birthday, Mother's Day, New Years, St. Valentine's Day, and Thanksgiving.

J. *Mother Goose Songs*

(See general bibliography at the end of this chapter for sources of Mother Goose songs and nursery rhymes.)

K. Songs from *Singing With Children* (Wadsworth), *New Dimensions-K,* and *This Is Music: K-N* concerning people and their work:

Clickety Clack (railroad)

We Are Good Musicians

Farmer in the Dell

Down By the Station (railroad)

Everybody Loves Saturday Night (people and customs) all from *Singing With Children*

The Dentist

Ice Cream Man

Johnny, Get Your Hair Cut   all from *New Dimensions-K*

Train Is A-Coming   *This Is Music: K-N*

I've Been Working on the Railroad (adapt)   in many books

Recordings

A. Family, Self-Awareness, and Feelings

Basic Awareness Through Music, K-3, by Lou Stallman. Album Ed 121-A-1, Educational Activities, Inc. Helps children relate to one another, achieve identity, and become aware of the world around them. Participation builds self-confidence.

Sounds All Around

Look Around

Animals on the Farm

Ten Fingers

My Name

It's Fun to Be

My Favorite Colors

Let's Act

Developing Understanding of Self and Others. American Guidance Service, Inc., Circle Pines, Minn. 55014.

Getting to Know Myself by Hap Palmer. Album AR 543-1. Educational Activities, Inc. Includes awareness of body image and the body's position in space; identification of body places; objects in relation to body planes; body part identification; movement of the body; laterality of the body, feelings, and moods.

Good Manners Through Music. Educational Activities, Inc. Fourteen original songs.

Rounds and Mixers Old and New. Records: ages 5-9. Bowmar.

Sensorimotor Training in the Classroom—K-3 by Linda Williams. Albums AR 5-32-1. Educational Activities, Inc. A program of carefully selected perceptual activities to develop: body image, laterality, space, directionality, basic movement, physical fitness, ocular training, auditory discrimination.

Won't You Be My Friend, by Patty Zeitlin. Educational Activities, Inc. A variety of musical styles are included—calypso, rock, folk, pop, and country. The music provides both structured and creative ways to express feelings through songs and body movements. The songs guide the child in emotional and social awareness; they make him feel good about what he is able to do by himself; assure him that others have fears, are angry, and sad also; includes songs and rhythm games to help children learn one another's names and taking turns. Titles included: What Makes Me Happy; I'm Afraid; Won't You Be My Friend; Angry Song; I Want You All to Myself; Twins; Sad Little Bird.

B. Community and Work

Action Songs for Growing Up—Pre k-3. Album K 3070-2. Educational Activities, Inc. The fifteen songs to sing and act out are all based on occupations that children have heard about; pilot, bus driver, doctor, cowhand, housewife, repairman, etc. Vocal and musical accompaniment are one side of the record; the other side has music only, the teacher and the children can create their own lyrics or adapt the ones provided.

Sing a Song of Home and Community, Bowmar.

C. Transportation and Machines

Mossolov: *Iron Foundry* on *Sounds of New Music,* Folkways FX 6160.

Train to the Zoo, Franson Corp, Children's Record Guild CRG 1001.

Villa-Lobos: *Bachianas Brasileiras No. 2,* "The Little Train of the Caipira," Adventures in Music 3, vol. 2.

D. People in Other Countries

Sing a Song of Neighbors, (Mexicans, Eskimos, Indians, Hawaiians, Africans). Bowmar.

Sing a Song of People. Includes Indian, Mexican, Oriental, and Black American songs.

E. Special and Holidays

Holiday Rhythms, Bowmar.

Holiday Action Songs. Educational Activities, Inc. Song and game activities for Christmas, Easter, Thanksgiving, and Hallowe'en.

F. Special Source

Best Records, Books, for Early Childhood catalog, Children's Music Center, Los Angeles, Calif. 90019. See actions titled "Self and Body Image," "Family and Home," "Friends," "Community," "Transportation," "Holidays and Celebrations," "Around the World," "Indian Children," "Japanese-American Children," "Living Together, U.S.A.," and "Lullabies."

Films and Filmstrips

A. Family, Self-Awareness, and Feelings

Filmstrip, "Jimmy's Family," SVE. 32 fr., c.; "The Happy Family," Eye Gate House, c.

Filmstrip, "Helping Each Other at Home," FOM, 30 fr., c.

B. Community and Work

Educational Activities, Inc. Set of six full-color filmstrips with recordings.

Your Neighborhood—The World

At Home

At School

The Community

Father's Work

My Daddy is a Carpenter

My Daddy is a Moving Man

My Daddy Works in a Shoe Store

My Daddy Works in a Supermarket

My Daddy Works in a Service Station

Mother Works Too

My Mother is a Waitress

My Mother Works in a Bank

My Mother Works in an Office

My Mother Works in the Home

"Let's Visit the Dentist," SVE 41 fr, c.

"The Grocer," McGraw-Hill, 40 fr.

Film, "The Mailman," EBF, 11 min., b & w.

Filmstrip, "Seven Little Postmen," McGraw-Hill, 32 fr., c.

Career Awareness, Grades K-3, by Phyllis Dolyin (ed.) Four full-color filmstrips, records, cassettes (fSR 430). Educational Activities, Inc. Careers starting with familiar territory of the school and then to hospital, construction, and airports. Makes children aware of the world of work.

Where Does It Come From? Group 1, 2 (Primary) Lyons. Each group has four color-sound filmstrips. Group I deals with lumber, milk, paper, and bread; Group II with textiles, meat, iron, and seafood. With records or cassettes.

C. Transportation and Machines
   "Travel in the City," Bro-Dart, c. Picture set.
   "Pedro, the Little Airplane," EBF, 50 fr., c.
D. People in Other Countries
   Discovering the World, 1850. Lorraine Music Co., Inc. A set of four filmstrips, four LP recordings, reading scripts, and teacher's guide. Parts 1 and 2: "The Universal Language of Children"; Part 3: "Cultural Dignity"; Part 4: "Masks." Ungraded.
   Visit a Country Series. Lorraine Music Co., Inc. 17321 *Denmark;* 17322 *Norway;* 17323 *Germany;* 17324 *Holland;* 17325 *Italy;* 17326 *England;* 17327 *Greece;* 17328 *Kenya;* 17329 *Japan;* 17330 *Mexico.*
E. Special and Holidays
   Holidays—American Style. Grades K-3. Educational Activities, Inc. Exciting, colorful, and original art and with musical background.
   "What Does Our Flag Mean?" Coronet, 11 min., c.
   "Stories of Great Americans" series, SVE, av. 33 fr. ea., c.

Finger Plays

(See finger-play sources listed in the general bibliography at the end of this chapter.)

A. Family, Self-Awareness, and Feelings
   New Nursery Book VI.
   "The Growing Child and His Family"
   "I Looked in the Cookie Jar"
   Anderson, Paul S. *Language Skills in Elementary Education,* 2d ed. New York: Macmillan Co., 1972.
   "Grandmother"
   "Pat a Cake"
   "Ready for Bed"
   Hildebrand, Verna. *Introduction to Early Childhood Education.* New York: Macmillan Co., 1971.
   "Little Boy"
   "Grandpa's Glasses"
   "Touch Game"
B. Community and Work
   Hildebrand, Verna. *Introduction to Early Childhood Education.* New York: Macmillan Co., 1971.
   "Fire Man"
C. Transportation and Machines
   Anderson, Paul S. *Language Skills in Elementary Education,* 2d ed. New York: Macmillan Co., 1972.
   "This is an Airplane Search Light"
   Hildebrand, Verna. *Introduction to Early Childhood Education.*

New York: Macmillan Co., 1971.
"Five Little Astronauts"
  D. Special and Holidays
McAfee, Oralie et al. *The New Nursery School, Learning Activities Booklet VI.* New York: General Learning Corp.
"Five Little Bells, Hanging in a Row"
"Santa Claus is Big and Fat"
"Little Jack Horner"

Poems

(See other poetry references listed in the general bibliography at the end of this chapter. Also Mother Goose and Nursery Rhymes.)
  A. Family, Self-Awareness, and Feelings
"Big Brother" and "A Diller, A Dollar," by Elizabeth Roberts. In *Gaily We Parade,* by Sara Brewton and John E. Brewton. New York: Macmillan Co., 1967.
"Girls' Names" and "Boys' Names," by Eleanor Farjeon. In *Eleanor Farjeon's Poems for Children.* Philadelphia: J. B. Lippincott Co., 1951.
"First Day of School," by Aileen Fisher. In *I Wonder How, I Wonder Why.* New York: Abelard-Schuman, 1962.
"Going to Sleep" and "I Never Hear," by Dorothy Aldis; and "Evening Song," by Fannie Davis. In *Poems to Grow On* by Jean M. Thompson. Boston: Beacon Press, 1959.
"Little," by Dorothy Aldis. In *Everything and Everybody.* New York: E. P. Dutton, 1927.
"My Family," by L. B. Scott and J. J. Thompson. In *Talking Time,* ed. by L. B. Scott and J. J. Thompson. St. Louis: Webster Publishing Co., 1951.
"Other Children," by Margaret Wise Brown (copyright 1937). In *Another Here and Now Story Book,* by Lucy S. Mitchell. New York: E. P. Dutton and Co., 1965.
  B. Community and Work
"Barber, Barber Shave a Pig." In *Barnes Book of Nursery Verse* by Barbara Ireson. New York: A. S. Barnes and Co., 1960.
"F is the Fighting Fire Truck," by Phyllis McGinley. In *Very Young Verses* by Barbara Geismer et al. Boston: Houghton Mifflin Co., 1945.
"Hippety Hop to the Barber Shop" (Mother Goose); "Barber's Clippers," by Dorothy Baruch; and "My Policeman," by Rose Fyleman. In *The Sound of Poetry* by Mary C. Austin and Queenie B. Mills. Boston: Allyn and Bacon, 1963.
"I Listen to the Whistles," by E. Scott and Chidsay; Riding in An Airplane," by Dorothy Baruch; and "Taking Off," by Mary H.

Green. In *Very Young Verses* by Barbara Geismer and Antoinette B. Suter. Boston: Houghton Mifflin Co., 1945.

"Moving," by Eunice Tiedjens; and "Moving Out," and "Moving In," by Edith Osswald. In *Poems to Grow On* by Jean M. Thompson. Boston: Beacon Press, 1957.

"The Postman." In *Favorite Poems Old and New*, ed. by Helen Ferris. Garden City, N.Y.: Doubleday & Co., Inc., 1957.

"Postman's Knock," by Eleanor Farjeon; and "Busy Carpenters," by James Lippett. In *Then There Were Three*, by Eleanor Farjeon. Philadelphia: J. B. Lippincott Co., 1965.

C. Transportation and Machines

"Boats Sail on the Rivers," by Christina Rossetti. In *Very Young Verses* by Barbara Geismer and Antoinette B. Suter. Boston: Houghton Mifflin Co., 1945.

"The Engineer" by A. A. Milne; and "The Freight Train" by Rowena Bennett. In *The Reading of Poetry*, by William D. Sheldon. Boston: Allyn and Bacon, Inc., 1963.

"Ferry Boats," "Trains," and "Engines," by James Tippett; "The Way of Trains," by David McCord; "Passenger Train," by Edith Chase; and "Song of the Train," by Rose Mary Cathrin. In *The Sound of Poetry* by Mary C. Austin and Queenie B. Mills. Boston: Allyn and Bacon, 1963.

"On a Steamer" by Dorothy Baruch. In *Favorite Poems Old and New*, ed. by Helen Ferris. Garden City, N.Y.: Doubleday & Co., Inc., 1957.

"Tug Boat," by L. B. Scott and J. J. Thompson. In *Talking Time*, ed. by L. B. Scott and J. J. Thompson. St. Louis: Webster Publishing Co., 1951.

"Stop-Go," by Dorothy Baruch; "Travel," by Edna St. Vincent Millay; and "Trams at Night," by Francis Frost. In *Time for Poetry*, by May Hill Arbuthnot. Chicago: Scott, Foresman and Co., 1951.

"Where Go the Boats," and "My Ship and I," by Robert Louis Stevenson. In *A Child's Garden of Verses*. New York: Franklin Watts, Inc., 1966.

D. People in Other Countries

"The Flag Goes By," by Henry Bennett; and "Marching Song" by Robert Louis Stevenson. In *Time for Poetry* by May Hill Arbuthnot. New York: Scott, Foresman and Co., 1951. (See other poetry anthologies for patriotic poems.)

Seeing the World Through Poetry (Grades K-3). Educational Activities, Inc. Two full-color filmstrips, record, cassette (FSR 402). Children explore the world of social studies through the exciting illustrated poetry of Ogden Nash, Ilo Orleans, James Tippett.

Community helpers, transportation, communication, food, clothing, and shelter become alive and meaningful to children.

E. Special and Holidays

"The Little Girl and the Turkey," by Dorothy Aldis. In *All Together: A Child's Treasury of Verse*, by Dorothy Aldis. New York: G. P. Putnam's Sons, 1952.

"Snow," by Dorothy Aldis; and "Thanksgiving," by Ralph Waldo Emerson. In *Everything and Anything* by Dorothy Aldis. New York: G. P. Putnam's Sons, 1955.

"Down Down" (autumn) by Eleanor Farjeon. In *Eleanor Farjeon's Poems for Children*. Philadelphia: J. B. Lippincott Co., 1951.

"Signs of Christmas," by Mary Justus. In *Winds A'Blowing*. Nashville, Tenn.: Abingdon Press, 1952.

Books

A. Family, Self-Awareness, and Feelings

Allen, Frances Charlotte. *Little Hippo*. New York: G. P. Putnam's Sons, 1971. After Little Hippo's mother gives birth to a baby sister, he is never lonely again. A short and simple animal story for children as young as two years of age.

Beim, Lorraine, and Beim, Jerrold. *Two Is a Team*. New York: Harcourt Brace Jovanovich, Inc., 1945. A black and a white boy settle their differences and combine resources to build a wagon. In the process they become good friends.

Berman, Rhoda A. *When You Were A Little Baby*. New York: Lothrop, Lee and Shepard Co., 1954.

Brown, Margaret Wise. *Runaway Bunny*. New York: Harper & Row, Publishers, 1942. Children who have thought about running away will identify with the runaway bunny and its mother.

Brown, Myra B. *Pip Moves Away*. Chicago: Children's Press, 1967.

Brownstone, Helen E. *All Kinds of Mothers*. New York: Lothrop, Lee and Shepard, Inc., 1965. A little boy remembers others' birthdays and in turn his is remembered.

Buckley, Helen. *Grandfather and I*. New York: Lothrop, Lee and Shepard, Inc., 1961.

Carton, Lonnie C. *Daddies*. New York: Random House, 1963. Rhymes about children and their daddies.

Clark, Nolan. *Mother's House*. New York: The Viking Press, 1941. A poetic book written from the point of view of Indian children about the everyday things that are so important in their lives.

De Regniers, Beatrice. *The Little Girl and Her Mother*. New York: Vanguard Press, 1963.

Ets, Marie Hall. *Gilberto and the Wind*. New York: Viking Press, 1963.

Flack, Marjorie. *The New Pet*. Garden City, N.Y.: Doubleday & Co., 1943. Dick and Judy ask for a pet. The pet happens to be a baby brother.

———. *Ask Mr. Bear*. New York: Macmillan Co., 1932. Danny asks Mr. Bear what to give his mother for her birthday.

Freeman, Dan. *Corduroy*. New York: Viking Press, 1968.

Green, Mary M. *Everybody Has a House and Everybody Eats*. Reading, Mass.: Addison-Wesley Publishing Co., 1961.

Hazen, Barbara S. *Animal Daddies and My Daddy*. New York: Western Publishing Co., 1968.

Hoban, Russell. *A Baby Sister for Frances*. New York: Harper & Row, Publishers, 1964. Watching her parents care for the new baby in the family, Frances feels alone and neglected.

House, Wanda Rogers. *Peter Goes to School*. New York: Grossett and Dunlap, 1953.

Keats, Ezra Jack. *Peter's Chair*. New York: Harper & Row, Publishers, 1967.

———. *Whistle for Willie*. New York: Viking Press, 1964. Peter, a small black boy, succeeds in learning to whistle. Now he will be able to call his dog, Willie. A story of patient effort and achievement.

Krauss, Ruth. *The Carrot Seed*. New York: Harper & Row, Publishers, 1945.

Lenski, Lois. *Papa Small* and also *At Our House*. New York: Henry Z. Walck, 1951 and 1959.

———. *When I Grow Up*. New York: Henry Z. Walck, 1960.

Lexan, Joan. *Benjie On His Own*. New York: Dial Press, 1970. Old enough to be in school for the first time, Benjie is faced with the problem of finding his way home in the large crowded city.

Schlein, Miriam. *Billy the Littlest One*. Chicago: Albert Whitman and Co., 1966. Billy finds many things he can't do because he is little but he is aware that he will not always be too small.

Shapp, Charles, and Shapp, Martha. *Let's Find Out About School*. New York: Franklin Watts, 1961.

Weisgard, Leonard. *Whose Little Bird Am I?* New York: Frederick Warne and Co., 1965.

Zolotow, Charlotte. *Do You Know What I'll Do?* New York: Harper & Row, Publishers, 1958.

B. Community and Work

Beim, Jerrold. *Country Mailman*. New York: William Morrow, 1968.

Dorian, Marguerite. *The Alligator's Toothache*. New York: Lothrop, Lee and Shepard, 1961.

Gergely, Tibar. *The Great Big Fire Engine Book*. Western Publishing Co., 1950.

Green, Carla. *I Want to be a Space Pilot*. Chicago: Childrens Press, 1961.

Kunhardt, Dorothy. *Billy the Barber*. New York: Harper & Row, Publishers, 1961.

Lenski, Lois. *Cowboy Small*. New York: Henry Z. Walck, 1949.

———. *The Little Fire Engine*. New York: Henry Z. Walck, 1956.

———. *Policeman Small*. New York: Henry Z. Walck, 1963.

Shapp, Charles, and Shapp, Martha. *Let's Find Out About Houses*. New York: Franklin Watts, 1962.

Shortall, Leonard. *The Hat Book*. New York: Western Publishing Co., 1965.

Vogel, Ilse-Margaret. *When I Grow Up*. New York: Western Publishing Co., 1968.

Windsor, Marie. *Let's Play Policeman*. Chicago: Follett Publishing Co., 1964.

———. *Let's Play Store*. Chicago: Follett Publishing Co., 1964.

C. Transportation and Machines

Charles, Nicholas. *How Do You Get From Here to There?* New York: Macmillan Co., 1962.

Dugan, William. *The Truck and Bus Book*. New York: Western Publishing Company, 1966.

Flack, Marjorie. *The Boats on the River*. New York: Viking Press, 1946.

Gramatky, Hardie. *Sparky, The Story of a Little Trolley Car*. New York: G. P. Putnam's Sons, 1952.

Kalish, Muriel, and Kalish, Lionel. *Planes, Trains, Cars and Boats*. New York: Western Publishing Co., 1963.

Lenski, Lois. *Little Sailboat*. New York: Henry Z. Walck, 1937.

Peters, Lisa. *Wonder Book of Trains and Wonder Book of Trucks*. rev. ed. 51 Madison Ave., 10010, New York: Wonder-Treasure Books, 1962.

Piper, Watty. *The Little Engine That Could*. New York: Platt and Munk, 1930.

Potter, Marian. *The Little Red Caboose*. New York: Western Publishing Co., 1953.

Scarry, Richard. *The Great Big Car and Truck Book*. New York: Western Publishing Co., 1951.

Shortall, Leonard. *Davey's First Boat*. New York: William F. Morrow, 1963.

Zaffo, George J. *The Big Book of Real Fire Engines*. New York: Grosset and Dunlap, 1964.

———. *The Big Book of Real Trains*. New York: Grosset and Dunlap, 1963.

———. *The Big Book of Real Trucks*. New York: Grosset and Dunlap, 1964.

———. *The Giant Nursery Book of Travel Fun: On a Train, On an Airplane to a Camp, in a Bus, on a Boat.* Garden City, N.Y.: Doubleday and Co., 1965.

D. People in Other Countries

Bemelmans, Ludwig. *Madeline.* Simon and Schuster.

Beskow, Elsa. *Pelle's New Suit.* New York: Harper & Row Publishers, 1929.

Association for Childhood Education International. *Told Under the Stars and Stripes.* New York: Macmillan, 1945. A collection of stories about children of many cultural origins.

E. Special and Holidays

Aliki. *George and the Cherry Tree.* Dial Press, 1964. A simple picture book dealing with special days and seasons.

Association for Childhood Education International. *Told Under the Christmas Tree.* New York: Macmillan Co., 1948. A collection of Christmas tales and legends to tell or read aloud. It broadens a child's concept of Christmas around the world.

Balian, Lorna. *Humbug Witch.* Nashville, Tenn.: Abingdon Press, 1965.

Battaglia, Aurelius. *The Reindeer Book.* New York: Western Publishing Co., 1965.

Carroll, Ruth, and Carroll, Latrobe. *Beanie.* New York: Oxford University Press, 1953. Beanie is the youngest member of a large mountain-farm family of Appalachia. He does not own a pet until he gets a puppy that he calls "Tough Enough," for his birthday. Excellent in showing love and affectionate family relationships.

Cassidy, Clara. *We Like Kindergarten.* New York: Western Publishing Co., 1965.

d'Aulaire, Ingrid. *Abraham Lincoln.* New York: Doubleday & Co., 1938.

———. *George Washington.* New York: Doubleday & Co., 1936.

Felt, Sue. *Contrary Woodrow.* New York: Doubleday & Co., 1958. Valentine's Day and kindergarten activities are discussed.

Hazen, Barbara S. *Rudolph The Red-Nosed Reindeer.* New York: Western Publishing Co., 1958.

Kaufman, Joseph. *The Christmas Tree Book.* New York: Western Publishing Co., 1966.

———. *The Toy Book.* New York: Western Publishing Co., 1965.

Monsell, Helen. *Paddy's Christmas.* New York: Alfred A. Knopf, 1942. A bear celebrates Christmas in a very delightful manner.

Moore, Clement C. *Visit from St. Nicholas: 'Twas the Night Before Christmas.* New York: McGraw-Hill Book Co., 1968.

Scarry, Richard. *The Santa Claus Book.* New York: Western Publishing Co., 1965.

Yashima, Taro. *Umbrella.* New York: The Viking Press, 1958. On Momo's third birthday he receives a new umbrella and red rubber boots, but it is several days before the rain arrives. Something very exciting happens to Momo when she carries the umbrella.

Music and Art

Music and art are different media; music is aural while art is visual. Yet it is believed that there are some genuine relationships between these dissimilar arts. Teachers utilize pictures to add interest to songs and recorded music; it is possible that they should do more with selecting songs to add interest to drawings, pictures, and paintings. When children dramatize the waves cresting at the seashore they are creating a picture in movement that can relate to a painting of that subject, and all of this can relate to a musical composition describing the sea.

Moods and colors in art can relate to these same concepts in music. Humanity has decided that there are cool and warm colors that can be visualized in art and heard in music. Patterns that are repeated, and patterns that are even and uneven can be seen in art objects and paintings; patterns such as these can be found in music. From this study can come the generalization that repeated shapes and patterns result in unity in art in the same general way that repeated patterns, phrases, and sections result in unity in music. This refers to the concepts of same and different, the basis of form, a principle strongly present in all of the arts. Simple musical forms can be drawn as a series of geometrical designs or presented as a series of pictures, some of which will be repeated: AA, AB, ABA, ABACA. Of course these can be danced in ways that illustrate the same-different principle of form.

Loud and soft in music can be reflected in children's finger painting with their palms, with large swirls for loud music and small swirls for soft music. The advantage is that children can see in their own painting the difference between loud and soft. Fast and slow in painting transfers to short and long lines while the same concepts in music refer to notes of short and long durations. Melodic contours of songs can be drawn. When working with these concepts the teacher must select both music and art that are very clearly illustrative of the concepts being dealt with.

Examples of the use of art in music textbooks include colored drawings in *Discovering Music Together: Early Childhood,* that assist visual recognition of the basic concepts high-low (p. 134), up-down (p. 138), even-uneven (p. 142), fast-slow (p. 147); and a concerted effort to relate music and art in *The Spectrum of Music: K,* in which most of the songs are accompanied by colored art illustrations.

An interesting study of forms and shapes can be accomplished with children's shadows. With lights placed behind children, their silhouettes are shown on a wall. They can use scarves, fragile plastic, or balloons and move creatively to lively, light music. They may discuss how the shadows made by these light objects differ from those made by their bodies, and how the music suggests movement. Through this activity the children become more aware of their bodies and who they are as well as learning about line, shape, patterns, and artistic configuration.

With the classroom somewhat darkened, flashlights with lenses covered with colored cellophane can be turned on and off by children in time with music or when the music changes in character. By using different selections of music, the children can perceive differences in tempo, and the flashing colors can help them to learn some relation between aural and visual arts.

Songs can be used that develop consciousness of colors in the environment—colors people wear, colors in nature, color of leaves, flowers, and grass in the spring and in the winter. Percussion instruments can be of different colors, and when children who hold instruments of a specific color can be asked to perform at appropriate places in recorded music or in songs. Recordings that assist in learning colors include Hap Palmer's *Learning Basic Skills Through Music* Vols. I and II, and *Basic Songs for Exceptional Children* Vol. I. Favorite songs from those albums include "Color Song" and "Parade of Colors." Songs can also be created by the children about colors attractive to them.

Songs

Songs have long been used to teach colors. One in which all colors are involved is "Rainbow Song" in *New Dimensions in Music: Music for Early Childhood,* American Book Company.

Invent other verses: example, blue shirt, red scarf, who's wear-ing green pants, etc. Notice that the song is an exercise in tone matching; the child's answering pitches are identical to those of the teacher's question.

Any songs that contain facts and concepts about shapes or patterns made from straight or curved lines relate to the basic understanding of all forms of art. Examples of songs that relate to art:

Mary Wore a Red Dress	*Birchard Music Series*: *K*, p. 17
Color Song	*New Dimensions*: *Beginning Music*, p. 74
Colors	*Hap Palmer Song Book, Vol. 1*
Jenny Jenkins	many sources
Parade of Color	*Hap Palmer Song Book, Vol. 2*
One Shape, Three Shapes	*Hap Palmer Song Book, Vol. 2*
Triangle, Circle, and Square	*Hap Palmer Song Book, Vol. 2*

Resources for Art-Music Relationships

Books

Bright, Robert. *I Like Red*. Garden City, N.Y.: Doubleday & Co., 1955.

Brown, Margaret Wise. *The Color Kittens*. New York: Western Publishing Co., 1950.

Fletcher, Helen J. *The Color Wheel Book*. New York: McGraw-Hill Book Co., 1965.

Gottlieb, Susanne. *What Is Red?* New York: Lothrop, Lee and Shepard Co., 1961.

Steiner, Charlotte. *My Slippers Are Red*. New York: Alfred A. Knopf, 1957.

Wolff, Janet. *Let's Imagine Colors*. New York: E. P. Dutton and Co., 1963.

For books about shape, see Mathematics bibliography.

Pictures

Kindergarten Picture Packet. Silver Burdett Company, Morristown, N.J. 07960. Twenty-two enlarged illustrations from *Making Music Your Own*: *Kindergarten Book* to improve picture-reading skills, stimulate creative expression, create social awareness, and expand vocabulary.

Music and Language

Some authorities believe that at first the teacher does not teach music but rather provides language arts experiences: experimenting with vocal sounds in the form of chanting, nonsense syllables and words, phonetic sounds of words that begin and end alike, proverbs, riddles, rhymes, all the communicative areas that music and language have in common. (Pratcher, 1968) The Carl Orff approach to music for children is in keeping with this belief.

As a means of expression, music is related to language. Most of the young child's early communication is nonverbal; and music and dance provide means by which he can exercise this normal communicative process. Research supports the belief that active physical involvement helps the very young child to develop language skills. As stated by the authors of *Beginning Music* of the New Dimensions in Music series (Choate et. al. 1970), "Music activities provide one of the most powerful tools in developing language use, as music places language in an enjoyable and satisfying context. For (young) children (and for those) whose language development is retarded and who lack verbal skills to articulate well in a discussion, music offers an opportunity to participate with the group without embarrassment while gaining proficiency."

Songs are used to stress children's names, names of familiar objects, colors, number concepts, right and left, fast and slow, loud and soft, and many other concepts useful in daily living. Music and language have much in common in mood, rhythm, and form. Descriptive music helps to expand vocabulary. Songs and finger plays, rhymes and poems, offer models for sentence patterns. They help children to learn new words, particularly those that express definite sounds and involve rhythmic action; the rhyming and alliteration characteristic of songs, rhymes, poems, and finger plays can further the child's capability for developing auditory discrimination. Experimentation with sound sources does this also. Music provides opportunity for children to become members of groups, and as they participate in group musical activities they are almost forced to develop verbal skills and concepts as they interact with each other and with the other elements in their environment.

There is more language expression when the children are encouraged to respond spontaneously to action words such as walking, running, jumping, hopping, sliding, bouncing, clapping, and singing. When the teacher arranges the various learning stations in the classroom to stimulate role-playing and self-expression, the children's involvement in using these stations to dramatize and reenact the activities, roles, and movements they have observed in their social and natural worlds serves to generate subject matter for the creation of rhythmic words, rhythms, chants, songs, rhymes, phrases, sentences, and stories. A free musical environment also encourages children to experiment and to express their understanding of various concepts.

Language and Concept Enrichment

Both the child's language facility and his background for learning to read later in formal reading situations are enhanced when appropriate songs and rhythms are chosen or composed to teach specific concepts. Children's learning of vocabulary and concepts is made more interesting and challenging through the use of rhymes, chants, singing games, and dialogue songs. For example, the teacher sings, "Who has the hammer?" and the child answers. "I have the hammer" or "Johnny has the hammer." By using dialogue of question-and-answer format children learn name, color, number, shape, notions of relative position and opposite situation, as well as concepts of different moods. "Billy, are you sad today?" "No, Miss Brown, I am not sad today." "How do you feel?" "I feel happy, thank you." Examples of concepts that can be introduced and learned through singing and composing songs, listening to recordings, and moving creatively to music are:

1. Concepts of relative position
   up-down
   over-under
   beside
   below
   between
   in-on
   inside-outside
   top
   bottom
   middle

2. Alike and different
   same size
   same sound
   same speed (fast, slow)
   same shape, etc.

3. Contrasting opposite situations
   loud-soft
   noisy-quiet
   fast-slow
   have-have not
   laugh-cry
   high-low
   light-heavy
   up-down

4. Relative number
   more than-less than

5. Relative weight
   heavy, heavier, heaviest
   light, lighter, lightest

Through the repetitive nature of song verses that allow for substitutions of names, people, objects, motions, shapes, colors, sizes, weights, textures, and odors, many other related language arts skills are introduced, used, and learned, such as listening to the question in order to respond, pronunciation and enunciation, oral expression, proper vocabulary usage, declarative and interrogative sentences and how to use them. A given idea such as square can be experienced in more than one context. Children may sing:
(instructional objective: to learn the concept of "square" by experiencing it in many contexts.)

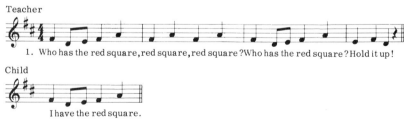

Teacher

1. Who has the red square, red square, red square? Who has the red square? Hold it up!

Child

I have the red square.

2. square box
3. square book
4. square clock
5. square shape

Listening and Auditory Discrimination

Listening to sounds is basic to both language development and musical awareness and growth. The sounds found in the environment, both musical and nonmusical, are used to assist the young child to become a sensitive and skilled listener. Children learn to listen when they have a purpose for listening and when they have the opportunity to explore, experiment, discuss, reproduce, and use what they hear. They may listen to a bird as he sings, and as the teacher guides them in their analysis of the bird's song through appropriate questions they may attempt to imitate the sound the bird is making and perhaps create a song that describes the experience. Through discussion they may determine whether the bird's sound is loud or soft, high or low. Other sources children can listen to as a basis for musical learning are motors of cars, airplanes, boats and motorcycles, horns, echoes, leaves on a tree in the wind, dry leaves in the fall, and so on. Various conventional and unconventional sound sources can be used successfully in experimenting with sound and for the enjoyment of producing and creating music. Children learn to listen to the drum in order that they will know whether to sing slow or fast. For other suggested activities for listening and dramatizing, see "Science" in this chapter, and "Listening to Sounds and Tones" and "Movement" in chapter four.

The child's ability to listen appreciatively and analytically is improved as he listens attentively to a song, singing game, finger play, rhyme, or story to do things in sequence; to follow directions to find out if he is to walk, run, or hop; listens to the teacher as she explains how to hold an instrument and when to sound it.

Listening is an essential skill that influences every aspect of the curriculum. The music program provides a meaningful and attractive setting for learning these skills. Children can classify the sounds they hear under headings such as soft, loud, high, low, harsh, squeaky, foot sounds, voice sounds, animal sounds, bird sounds, machine sounds, music sounds, insect sounds, and so on.

Listening activities stressing accuracy of pitch should be employed to teach auditory discrimination. Clapping and chanting of rhythmic syllables can be used to denote rhythm patterns and auditory sequencing. Use of a magnetic board or flannel board with appropriate figures to demonstrate or evaluate a child's ability to illustrate a song, rhyme, or poem in sequence is an effective activity. Instrumental and/or song selections should be used to assist the child in detecting likenesses and differences— high and low tones, fast and slow tempos, loud and soft sounds. Songs should be selected that contain rhyming words, words that begin or end with the same sounds, and vocabulary words that are relevant to the child's interests, needs, and capabilities. Through such activities the teacher is not only teaching musical skills, knowledges and appreciations, but also reading skills—phonetic analysis, vocabulary, pronunciation, enunciation, ways to express ideas creatively and colorfully through music. Thus the difficult task of learning to read and to use language is simplified. The child listens first and then responds to various musical situations or he listens to masterworks for sheer enjoyment and appreciation. Having the child listen so that he can respond in unique and spontaneous ways to show how he feels is one of the most valid methods of teaching the greatly needed skill of discriminating and appreciative listening. When listening is followed by imagery, expression through the use of instruments, words, and creative dance is a natural outgrowth.

Suggestions for Teaching

Have a small group of children tape their voices repeating a Mother Goose rhyme such as "Jack be nimble, Jack be quick, Jack jump over the candle stick." Then the group listens to the tape and identifies each of the voices. Tape words that begin or end with the same sounds; also tape sounds of various instruments. The children are to decide which words rhyme and which instrument they are hearing. Precede or follow this activity with discussion. Present pictures of instruments and have the children (child) match the picture with the instrument that is sounding on the tape. Children enjoy comparing and discussing the sounds made by two instruments, as to how they are alike and different.

When a teacher is always ready to listen to a song a child has created she is setting a good example for the children to follow.

The teacher listens to the child's song, sings it back to him, then helps him share it with the listeners and singers around him.

The teacher reads books and plays recordings that assist the children to hear and identify sounds and to develop an awareness of what is happening and what is going to happen next.

When a child brings a new song to sing, it can be used as a listening experience.

The teacher can use questions concerning music to stimulate discussion: What is music? Where do musical sounds come from? What do we use music for? How is music made? How does (this) music make you feel? How do you learn music? How do people invent their own music?

Music and Handwriting

In order to be able to write, a child needs prior use of all muscles of the body in many types of movement and positions to develop muscular and hand-eye coordination necessary for writing successfully. Rhythmic body movement in expressive and creative activities such as bouncing and catching a ball, or by imitating the rhythm and movement of an elephant in time to a musical accompaniment, provides opportunity for this development. No other area in the curriculum makes such adequate provision for this growth. In the music program children usually learn to sing the ABCs and learn to recognize them in music before attempting to physically write letters or words that contain them.

As children create their own songs and chants they observe the teacher as she records them in manuscript on the chalkboard or on charts. Thus they experience the use of written symbols to record what one says in the form of songs, poems, and stories. These experiences serve as a starting point for the learning of the skill of handwriting at a later date.

Music, Speech and Non-verbal Communication

Rhythm is innately a part of young children; this is evident in their free and creative movements. All speech contains rhythm. Some speech is effectively and beautifully produced whereas other speech rhythms are less pleasant. "Freedom in bodily movement leads to freedom in speech. A controlled body is essential to effective speech. Bodily movement, gestures, pantomime, and dramatic play afford a natural introduction to oral language. Not only does creative movement and dramatic play promote freedom in bodily action, it enhances the spoken word and reduces the inhibitions children feel in speech activities." (Logan, Logan, and Paterson, 1972)

Chants, nursery and nonsense rhymes, songs, and singing games provide natural avenues through which to improve a child's speech. Children are instinctively attracted and motivated to learn through movement and rhyme. As a child uses his body in rhyme and song and in dance and instrumentation he is readily involved in experimentation and discovery. This involvement creates interest and challenges him to attempt increasingly more difficult speech. When the child receives proper encouragement and assistance from a competent teacher he develops a sensitivity to and an understanding of increasingly more complex rhythmic patterns that he observes and experiences in his environment. He progressively acquires the skill to relate this knowledge of rhythm patterns to more formalized types of music as he becomes involved in performing physical responses to music: in singing, and in playing instruments.

Chanting flows from a child naturally as he works and plays—as he swings, climbs, hammers and saws and as he participates in activities in the various learning stations both inside and outside the classroom. He chants about anything that moves and things he can use in imaginary play. Chanting is an integral part of a young child's play and speech development; most children enter into it with interest and pleasure. Through it they exercise their speech organs, invent and use sounds, and new words, and sentences. Through guided chanting the child develops understanding and interest in melody and rhythm. Words can become more meaningful and picturesque, and the quality of speech can be improved. Proper pronunciation and enunciation of words are necessary for precise meaning and use of words in oral expression. High-low in pitch, loud-soft in dynamics, rhythm, and meter in music can have positive influence on speech. Many young children are not aware of speech accents and the varying lengths of word syllables. Good music teaching produces sensitivity to sounds, and this relates to good enunciation and correct pronunciation of words.

Music can be integrated into the many forms of literature. Children can be helped to clap hands to develop the feel of rhythm of speech in rhymes, poems, songs, and stories. A child can use the various parts of his body as an instrument to accompany, when appropriate, a chant, recording, or story. He can clap, stamp, snap fingers, or use his entire body to emphasize different tempi (fast, slow), dynamics (loud, soft), and rhythm patterns (beat and its divisions). Children can also choose appropriate instruments and use them to enrich and add meaning and interest to a poem or story. When a child manipulates objects and moves his body rhythmically to interpret music and literature his interest and enjoyment in these areas are greatly extended and his ability to listen and attend to the activity at hand is improved. Through the use of rhythmic body responses, if these responses serve as a stimulus for the child to use his body in unique and creative ways, the child can express his interpretation and understanding of speech, poetry, music, and stories.

According to Wheeler and Raebeck (1972) "Percussion instruments as an adjunct to speech experiences has infinite value: it gives a feeling of rhythmic stability, underlines the basic pulse, gives contrasting rhythm patterns and color, gives experiences in independent parts as well as ensemble experience, and bridges the gap between rhythm and melody. The imaginative use of percussion instruments can not only provide a simple background of texture, it can create and maintain changes in mood and atmosphere as well."

Shumsky (1965) gives an account of a teacher of young children presenting a lesson on the rhythmic patterns of children's speech. Since rhythm is inherent in speech, the teacher predicted that many valuable ideas would come from the children. She used the familiar and popular topic of food. A child's reply to the teacher's question concerning food he liked was, "Cookies and milk." At this, the teacher encouraged the child to chant those words in rhythm. Another child said, "Bananas and milk," and this was treated similarly. When "Pretzels and milk" was suggested, it was compared with "Cookies and milk" in an attempt to determine whether the rhythm pattern was identical for both. Eventually the chant became, "Cookies and milk, cookies and milk, taste very nice!" They experimented with performing this in several ways, combining or alternating chanting with clapping, beating on the floor, making mouth sounds and movements of the body or its parts. The group later had more sessions on rhythmic speech patterns, using original sentences, poetry fragments, song phrases, and original percussion patterns.

Music and Dramatization of Literature

Through dramatic play, song, and movement, children reenact the daily drama of life spontaneously, and creatively become the mailman, the postman, the doctor, the father, the mother, and other people with whom they come in contact; then act out their roles as they understand them. Similarly, they act out movements, sounds, and roles of animals, machines, weather, and plants. Therefore, through use of movement, rhythmic response, and dramatization they are attempting to interpret, understand, and appreciate everything in their known environment. See suggested sounds and movement dramatization activities in sections on Science and Social Studies, in this chapter.

Dramatic play may be instigated by any occurrence or experience in a child's home, neighborhood, or school. It may occur from reality of the moment or it may be stimulated by different forms of literature—poem, rhyme, song, instrumental music, and story. Whitehead recites an example of how dramatic performance arose from an experience in literature: "After reading the story of *Little Toot* by Hardie Gramatky one teacher asked her class, 'Who can steam out of the harbor like Little Toot?' Thirty-five little toots steamed out of the harbor, but with each making a different toot." (Whitehead, 1968)

The young child seems to possess a compulsion to apply rhythm to his movement and rhyming responses. Movement and rhyming are closely joined when the child uses his body as a means of expression. Chants of various types and lengths result automatically from his involvement in rhyming activities, thus simple chants and songs with differing tempos and accents are created.

The teacher's prime responsibility in teaching creative rhythms consists of serving as an assistant and guide—of freeing the children to use their own feelings and creative imaginations. When appropriate, the teacher should assist children's rhythmic responses by accompanying their interpretations with suitable musical instruments. Instruments may be used to accompany the child's pantomime or rhythmic movements to depict the tripping across the bridge in "Three Billy Goats Gruff," for example, or as poems or stories are read or records played and listened to that describe the habits and movements of kangaroos. Some children may become kangaroos and hop like kangaroos while others may accompany them by playing a percussion instrument. Often the drum will be chosen or they will use their bodies as instruments and clap or stamp to the rhythm of the kangaroo's hop.

According to many authorities children of this age enjoy interpreting Mother Goose and nursery rhymes, poems, and stories through dramatic play, or pantomime. They do it automatically and reenact their world as they comprehend it. They also enjoy the use of simple puppets in their dramatization of the realistic and meaningful activities they have experienced. Shadow plays for the young stimulate them to move and act. Puppets can be employed to introduce a new song, poem or story, or they can inspire children to create songs, poems, and stories. There are many visual materials that may be used to teach a poem, rhyme, song, or story. The magnetic board, as well as the flannel board, serves as an avenue for presenting or repeating the content and sequence of literature.

Some suggested Mother Goose rhymes to dramatize are:
This is the Way the Ladies Ride
Rock-a-bye Baby
Jack and Jill
Georgie, Porgie
Three Little Kittens
Baa Baa Black Sheep
Old King Cole
Old Mother Hubbard
Jack Be Nimble
Wee Willy Winkie

Simple puppets or flannel board figures can also be used in dramatizing the above rhymes. After the young child has had experience in dramatizing rhymes and songs, he should then be interested in and capable of dramatizing stories containing lines that rhyme and that have a definite plot with greater variety of action. Stories and poems written in simple format and that contain much repetition and action are more suited for the young child, but if we know the children under our direction we must match the type and difficulty of an activity and the content of a poem, song, or story to the interest and maturity of each child.

A suggested list of stories that might be used for dramatization and creative musical interpretation follows:

Cinderella
Chicken Little
The Elves and the Shoemaker
The Little Brown Hen
The Little Red Hen
The Old Woman and Her Pig
Peter Rabbit (Beatrix Potter)
The Snowy Day
The Three Bears
The Three Billy Goats Gruff
The Three Little Pigs

The above stories are suited for telling as stories, and for use with dramatization done by children or with puppets. They encourage body response and interpretation through creative dance, the creation of original words and music, and the selection and use of instruments to accompany each story.

Music and Finger Plays

Finger plays consist basically of rhythmic activities that involve physical movement of the fingers and hands. They serve as an avenue through which rhymes, rhythm, sound and phonics, enunciation, pronunciation, and vocabulary, as well as the skills of following directions and making accurate responses, can be enhanced and taught. Possibly one of the most fascinating experiences of young children is the process of discovering what they can do through rhythmic body movement and by moving their hands and fingers. There are many finger plays that assist them in this discovery. Eventually, however, one of the teacher's major objectives should be that of guiding the children toward developing the ability and interest in creating their own finger plays that spring forth as they participate in various activities. Such activities can serve as a basis for developing an interest in and a facility for writing creatively in later years.

Finger plays and the flannel board can be used to interpret literary stories, poems, and musical selections. Like music, finger plays always contain rhythm, and when music is combined with the words in finger plays, a child's learning of vocabulary, enunciation, pronunciation, and communication is made more meaningful and easier to master. As the child uses creative rhythmic movement with music to interpret the finger plays, coordination is improved, and music can become an interesting and exciting means of self-expression and interpretation.

According to Whitehead, finger plays "require minimal materials and effort including (1) simple finger properties, (2) a brief, quickly memorized verse from a story, poem, or song, (3) an enthusiastic finger pantomimist—all one needs is two hands, ten fingers and the door to stories . . . poetry (and songs) is open." (Whitehead, 1968)

Music becomes an integral part of finger plays and vice versa when teachers observe Whitehead's suggestions. Finger plays are available for teaching concepts in all areas of the curriculum. (See sources of finger plays in the bibliography at the end of this section of the chapter.) However, Anderson (1972) warns that, "In using action plays, it is better to use too *few* than too many. The fun seems to be in repetition of familiar favorites."

When presenting finger plays the teacher should consider strategies such as:

Choose a rhyme, poem, song, or story that is appropriate for young children and that contains action, rhythm, dialogue, and content worthy of being taught. (How does the finger play assist in realizing the stated objectives?) The teacher will need to adapt songs, poems, and stories for a child or for a small or large group of children.

The teacher first demonstrates the entire verse, then one or two children should be chosen to do the verse with her. Following this, each line is done by a child or by the group and repeated until an individual or a few of the children in the group has mastered the finger play.

The optimum aim of the teacher should be to free and encourage children to eventually create their own finger plays, both the words and actions.

Interest in rhythm, action, and concepts contained in finger plays can be increased through the use of finger puppets. They are available in many forms including the ring and finger types.

See finger plays, poetry and Mother Goose rhymes, songs, and stories (at the end of this section of the chapter) for use with finger play and musical activities. Many of the Mother Goose rhymes can be converted into finger plays, dramatic action, and songs.

Listed below are titles of finger plays that are commonly used with young children (included in many of the sources listed at the end of this section):

Five Little Squirrels
Two Dickey Birds
Little Turtle
Caterpillar
Itsy Bitsy Spider
Grandmother
Grandfather
Ready For Bed
Five Little Pumpkins

Finger plays aid children in extending their vocabularies and understanding of various concepts of space, number, seriation, ordinals in number sequence, time, direction, and mood. A child as he involves his body, as he speaks and pantomimes finger plays, becomes less self-conscious and is freed to express himself in both verbal and nonverbal ways. He receives recognition and feedback from both teacher and peers which stimulate him to attempt inquiry and creative involvement in all aspects of learning.

Music and Poetry

Music and poetry have much in common. The main objective in teaching poetry, as in music, is to develop interest in poetic and rhythmic effects.

Little time should be devoted to analyzing poetry or musical compositions at this age. Instead, time should be given to listening, responding, and discussing music and poetry. Many poems, because of their rhythmic quality, have been set to music and can be used to demonstrate the relationship between musical and poetic forms. "Music amplifies and extends poetry and dominates many settings, from the love song and the lullaby to the miracle play and the chant of worship. Thus, for thousands of years, music has been used in everyday living and it has been combined with other art forms." (Aronoff, 1969) When children develop a feeling for music and poetry during the early years of music and language instruction, they participate in different types of learning.

The chant of nursery rhymes and the rhythm found in poetry are instinctive interests of the young child. One can notice the natural lilt of a child's voice as he spontaneously arranges words into stressed and unstressed syllables, and with accents of varying durations. Rhymes are automatically converted into chants with varying pitches that lead the child to create short and easy songs. Wheeler and Raebeck (1972) write that "It is the child's natural affinity to rhythm which is present in all living organisms and is felt not only in breathing, eating, walking and playing that expresses itself so superbly in speech and thus makes rhythm the logical cornerstone for all speech and further rhythmic experiences." (Wheeler and Raebeck, 1972)

For many years leading literary figures have attempted to define poetry. As will be noted in the following quotations, poetry and music are closely allied. (Hennings and Grant, 1973)

Poetry is the music of the soul; and above all, of great and feeling souls.—Voltaire
Poetry is that fine particle within us that expands, rarifies, refines, raises our whole being.—William Hazlitt
Poetry then begins with music in the soul, a feeling, an expression of our being, an explanation of life too swift for explanation, but it is music, a feeling, an expansion, an explanation clothed in the beauty of words.—Edgar Allen Poe
In essence the poet paints his idea with a radiance of words that sing, shout, bubble, and burst forth upon the ear.—Plutarch

Little children, like poets, take ordinary everyday events and through their creative chants, verse, and song, add new dimensions to them. They create their own images by observing closely the objects and events nearest to them and then formulate words into new and picturesque patterns that flow spontaneously as they combine them with rhythm and song. The sound of the words they use are basic to their creation of poetry and song. There is almost always a musical lilt to the poetry of young children. They enjoy this same lilting and rhythmic quality in poems read and sung to them. (See the bibliography at the end of each section of this chapter for sources of poetry.)

Nursery Rhymes   A child's first experience with poetry is usually that of Mother Goose rhymes. Anderson (1972) tells us "when using nursery rhymes, children's names may be substituted for the rhyme or song characters. Let each child select the person he wants to be, but avoid this being used in a way that might hurt the child. Let children join in on repeated refrains. This may be done in a story such as "Little pig, little pig, let me in; No, no, no, not by the hair of my chinny chin chin."

Choral Speaking   Simple choric speaking is another form of poetry that can be used as a medium of artistic expression. However, care should be taken to select Mother Goose and other rhymes and poems with simple refrains that young children can repeat with ease. Interest and social abilities of the children must be considered to avoid involving them for extended periods of time. Thus the material should be appealing and enjoyable and on the child's level of maturity and understanding, otherwise the children learn negative feelings and attitudes toward poetry rather than the enjoyment and interest in it that should be theirs.

If poetry and song are image and word beauty wrapped in one, then we are asking children to search for unique images through which to express their ideas, thoughts, emotions, and explanations of the experiences they have in their world. We set the stage and encourage them to experiment with imitation and the creation of words that communicate their natural feel for the poetic and the rhythmic. As they explore in a rich, open, positive, and accepting environment, they freely create, compare and enjoy their own poems, chants, songs, and dances.

Creating Poems, Chants, Songs, and Dances   In assisting and directing children to experiment with the creation of poems, rhymes, songs, and dance, a teacher can encourage them to imagine and reproduce their own sounds to accompany activities of tools and machines, growing plants, animals, and people. As a teacher repeats chants and sings back to the child the words of his own lilting compositions he is encouraged to experiment with ever-increasing varieties of sounds, words, and word combinations. He imitates and reproduces the sounds and movements of things, people and activities that he observes, such as how it

moves, its color, size, weight, how it eats
feels—warm, cold, softlike
makes a sound
behaves

As he imitates the sounds through his own syllable, word, phrase, or sentence creation, he almost always accompanies these sounds with his song and rhythmic interpretations.

Summarizing the Integration of Music and the Language Arts

Leeper (1968) states that "music can contribute in many ways by offering opportunities for listening, creating, singing, rhythmic responses, and playing instruments. Through these activities the child experiences pleasures, joy, creative expression; develops listening skills and auditory discrimination; gains in physical development and use of his body; and increases the range and flexibility of his voice. The child grows in his appreciation of music and can learn to discriminate in his choices."

A child who has participated in a program where music and literature are related and integrated usually profits in the following ways:

—Shows progressively more interest in listening to and participating in a greater variety of music forms and types of literature—poetry and stories.

—Is more interested in listening to and/or participation within small groups as well as individually, dramatization, dance, creation of songs, and the use of instruments.

—Enjoys realistic, familiar, and repetitious content in songs, poems, rhymes, and stories when they are selected in terms of his maturity, needs, and interests.

—Shows increasing interest in poems, songs, and stories about moving objects: animals and machines, plants, weather, and things.

—Enjoys sharing learned poems, stories, songs, and dances with peers and adults. Attempts to read songs, poems, and stories from books.

—Is becoming aware that familiar things and events in his environment are contained in poems, books, songs, and radio and television—musical and other types of programs.

—Enjoys familiar and enjoyable pictures that are closely related to the song, poem, rhyme, or story.

—Shows an interest in poems, stories, and songs that first introduce him to a friendly and happy world.

—Is beginning to think in simple abstractions and can therefore relate a limited number of new encounters with a familiar one.

—Absorbs new words and concepts slowly as they are presented in a variety of interesting and repetitious ways that help him understand and enjoy literature and music.

—Begins to show improved attitudes concerning acceptance.

—Is fascinated with imaginative poems, stories, songs, and dances.

—Is usually highly interested in poems, stories, and songs that involve nonsensical words and phrases, guessing and riddles.

—Shows increased awareness and interest after hearing poems, stories, and songs by requesting their dramatization, thus asking for time to dramatize them through pantomime and dance.

—Shows greater appreciation and understanding of literature and music by asking that poems and stories be reread or retold and that songs and musical recordings be resung and replayed with no alterations from the original presentation.

—Shows growth in ability to verbalize and relate concepts as songs, poems, and stories are being listened to and as the children discuss them. New awareness is also shown as children interrupt the teacher while she reads a story, poem, or as she sings a song to and with them.

—Shows evidence of an expression of his understanding and acquisition of information and concepts presented in literature and music by asking relevant questions and by asking for other selections dealing with the same subject or content.

Resources for Language Arts-Music Relationships

Music and language arts permeate all areas of the curriculum, therefore any source listed in this entire chapter can be used in some manner to teach music and language arts skills and concepts. The materials and sources listed below have been selected to assist the teaching of specific music and language arts skills, knowledges and appreciations.

Songs

Because songs have words and are generally based on poems, and because they usually emphasize or reflect rhythmic speech, they can be used advantageously to enhance language arts study. There are songs dealing with the alphabet with traditional words sung to various melodies. "Bingo" is an example of a song that features spelling and omitting letters in the name Bingo. Sometimes the classified indexes of music textbooks can assist the teacher in finding songs that are particularly appropriate for meeting her objectives in this area.

A songbook containing forty-four songs by Denise Bacon, *Let's Sing Together!* is composed for nursery school children. It contains a large number of Mother Goose and other nursery rhymes and poems set to melodies of limited vocal range. Finger plays are included, and movement and dramatization are suggested.. It is obtainable from Boosey and Hawkes, Oceanside, New York 11572. Commonly found songs for five-year-olds that illustrate music and language arts relationships include:

Chumbara	Canadian nonsense song
Bingo	spelling
Alphabet Song	ABCs
Pawpaw Patch	word rhythms
John Jacob Jingleheimer Schmidt	tongue twister (in *Spectrum of Music-K*)

A. Recordings
   Refer to these catalogs:

   Best Records, Books, for Early Childhood, Children's Music Center, Los Angeles 90019. See section "Alphabet Concepts."

   RCA Records School and Library Catalog, Educational Dept., 1133 Avenue of the Americas, New York, N.Y. See "Language Arts—Elementary" section. Much is suitable for young children and is age-rated as such. Other sections are of interest: "Songs and Music Children Like," "Music to Relax By," and "Features for Little Creatures."

Action and Rhythm Records

Franson Corporation
A Visit to My Little Friend CRG 1017
Creepy, Crawly Caterpillar CRG 5019
Jingle Bells and Other Songs for Winter Fun YPR 718
My Playful Scarf CRG 1019
Nothing To Do CRG 1012
Rainy Day YPR 712

Bowmar

Rhythm Time Album 1 and 2, 023 and 024
Decca Records
Mother Goose Playtime Songs 1-100
Children's Music Center
ABC, 1 to 10, Frank Luther. MC-C534. Alphabet in songs and sounds, counting rhymes.
American Game Songs for Children, Pete Seeger. CE9R. Counting, nonsense, and repeated words.
Educational Activities, Inc.
Learning Basic Skills Through Music, Vol. 2 *Game Songs,* Hap Palmer includes songs that develop vocabulary, concepts, and reading readiness.

Listening and Participation Records

Franson Corporation
Building a City YPR 711
Eensie-Beensie Spider CRG 1002
Musical Mother Goose CRG 209
Train on the Farm CRG 1011 or YPR 1000
Train to the Zoo CRG 1001 or YPR 1001
Little Gray Ponies YPR 735
The Sleepy Family YPR 10011

Bowmar, Glendale, Cal.

Little Favorites 006
Nursery and Mother Goose Songs 007

Decca

Mother Goose Singtime Songs 1-101
Mother Goose Storytime Songs 1-102

B. Mother Goose Sources

Books

Anglund, Joan Walsh. *In a Pumpkin Shell*. New York: Harcourt Brace Jovanovich, Inc. 1960. An ABC book of rhymes.

Austin, Margot. *The Very Young Mother Goose*. New York: Platt and Munk, 1963.

Briggs, Raymond. *Ring-a-ring o' Roses*. New York: Coward-McCann, Inc., 1962. One of the more effectively and appealingly illustrated rhymes from Mother Goose.

Brown, Marcia. *Peter Piper's Alphabet*. New York: Charles Scribner's Sons, 1959. Tongue-twisting nonsense rhymes are used to represent the sounds of the alphabet.

De Angeli, Marguerite, compiler. *Book of Nursery and Mother Goose Rhymes*. Garden City, N.Y.: Doubleday & Co., Inc., 1954. Contains 376 of the most popular rhymes.

De La Mare, Walter. *Rhymes and Verses*. New York: Holt, Rinehart & Winston, 1947.

Rojankovsky, Feodor. *The Tall Book of Mother Goose*. New York: Harper & Row, 1942. Whimsical, humorous cartoon-type pictures.

Tudor, Tasha. *Mother Goose*. New York: Henry Z. Walck, Inc., 1944. Contains seventy-seven well-known verses.

Werner, Jane. *The Giant Golden Mother Goose*. New York: Western Publishing Co., 1948.

Wright, Blanche F., and Arbuthnot, May Hill. *The Real Mother Goose*. Chicago: Rand McNally & Co., 1944. Presents the origins of Mother Goose.

Records and Filmstrips for Teaching

Mother Goose Songs and Children's Songs (two kits), Bowmar. Sound filmstrips, art prints, minibooks, verse cards, vocabulary cards, teaching suggestions. Kits available separately.

Mother Goose Stories with a Rock Beat, Educational Activities, Inc. Twelve stories with modern music and adapted lyrics. Album K 7015 (records).

Musical Mother Goose, Golden Records LP 65.

Nursery Rhymes for Dramatic Play, Educational Activities, Inc. Mother Goose sung so that children learn rhymes by dramatizing them.

C. Teaching Poetry and Rhyme

Books and Anthologies

Arbuthnot, May H. *Time for Poetry*. Chicago: Scott, Foresman and Company, 1951. A representative collection for all ages.

Association for Childhood Education International, *Told Under the Blue Umbrella*. New York: Macmillan Co., 1962. Short, simple stories for very young children. Excellent as a source of tales for story-telling. *Told Under the Magic Umbrella*, 1939. Modern fairy tales portray a kind of fantasy found in the everyday life of a child. *Sung Under the Silver Umbrella*, 1962. Collections of poetry for young children. Poets such as Robert Louis Stevenson, Edna St. Vincent Millay, Christina Rossetti, and Eleanor Farjeon are represented. *Told Under Spacious Skies*, 1952. Stories about people of various races, colors, creeds, cultures, and backgrounds, but all are American.

Brown, Margaret Wise. *Where Have You Been?* New York: Scholastic Book Services, 1966. Delightful preschool poems.

Ferris, Helen, ed. *Favorite Poems Old and New*. Garden City, N.Y.: Doubleday & Co. An excellent comprehensive collection.

Frank, Josette, ed., *Poems to Read to the Very Young*. New York: Random House, 1961.

———. *More Poems to Read to the Very Young*. New York: Random House, 1968. Poems about the life of a young child.

Hoffman, Hilde. *Green Grass Grows All Around*. New York: Macmillan Co., 1968. Illustration of the traditional folk song.

The House That Jack Built. New York: Lothrop, Lee and Shepard, 1968. Traditional rhyme. Illustrated by Joe Rogers.

Junker, Florence. *Come With Me*. Minneapolis, Minn.: T. S. Denison & Co., Inc. Children's guessing and dancing poems.

Lear, Edward. *Nonsense Verse*. Boston: Little, Brown and Co., 1950.

Lewis, Richard, ed. *In a Spring Garden*. New York: The Dial Press, 1965. Haiku illustrated by Keats. They involve values and provide opportunities for the child to express his feelings.

Merriam, Eve. *Catch a Little Rhyme*. New York: Atheneum Press, 1966. Poems that express a child's feelings.

Milne, A. A., *When We Were Very Young*, 1966 and *Now We Are Six*. rev. ed., 1970. New York: E. P. Dutton Co.

Oberhansli, Gertrud. *Sleep, Baby, Sleep*. New York: Atheneum Press, 1969. Gertrud Oberhansli illustrated the familiar cradle song.

Rossetti, Christina. *Sing-Song*. New York: Macmillan Co., 1924.

Segal, Edith. *Be My Friend*. Secaucus, N.J.: Citadel Publishers, 1964. Poems designed to open the door to friendship and people.

Thompson, Jean McKee. *Poems to Grow On*. Boston: Beacon Press, 1957.

Withers, Carl. *A Rocket in My Pocket*. New York: Holt, Rinehart & Winston, 1948. Rhymes and chants, counting and playground games, and jump rope chants.

Recordings and Filmstrips
A Child's Garden of Verse NS 5067. Lyons: Elkhart, Ind. All of Robert Louis Stevenson's favorites are included.

Poems LB 7611. Lyons. Quiet time listening for very young children. Beautifully spoken poems illustrating the beauty of sound and music.

Poems for the Very Young. Bowmar. Interpretive readings with incidental music.

We Move to Poetry (K-3) Albums K 9025 and K 9035. Educational Activities, Inc. Each poem is read, then a musical interlude follows in which children can interpret it through movement. Weather, things, personal experiences, animals, and ways of having fun are included.

We Sing Poetry. 2 color filmstrips, 2 records or cassettes, guide. Educational Activities, Inc. "Wynken, Blynken and Nod"; "I Have a Little Shadow"; "O, How I Love to Go Up in a Swing"; "The Owl and the Pussycat"; "If"; "Spider and the Fly"; "Nine Little Goblins"; "Little Boy Blue"; "Land of Storybooks"; "If You Go to Fairyland"; "The Pussycats Tea Party"; "Little Lamb"; "Lullabye Town."

D. Teaching Finger Plays

Books

Carlson, Bernice Wells. *Listen and Help Tell the Story.* Nashville, Tenn.: Abingdon Press, 1965.

Ellis, Mary Jackson and Lyons, Frances. *Finger Playtime.* Minneapolis, Minn.: T. S. Denison, 1960. Finger plays suitable for various areas of curriculum.

Grayson, Marion F. *Let's Do Fingerplays.* Washington, D.C.: Robert B. Luce, Inc., 1962.

Jacobs, Francis S. *Finger Plays and Action Rhythms.* New York: Lothrop, Lee, 1941.

Matterson, Elizabeth. *Games for the Very Young.* New York: American Heritage Publishing Co., 1969.

Owens, Ruby. *Musical Finger Plays.* 7225 Carmenita Rd., Lemon Grove, Calif. 92045, 1970.

Pierce, June. *Wonder Book of Finger Plays and Action Rhymes.* New York: Wonder Books, Inc., 1955.

Poulsson, Emile. *Finger Plays for Nursery and Kindergarten.* New York: Lothrop, Lee and Shepard Co., 1971.

Scott, Louise B., and Thompson, J. J. *Rhymes for Fingers and Flannel Boards.* New York: McGraw-Hill Book Co., 1960.

———. *Talking Time.* 2d ed. New York: McGraw-Hill Book Co., 1966.

Records

Children's Creative Play Songs EC96. Available from Children's Music Center. Finger plays and play songs sung by children for language and body play.

Finger Games Album HYP 506. Educational Activities, Inc. Rhythmic verse, hand motions, with directions on the record. Contains rhythmic movement and imaginative song patterns. Listening, learning concepts, and coordination are by-products of enjoyable games.

Sing a Song of Action, Vol. 1. Album K 3600. Educational Activities, Inc. 2 records. Twenty-three progressive songs to be acted out rhythmically through finger play and games.

E. Teacher's References

Books for Literature and Language Development

Anderson, Paul S. *Flannelboard Books for the Primary Grades.* Minneapolis, Minn.: T. S. Denison & Co., 1962.

———. *Storytelling With the Flannelboard.*

Arnott, Peter D. *Plays Without People.* Bloomington: Indiana University Press, 1964.

Bailey, Carolyn S., ed. *Favorite Stories for the Children's Hour.* New York: Platt & Munk, Publishers, 1965. Anthology of favorite folk tales, fables, and legends. Also *Merry Tales for Children,* 1943. Humorous short stories divided into subject categories: Home, animal, folk, and holiday.

Bain, Geraldine, ed. *Children's Literature for Dramatization: An Anthology.* New York: Harper & Row, Publishers, 1964. Fifty-six stories and eighty-two poems for dramatic presentation.

Baird, Bil. *The Art of the Puppet.* New York: Macmillan Co., 1965.

Child Study Association of America. *Read-to-Me Story Book.* T. Y. Crowell, 1947. Stories and poems about weather, animals, daddies, and transportation.

Dobbs, Rose, ed. *Once Upon a Time.* New York: Random House, 1950. A collection of old tales that have been favorites for many years. The stories are easy to prepare for storytelling.

Evans, Pauline, ed. *The Family Treasury of Children's Stories,* Book 1. Garden City, N.Y.: Doubleday & Co., 1956. A collection of poems and stories for children. It begins with Mother Goose and simple tales for very young listeners.

Gruenberg, Sidonie. *Let's Read a Story.* Garden City, N.Y.: Doubleday, 1957. Selected stories about real boys and girls.

Hutchinson, Veronica, ed. *Chimney Corner Stories.* New York: Minton, Balch & Co., 1925. Includes sixteen of the world's favorite tales.

Kramer, Nora, ed. *Nora Kramer's Storybook.* New York: Gilbert Press, Inc., 1955. Collection of story and verse from contemporary literature selected for children ages three and four.

Lionni, Leo. *Frederick.* New York: Pantheon Books, 1967. A mouse who stores up words and colors instead of nuts and grain as the other mice do. During the winter he tells stories so well that the others can see the colors as clearly as if he had painted them in their minds.

Martignoni, Margaret E., ed. *A, B, C, Go!* New York: Crowell-Collier Publishing Co., 1962. A well-illustrated classic collection of poems and stories for childhood.

Mitchell, Lucy S., *Here and Now Story Book.* New York: Dutton, 1948. How to create and tell stories to children ages two to seven years.

Roy, H. A. *Anybody at Home?* Boston: Houghton Mifflin Co., 1942. Each short rhyme is followed by a question.

Sandberg, Ingar, and Sandberg, Lasse. *Little Anna and the Magic Hat.* New York: Lothrop, Lee and Shepard, 1965. An imaginative story about everyday things like shoes and dolls.

Sawyer, Ruth. *The Way of the Storyteller.* New York: Viking Press, 1962.

Scarry, Richard. *The Gingerbread Man.* New York: Western Publishing Co., 1953. Also *Scarry's Best Word Book Ever*, 1963.

Schaer, Julian, and Bileck, Marvin. *Rain Makes Applesauce.* New York: Holiday House, 1964. Silly talk enjoyed at this age.

Showers, Paul. *The Listening Walk.* New York: T. Y. Crowell, 1961.

Steiner, Charlotte. *My Bunny Feels Soft.* New York: Alfred A. Knopf, Inc., 1958. A first book of definitions.

Vance, Eleanore G. *Jonathan.* Chicago: Follett Publishing Co., 1966. Excellent for reading to preschool children.

Books About ABC's

Crews, Donald. *We Read A to Z.* New York: Harper & Row, 1967. Each letter of the alphabet introduces a concept illustrated with a colorful design. "A is for almost" "Z is for zigzag."

Gag, Wanda. *The ABC Bunny.* New York: Coward-McCann, 1933. A favorite ABC book for many years. Adventures of a small bunny.

Larrick, Nancy. *First ABC.* New York: Platt & Munk, 1965. Suggestions for parents and teachers on how to use the book.

Lionni, Leo. *The Alphabet Tree.* New York: Pantheon Books, Inc., 1968. The letters of the alphabet on the leaves of the alphabet tree are there with no purpose until a word bug comes and teaches them to group themselves to form words.

Sendack, Maurice. *Alligators All Around.* New York: Harper & Row, 1962. A delightful nonsense book.

Tudor, Tasha. *"A" Is for Anabelle.* New York: Henry Z. Walck, 1954.

Records and Filmstrips for Teaching Children Stories

Rhythms to Reading, Bowmar. 12 records, 12 books, picture song book (obtainable separately). A set in which "The music commands involvement."

Call and Response, by Ella Jenkins. Children's Music Center.

Franson Corporation. Source of Children's Record Guild and Young People's Records:

For Ages 2-4

The Carrot Seed, CRG 1003
The Four Bears, CRG 1009
Peter, Please, Pancakes, CRG 1026
Noah's Ark, CRG 1035
For Ages 2-5
Muffin in the City, YPR 601
Muffin in the Country, YPR 603

For Ages 5-8

The Golden Goose, CRG, 5002
Hot Cross Buns, CRG 5005
Mr. Grump and the Band, CRG 5007
Billy Rings the Bell, CRG 5008
Creepy, Crawley, Caterpillar, CRG 5019
Circus at the Opera, CRG 5022
The Eagle and the Thrush, CRG 5024

Golden Records

Frosty the Snowman, 00179
Gingerbread Man, 00164
Little Red Caboose, 00159
Little Red Hen, 00166
Peter Rabbit, 00173
Three Bed Time Stories: Three Little Pigs, Three Kittens, and Three Bears, 00157

Learning Basic Skills Through Music: Building Vocabulary, by Hap Palmer. Educational Activities, Inc., Album AR 521, record or cassette. Children learn by doing; they learn safety vocabulary, kinds of food, parts of the body, forms of transportation, and objects.

Learning Basic Skills Through Music, Vols. 1 and 2, by Hap Palmer. Educational Activities, Inc., Album AR 514, record or cassette. Numbers, colors, the alphabet, and body awareness are presented.

Laban, Walter, and Watkins, Lillian. Bowmar. *The Best in Children's Literature, Series One.* Records or cassettes (D-47 or 526). Contains such records as: Halloween Tales, Thanksgiving and Easter, Christmas Stories, Classics for Children, Child's World of Sounds, Transportation, Community Helpers, Fun With Language. *Series Two,* records 062 or cassettes 527. Contains such records as: Famous Classics, Animals, Numbers and Time, Fables, World of Nature, Say-Along Stories, Favorite Folk Tales, Science Concepts, Night, Seasons.

Listening Activities Record Album. Scott, Foresman and Co., Glenview, Ill. 60025. Song, dance, pantomime, mood music, poetry, dramatization, auditory discrimination game, and sound stories.

Magic of Story Telling. Lyons, Elkhart, Ind. Six sets consisting of six filmstrips, three records or cassettes, with story, art packet, and guide. All-time favorites.

Music to Tell a Story By. RCA Records. Vols. 1 and 2. (For pre-K-4). Cassettes.

Old Tales for Young Folks. Filmstrip set NS 8099, Lyons. The Three Bears, Three Billy Goats Gruff, Three Spinners.

Nursery Rhymes, Columbia Record CC70003. 45 rpm.

Singing Sounds, Bowmar. Two records with accompanying books. Phonics.

Who Am I? Children's Music Center. Games and songs for "I am a person." (Story records and books in combination present aural-visual experiences to stimulate joy in listening and an eagerness for reading. See the catalog *Best Records, Books, Rhythm Instruments for Early Childhood.* Children's Music Center. "Story Records, Book Combinations" section.)

Fun and Fantasy Sources

Children's Music Center. The early childhood catalog of this company lists a number of books that can be used as a stimulus for creative language, poems, dance, and instrumentation:

If I Were	Children's fantasies in brilliant color.
I Can Fly	"I can play I'm anything."
The Day Everyone Cried	
The Two Giants	Riotous illustrations.
Puzzles	
Some Frogs Have Their Own Rocks	They sit, think, leap, and sing high, low, loud, and soft.
The Moon Jumpers	Beautiful pictures of children playing in the moonlight, full of wonder at the moon.
Did You Ever?	Get into bed and feel like a tiger? Get under a blanket and become a turtle? Lead an orchestra? Get all mixed up?
Let's Walk Up the Wall	Absurdities to help children discover what animals can do that people cannot. Can you fly? make honey? carry your house on your back? But, we can think.

That's What Friendships Are For	Each animal gives advice according to his own body movement. A very funny story.
Are You My Mother?	A funny story about Marini; a picture dictionary in English and Spanish.
Everyone Has a Name	Fourteen animals are described and identified. Some bark, some have four legs, and none are the same. This is why everyone has a name.

(Children's Music Center catalog also lists fun and fantasy records for developing music and language arts, including those cited below.)

I Wish I Were	What I could be if I were very big or very little; includes rhythms.
Activity Songs by Marcia Berman	Original songs about being tall, a cow in the house, rain, bees, trains, the ocean, etc.
Amusing Animals	For listening, singing, and responding.
Our House Is Upside Down	Whimsey with Marais and Miranda.
Let's Go to Fairy Tale Land	Traditional fairy tales and Mother Goose rhymes with satisfactory conclusions.

Spanish and English Language Development Sources
Children's Music Center catalog lists:

Books

> *What Do I Say?*
> *What Do I Do?*

Records

> *Spanish-American Children's Songs* from Mexico and New Mexico.
> *Songs in Spanish for Children* dealing with counting, animal sounds, months of the year, shopping, and resting. English words also.
> *Cantemos Ninos*, record and book, contains Mexican singing games, folk songs, and dances for young children, sung in Spanish. English words also.
> *Learning Basic Skills Through Music*, by Hap Palmer, sung in Spanish. Building Spanish vocabulary through music.

Suggested Activities

1. After establishing from research a set of criteria to use in evaluating your performance, select, prepare, and present a related song, poem, and story appropriate for a group of four- or five-year-old children.
2. Select a song appropriate for use with puppets or flannel board figures and present it to the class.

3. Begin to keep a file of songs, poems (rhymes, finger plays), and stories. Using these categories, select and file several titles under each that are appropriate for teaching musical skills, concepts, and appreciations and concepts from the other curricular areas: science, mathematics, art, language arts, and social living.

4. Select one holiday that comes during the school year and prepare a song, a poem, and a story suitable for a four- or five-year-old child or group; then present them in the college class or to a small group of children.

5. Organize a panel to discuss in class ways music can be used to teach values and intercultural understanding.

6. State some suggested musical experiences that can be used to teach mathematical concepts to young children. Demonstrate these to the class.

7. Select a song, poem, and story about health and safety. Analyze them to indicate what safety or health concepts can be taught along with music skills, knowledges, and appreciations.

8. Discuss in class the value of music for young children in all areas of the curriculum: cognitive, psychomotor, and affective areas.

9. Analyze recordings, song collections, and music textbooks for ages three, four, and five to determine if there is sufficient attention given to the different cultural groups and to the male and female gender.

10. Tell a nursery rhyme, children's story, or create your own story. Use the piano, Autoharp, or percussion instruments to make sounds appropriate to the story.

11. Create a musical story, possibly with songs and sound effects, for young children and share it with the class.

References

Music

Film Guide for Music Education. Reston, Va.: Music Educators National Conference. Revised periodically.

Jacques-Dalcroze, Emile. *Rhythm, Music and Education.* Trans. by Harold F. Rubenstein. New York: G. P. Putnam's Sons, 1921.

Jones, Bessie, and Bess L. Hawes. *Step It Down.* New York: Harper and Row, Publishers, 1972. A book of games, songs, stories, rhymes, and plays about Afro-American children.

Landis, Beth, and Polly Carder. *The Eclectic Curriculum in American Music Education: Contributions of Dalcroze, Kodály, and Orff.* Reston, Va.: Music Educators National Conference, 1972. For elementary school, but a valuable source of information.

Nash, Grace, et. al. *The Child's Way of Learning: Do It My Way.* Sherman Oaks, Calif.: Alfred Publishing Co., 1977. Music in an integrated curriculum K-6.

Nye, Robert, and Bjornar Bergethon. *Basic Music: Functional Musician-ship for the Non-Music Major,* 4th ed. Englewood Cliffs, N.J.: Prentice-Hall, Inc., 1970.

Nye, Robert E. and Meg Peterson. *Teaching Music with the Autoharp.* Evanston, Ill. 60202: Music Education Group, 1973. How to play and use the instrument in teaching.

Sheehy, Emma D. *Children Discover Music and Dance.* New York: Teachers College Press, 1968.

Smith, Robert B. *Music in the Child's Education.* New York: Ronald Press Co., 1970.

Early Childhood Education

Bearley, Molly, ed. *The Teaching of Young Children.* New York: Schocken Books, 1970. A guide for teachers in music, movement, language, and art, applying Piaget's learning theories.

Bentley, William. *Learning to Move and Moving to Learn.* New York: Scholastic Book Service, 1970. A concise and inexpensive manual for use with children in small groups.

Chandler, Martha A. *A Bibliography of Books for Young Children.* Medford, Mass.: Eliot Pearson Department of Child Study, Tufts University, 1970. For ages two to seven.

Chenfield, Mimi B. *Teaching Language Arts Creatively.* New York: Harcourt Brace Jovanovich, Inc., 1978.

Chukovsky, Kornei. *From Two to Five.* Berkeley, Calif.: University of California Press, 1963. Language in its beauty, use, and pleasure is explored through children.

Coody, Betty. *Using Literature with Young Children.* Dubuque, Iowa: Wm. C. Brown Co. Publishers, 1973. Concise resource book.

Frazier, Alexander. *Open Schools for Children.* Washington, D.C.: Association for Supervision and Curriculum Development, 1972.

Frost, Joe L. *Early Childhood Education Rediscovered—Readings.* New York: Holt, Rinehart and Winston, 1968. See also the 1973 edition.

Gerhardt, Lydia A. "The Role of Body Movement in the Child's Conceptualization of Space." Ed. D. dissertation. New York University, 1970.

Gray, Vera, and Rachel Percival. *Music, Movement, and Mime for Children.* London: Oxford University Press, 1962.

Griffin, Louis, comp. *Multi-Ethnic Books for Young Children.* ERIC-NAEXC Publication in Early Childhood Education. Washington, D.C.: National Association for the Education of Young Children. Excellent annotated bibliography of multi-ethnic books.

Hartley, Ruth E., Lawrence K. Frank, and Robert M. Golden. *Understanding Children's Play.* New York: Columbia University Press, 1952. One chapter includes specific observations and analyses of children's behavior during music and dance experience.

Lavatelli, Celia S. *Piaget's Theory Applied to an Early Childhood Curriculum.* Boston: American Science and Engineering, 1970.

Nimnicht, Glen, et. al. *The New Nursery School.* New York: General Learning Corp., 1969. Six pamphlets with educationally sound suggestions for every aspect of the curriculum. Thorough description of a program.

Sinclair, Caroline B. *Movement of the Young Child.* Columbus, Ohio: Charles E. Merrill Co., 1973. Answers questions about the development of young children; how they should move; and what movement experience should be provided.

Smith, James. *Setting Conditions for Creative Teaching.* Boston, Mass.: Allyn and Bacon, 1967.

Todd, Vivian E. *The Aide in Early Childhood Education.* New York: Macmillan Company, 1973. Handbook to assist aides and parents; has practical suggestions.

Todd, Vivian E. and Helen Heffernan. "Developing Communication Skills" and "Stories for Preschool Children," Chapters 11 and 12. In *The Years Before School,* 3rd ed. New York: Macmillan Company, 1977.

Weber, Lillian. *The English Infant School and Informal Education.* Englewood Cliffs, N.J.: Prentice-Hall, Inc. 1971.

6 Parents and Teachers: Partners in Teaching Music

In the history of American society, the family was the one closely-knit unit that established the foundation for all types of learning. The children were taught to identify with a task, and then to persist with it until a certain degree of mastery was achieved. When values, sensitivity to beauty, and positive attitudes toward life and people were attained they were acquired in the home, because the school concentrated primarily on teaching the three R's. Much of what the children learned was accomplished by observing the behavior of adults and modeling themselves accordingly. However, in the modern industrial and technological societies of today where both parents often work outside the home, the schools have tended to become a substitute for the parents by expanding the curriculum to include the knowledges, skills, attitudes, and values that were formerly learned in the home. In order to make these learnings relevant and more meaningful to young children, the basic content of music and other areas of the curriculum for young children should be drawn from, or closely related to, the life and music of their home and community.

For many years we have known that at the very base of an effective music program, or at the base of any other effective program, for that matter, has been cooperative home-school relations and communications. Nevertheless, until recently many teachers have failed to work closely with parent and community groups in planning and implementing relevant and improved school curricula. This neglect has resulted in some parental demands to be involved at the decision-making level concerning the education of their children.

In evaluating the Head Start programs, it appeared quite evident that staffs of those that worked closely with parents who wanted to be involved in the education of their children in school and also in ways they could improve the health and educational environment of their home, proved to be quite effective, whereas those working with parents who were not directly involved proved to be of little value the children. As a result of these and similar research findings, the values resulting from parental involvement are generally accepted by leading educators, particularly those who decide upon the types of educational programs to be funded by the federal government. There are specific stipulations set forth as guides for the funding of many proposals for early childhood education. One such stipulation includes the different ways parents are to be involved in the planning and implementing of the proposed early childhood education project. Some of the types of parent participation suggested as necessary for designing an effective program are:

1. Planning and making suggestions concerning the types of programs and how they might be implemented.
2. Becoming involved in the classroom and school as paid aides and volunteers.
3. Making plans for initiating a cooperative home-school program.
4. Assisting and observing teachers and children in school.

It is the obligation of the school and the parents to plan viable ways for working cooperatively in the education of children. People who have children attending school are the most deeply involved and should therefore be active in deciding what takes place. Teachers, on the other hand, must work closely enough with parents to know what happens to the child while he is not in school. If significant and appropriate learning experiences are to be provided for children in the classroom, the teacher must plan ways to assist parents with problems occurring during the child's out-of-school hours as well. Parent and community involvement in every aspect of the child's education is a necessity and an obligation in the schools of a modern complex society.

In explaining the importance of teacher explanations concerning the mental growth of children, and parental responsiveness, J. McVicker Hunt (1964) quotes Baldwin, Kalhorn and Breese, who found that "the I.Q.'s of 4- to 7-year-old children tend to increase with time if parental discipline consists of responsive and realistic explanations but tend to fall if parental discipline consists of nonchalant unresponsiveness or of demands for obedience for its own sake, with painful stimulation as the alternative."

In like manner, the home has an equally strong influence upon the language and the aesthetic learning of the child, his concerns for the feelings and rights of others, and his values. The home can be used as a source of valuable learnings and as a stabilizing and enriching influence. Too, the home is needed to reinforce music instruction and to encourage the child's music participation. The teacher should strive to assist parents in obtaining an understanding of the goals and learning experiences of the school music program. Through conferences and home visits with parents, she can keep them informed of their child's progress and interest in music. Parents and teachers may plan what each can do in the home and school to reinforce each other's efforts to improve the child's music accomplishments.

How the Teacher Can Communicate with Parents

Listed here are suggested ways the teacher may keep the parents informed about what is being accomplished in the music program, and suggest what parents can, for their part, do in the home. You may wish to add to this list.

- Arrange for parents to observe the teacher as she teaches music.
- Make telephone calls to inform the parents of the child's needs and progress.
- Make notes to parents with comments about child's music accomplishments and interests.
- Visit homes. Take music instruments to play and demonstrate their use; take song books with appropriate and easy songs to sing; sing the songs with the members of the family.
- Attend parent study groups; demonstrate ways of working with young children.
- Make tapes of the child's musical performance—to be sent home with the child.
- Work with parents to help them prepare to perform a dance, sing a song, or play an instrument for the children.
- Work cooperatively with parents in choosing recordings for home use.
- Assist parents in selecting appropriate television and radio musical programs for children.
- Attend room mother's programs, teas, or coffees.
- Send parents a list of those songbooks, recordings, tapes, instruments, and machines (tape recorders, phonographs, projectors, etc.) that are available for home use.
- Send parents examples of their child's creative compositions.
- Invite parents to assist in class music programs.
- Invite parents to help plan ways for enhancing a child's self-concept by the way in which they respond to the child and his music.
- Organize a "Music Night" at school where parents learn to play an instrument, do folk dances, or learn songs to use in the family music program.
- Provide parents information about child's performance—singing, creating and learning songs, rhythms, playing instruments, learning skills and concepts of music, and brief them about the way music is taught as a part of all subject areas.

How Parents Can Help Their Children in Music

- Read storybooks about music to the child; and assist him with the selection of books about music.
- Present poems, nursery rhymes, finger plays and stories, and encourage children to learn the rhythm of words by participating in

repetitious parts and by interpreting the content through rhythmic and creative movement and pantomime.

- Sing songs throughout the day that express moods, interests, and that relate to the various everyday problems which arise in and about the home.
- Encourage the children to create their own songs.
- Assist the child in selecting, listening, and responding to recordings and tapes.
- Make available a library of well-chosen recordings. Discuss with the child what he likes or dislikes about the recordings and how each makes him feel. Since the very young child has difficulty in explaining his feelings verbally, he may communicate through movement of the body how the music makes him feel.
- Call the child's attention to the sounds of people, animals, and things. Help him to identify high, low, fast, slow, short, long, loud, and soft sounds. Have him imitate them. He can compare one sound with another. He can identify and compare the sound of an airplane with that of a train. Discuss how they are alike and different. He can also identify and categorize (group) the things that make high sounds, low sounds, and loud sounds.
- Call the child's attention to the different ways people, animals, and things move. Help him determine how they move, and to categorize as fast, slow, quick, quicker, up and down, beside, behind, below, between, under, over, walk slowly, fast, run, jump, crawl, squirm, hop, skip, lope, trot, and long or short steps. Have him compare the way a rabbit moves with that of a cat. How are their movements alike and different? Why does the cat move this way? Show how a snake moves. How does it feel to move like a snake?
- Sing often with the child.
- Know the songs, recordings, or tapes to which he is experimenting and rhythms he has been creating, and help him with these activities. Discuss his accomplishments at school and at home.
- Show enthusiasm and interest in the child's musical efforts. A short special time each day should be designated when a parent and the child can share music. Of course, music can be engaged in throughout the day, but this special time gives dignity, importance, and emphasis to the significance and joy of music in a child's life endeavors. Such parent participation and involvement as indicated above reinforce a child in his musical efforts and encourage him to make music an important part of his life.
- Assist the child in discovering objects or materials that will produce different types of sounds. These can be readily found around the home. Also, make simple percussion instruments for the child; learn how to make them in a parent work-study group

at school, and make those that will produce a musical sound or tone.

- Involve the child in the selection of some musical television programs.
- Play and sing well-chosen selections for the children often. They tend to like and to develop a musical taste for the types of music they become aurally familiar with in the early and formative years.
- Choose with care movies that include good music. (Some films are too long for very young children.)
- There are excellent children's concerts available in most cities. The programs usually are not too long and include enough action and appropriate movement for most preschool children. Be sure that the child views excerpts of children's concerts on television or sees live concerts on the stage. This is part of giving the child rounded and balanced experiences in a variety of types of music.
- Provide space in the home, if possible, for children to experiment with instruments and sound-producing materials as well as space both inside and outside for movement exploration. Since children's fine and small muscles are underdeveloped, they need ample space with which to move as they use their large muscles.
- Encourage the entire family—mother, father, sister, brother, and their friends—to sing, dance and play together. In this way they share enjoyment of musical experiences with the child.
- Parents who play an instrument may take it to school, explain how it is made, answer children's questions and demonstrate how to play it.
- Parents who know folk dances (from their younger or present days), or who can contribute them from another cultural community can share these with children in school by demonstrating and explaining the dance and possibly teaching the children a short and simple part of it.
- Obtain music series books for nursery school and kindergarten or other song collections for this age, and periodically teach children new songs that relate to particular daily events or special interests of the child.
- Participate in the community education center, listen to recordings, learn to sing and to play simple instruments, and practice doing simple dances or rhythms. Parents can work with the director or teachers in the school to learn ways to relate to their child by reinforcing and encouraging his musical efforts, in order to demonstrate to him that he is accepted as a unique and worthy individual.
- Become involved in teaching a music lesson which relates the learning of music to another area of the curriculum. Plan the lesson carefully with the teacher, and evaluate the results of your efforts. There is no better way to learn to accept children and to en-

courage them in their learning efforts than to teach them. Mothers and fathers involved as observers or teaching aides learn techniques that they can use in the home as they guide the musical learning of their own children. As a parent participates in a formal program of music instruction, the classroom teacher usually assists him in planning his teaching strategies.

Teachers have the professional responsibility for assuming leadership in designing programs for children since the former are expected to possess such skills. Spodek (1972) states, "The judgment of parents can be considered another source of information about the effectiveness of the program. Parent grievances should be considered as well as other data in making school decisions and teachers should always be receptive to parents' ideas and criticisms. Changes should not be instituted merely as a way of placating parents, however. Teachers should feel strong enough in their professional role to be able to justify their acts in school and to stand by programs they believe constitute sound professional practice."

Parents should be encouraged to participate in plans for a continuously improving music program and be allowed to become involved in the initiation and evaluation of plans for improvement in both the home and the school. For too long teachers have functioned as if they had to tell parents what to do. Many parents are competent and well-informed and should be encouraged to make suggestions for improving the school music program. In order to know the children they teach and to teach each child at his experience level, the teacher must know the home, and the parent must know the school. For children to achieve maximum success in music, teachers and parents must plan ways to work together cooperatively. When this happens, frustrations and contradictions are lessened for the child as well as for the parents and teacher, thus providing a more positive and receptive climate for learning music.

Teachers, Parents, and Children with Special Learning Problems

As has been stated earlier, children with special needs can frequently be taught with the same strategies, activities, and materials that the majority of children encounter, although often the instruction of the former proceeds at a slower pace, in a more structured setting, and with some emphasis on how to accommodate such children at this time, because it is relatively new to many teachers.

The teacher of children with special needs, regardless of their handicapping condition, will first need to become knowledgeable concerning every aspect of the child's problem, especially how the child is like and different from the others in the class. Furthermore, she will need to diagnose carefully the child's strengths, limitations, levels of performance in cognitive, social, and affective development.

The next logical step is to investigate, formulate, and create individualized ways to involve each child in musical activities that develop his full musical potential. The third step is to identify goals and attainable objectives for each child, together with specific activities appropriate for the realization of the specific performance objectives. Subsequently, it is necessary to assess the changes that have resulted from the planned objectives and activities and to adjust the program accordingly.

A teacher of special children will need to master the skill of observing behavior accurately. This will require the time and effort to know a child's operational and functional level. But it is a necessary step in assimilating important data to use as a guide for designing appropriate individualized objectives, activities, materials, and assessment tools compatible with the child's learning style. Learning experiences for special children must be carefully identified, planned and directed. Even though process learning and discovery learning strategies will be used, more time will be given to direct instruction and teacher-directed learning then is used with the majority of children in a regular classroom.

As an outgrowth of working with special children and their parents, values such as described by Brown and Lasher (1978) may accrue:

- an appreciation of the complexity of the human condition—its biological family and community interrelatedness. The teacher will learn to utilize the various resources in the community to build an understanding of the needs of each child and how through cooperative effort and utilization of these resource the child can be helped.
- a sensitivity to the uniqueness of each child, who has a variety of interests, skills, and relationships.
- improvement in relationships with parents; development of interpersonal communicative skills. The teacher must learn to listen and question.
- growth in ability to respond to others, regardless of their level of performance.
- growth in ability to identify and specify strengths and to help the individual with limitations and needs.

Parents and Special Children

When working with special children it will be necessary to work closely and consistently with parents. Parents usually feel uncertain about entering their child with his special problems in a regular classroom. They may feel threatened and often have an undefined feeling of guilt for their child's condition. This may be the first time their handicapped child has been in a situation where he is compared with more normal children. Of course, many of these parents are fearful of what the other children might say and do to hurt their child.

Parents of special "mainstreamed" children often need assistance with their child's problem at home. The following activities have been used successfully with parents by many teachers of young "mainstreamed" children.

- Regular telephone calls
- Parent-teacher conferences
- Discussion of special problems and topics
- Parent meetings and activities among parents with common problems and/or interests
- Provision of films on how to teach and aid a child with a special handicap or learning disability
- Home visitations and demonstrations on how to teach a song, to play an instrument and how to respond and give positive feedback to a child
- Interchange between parent and teacher—each asks the other to continue and enrich a musical activity begun either at home or at school.
- Discuss how to pace learning activities and what to expect from the special child.
- Oftentimes parents do not know what to look for while observing their child. Teacher and parent can observe the child simultaneously in the home and then validate each other's observations. Plans of action can then be designed, based on observation data.
- A teacher must know the cognitive, socio-emotional and physical developmental characteristics of so-called "normal" young children, then teach parents these and how to use them in assessing the levels of maturity and behavior of their child.
- Assist parents with ways to respond constructively to the child's behavior.
- Provide opportunities for parents to discover the relationship between the child's dramatic movement, play, and learning.
- How to use music to cope with the child's fears, listening problems, taking turns, etc.
- Ident.fy specific ways the parent can become involved in the classroom.
- Coach the parents in how to assist the child in school work at home.
- Offer concrete strategies to use with their child in the home. Give encouragement and feedback to parents in their efforts.
- Encourage parents to think of and share ideas or solutions to problems.
- Use home visits to draw up a working contract between teacher and parent.
- Introduce parents of handicapped and learning disabled children to other parents with the same problems.

Most children with learning disabilities are deficient in dealing with problems or learning situations that involve *directionality* and *laterality;* they also experience an inability to focus on musical tasks. Often these skills can be strengthened or taught through the use of creative movement for those who can use their bodies in movement, singing songs and performing rhythms which involve experience through body activity. The concepts involved in *directionality, laterality,* and following directions can be learned from music activities. The understanding of these concepts is gradually developed over a period of time which varies from child to child; it should not be abnormally stressed to the point that children become overly anxious. The teacher can work cooperatively with parents in identifying and utilizing activities that gradually develop the child's abilities in these skills. Most children with learning handicaps are deficient in the understanding and use of hand (manual), eye (visual), and foot (pedal) functions. (Kephart 1971)

Summary

In the "mainstreamed" classrooms or in homes of special children the music program is usually more personalized than in regular classrooms. Seldom will one find a sequence of music activities that is appropriate for all children. The teacher and parents of special children should be capable of assessing the developmental and performance level and evaluating the mastery level of each child.

Some children will employ visual skills when they are deficient in auditory ability. Others will learn through involvement in sensory-motor activities, while some will have more facility in the use of verbalization as a way of learning. The teacher must be able to identify each child's strengths and weaknesses, determine his performance level, style of learning, then set individualized goals and use these in developing and implementing a music program for each child and for the class group. Since young children spend only a short period of time each day in school, the teacher works closely with parents and assists them in extending, continuing and reinforcing what she initiates in school.

The use of performance objectives serve as a device for detailing in specific terms what the child will learn; it also provides a base for assessment and quick feedback to the child. For a child who learns slowly it is a way of limiting the amount presented in one lesson or activity.

Suggested Activities

1. Interview a nursery or kindergarten teacher about methods she uses to involve parents in teaching music.
2. Obtain permission to observe a parent-teacher conference. Make note of strategies the teacher uses to make the parent feel more at ease.

Record the type of information exchanged and determine how you could use the information obtained to improve the child's learning.

3. Observe the comments and concerns shared in a nursery school or kindergarten parent meeting concerned with music. Record the types of questions the parents ask about providing a favorable climate for music for their children.

4. Be present in a nursery school or kindergarten when parents bring their children to school. Observe the types of interaction between parent-teacher, parent-child, and teacher-child. Record types of information exchanged and determine how you think this information can be used for further understanding of a child's behavior in school.

5. Determine ways that might be used to get the father as well as the mother interested in participating in music with he child.

6. List and describe ways in which teachers, parents, and interested members of the community can work cooperatively to equip the school with adequate music materials, equipment, and instruments.

7. List and describe strategies you might use to assist parents in teaching and sharing music in the home.

8. After careful research, formulate a list of appropriate songs, recordings, and instruments that could be shared with the home.

9. Assist a parent in selecting and teaching a rhythm or song to the child.

10. Preview films that contain information and strategies helpful to parents in teaching music in the home or in assisting music teaching in the school.

11. If a music consultant offers a parent workshop for making or learning to use music instruments, ask to become a member of the group.

12. How can parents help the child with movement development in the home?

13. Prepare instructions for parents to use when they observe their child and formulate specific observation guidelines.

References

Finnie, Nancie R. *Handling the Young Cerebral Palsied Child At Home,* 2nd ed. New York: E. P. Dutton, 1975.

Ginott, Haim G. *Between Parents and Child.* New York: Avon Books, 1969.

Gordon, Ira J. *Early Childhood Education.* Chicago: The University of Chicago Press, 1972. (Part Two of the Seventy-first Yearbook of the National Society for the Study of Education.) Emphasizes the importance of parent involvement in early childhood education.

Golick, Margaret. "A Parent's Guide to Learning Problems." *Journal of Learning Disabilities,* 1 No. 6 (June 1968): pp. 366-77.

Grim, Janet, ed. *Training Parents to Teach.* Chapel Hill, N.C.:TADS n.d.

Heisler, Verda. *A Handicapped Child in the Family.* New York: Grune and Statton, 1972.

Hess, Robert, and Doreen Croft. "School and Family: Partners or Competitors?" and "Parents and Teachers as Collaborators," Chapters 4 and 5 in *Teachers of Young Children*, 2nd ed. Boston: Houghton Mifflin, 1975.

Hildebrand, Vernia. "Teacher-Parent Relations" in *Introduction to Early Childhood Education*, 2nd ed. New York: The Macmillan Company, 1976.

Honig, Alice S. *Parent Involvement in Early Childhood Education*. Washington, D.C.: National Association for the Education of Young Children, 1975.

Jones, Beverly, and Jane Hart. *Where's Hannah?: A Handbook for Parents and Teachers of Children with Learning Disorders*. New York Hart Publishing, 1968.

Project Head Start. *Parents Are Needed*. Washington, D.C.: U.S. Government Printing Office, 1967.

———. *Points for Parents*. Washington, D.C.: U.S. Government Printing Office, 1967. How parents can participate (50 suggestions).

Read, Katherine H. "Home-School-Community Relations." In *The Nursery School: A Human Relationship Laboratory*. Philadelphia: W. B. Saunders, 1971.

Taylor, Katherine Whiteside. *Parents and Children Learn Together*. New York: Teachers College Press, Columbia University, 1968.

Todd, Vivian E. *The Aide in Early Childhood Education*. New York: Macmillan Company, Inc., 1973.

Todd, Vivian E. and Helen Heffernan. "Parent Development," Chapter 16. In *The Years Before School*, 3rd ed. New York: Macmillan Company, Inc., 1977.

References

Anderson, Paul S. *Language Skills in Elementary Education,* 2nd ed. New York: Macmillan Co. 1972, p. 140.

Andress, Barbara L. et al. *Music in Early Childhood.* Reston, Va.: Music Educators National Conference, 1973, pp. 48-52.

Aronoff, Frances W. *Music and Young Children.* New York: Holt, Rinehart and Winston, 1969. p. 6, 15.

Baker, Katherine Read, "Extending the Indoors Outside," in *Housing for Early Childhood Education.* Washington, D.C.: Application for Childhood Education International, 1968. p. 59.

Bacon, Denise, *Let's Sing Together!* New York: Boosey & Hawkes Publishers Ltd., 1973.

Biasini, Americole, Ronald Thomas, and Leonore Pogonowski, *MMCP Interaction,* 2nd ed. Bardonia, N.Y.: Media Materials, Inc. n.d. pp. v-vi, 117-19, 24.

Bowmar, Inc., Early Childhood Brochure. Glendale, California, 1973.

Bruner, Jerome S., "The Course of Cognitive Growth." *American Psychologist,* 1964, (34). pp. 1-15.

———. *The Process of Education.* Cambridge, Mass.: Harvard University Press, 1960.

Burns, Paul and Betty Broman. *The Language Arts in Childhood Education.* Chicago: Rand McNally College Publishing Company 1975. p. 115.

Carswell, Evelyn M. and Roubinek, *Open Sesame: A Primer to Open Education.* Pacific Palisades, Calif.: Goodyear Publishing Co. p. 191.

Cherry, Claire, *Creative Movement for the Developing Child,* rev. ed. Belmont, Calif.: Fearon Publishers, 1971. p. 6.

Choate, Robert A. et al. *Beginning Music.* New York: American Book Co., 1970. p. vii.

———. *Music for Early Childhood.* New York: American Book Co., 1970. p. v.

Chenfeld, Mimi B. *Teaching Language Arts Creatively.* New York: Harcourt Brace Jovanovich, Inc., 1978. p. 189.

Coleman, Satis. *Creative Music for Children.* New York: C. P. Putnam's Sons, 1922. p. 169.

Crosby, Muriel, ed. *The World of Lanuguage, Book Y, Teachers' Edition.* Chicago: Follett Publishing Co., 1972. p. 115.

Eliason, Claudia F. and Loa T. Jenkins. *A Practical Guide to Early Childhood Curriculum.* St. Louis: The C. V. Mosby Company, 1977. p. 257-58.

Frost, Joe L. and Joan B. Kissinger. *The Young Child and the Educative Process.* New York: Holt, Rinehart and Winston, 1976. p. 272.

Gagne, Robert. "Contributions of Learning to Human Development." *Psychological Review*, 1968. 73 (3). pp. 177-185.

Gesell, Arnold and Francis Ilg. *Child Development.* New York: Harper & Row Publishers, 1949. p. 26.

Gerhardt, Lydia A., *Moving and Knowing: The Young Child Orients Himself in Space.* Englewood Cliffs, N.J.: Prentice-Hall, Inc., 1973. pp. 164-65.

Gibert, Janet P., "Mainstreaming in Your Classroom: What to Expect," *The Music Educators Journal,* February, 1977. pp. 64-68.

Hanshumaker, James, "The Arts and Educational Development,' a report reprinted by San Diego County (Calif.) Schools, n.d.

Hennings, Dorothy D. and Barbara Grant. *Content and Craft: Written Expression in the Elementary School.* Englewood Cliffs, N.J.: Prentice-Hall, Inc., 1973. pp. 165-66.

Hess, Robert D. and Doreen J. Croft. *Teachers of Young Children.* Boston: Houghton Mifflin Co., 1972. p. 5.

Hunt, J. McVicker. "The Implications of Changing Ideas on How Children Develop Intellectually.' *Children,* May-June, 1964.

Kodaly, Zoltan. *Fifty Nursery Songs,* trans. P. M. Young. New York: Boosey & Hawkes Publishers Ltd., 1964.

Leonard, Charles and Robert House. *Foundations and Principles of Music Education.* New York: McGraw-Hill, 1959. p. 123.

Leavitt, Jerome E., ed. *Nursery-Kindergarten Education.* New York: McGraw-Hill Book Co., 1958. pp. 131-133.

Leeper, Sarah H. et al. *Good Schools for Young Children.* New York: The Macmillan Co., 1968.

Logan, Lillian, Virgil Logan, and Leona Paterson. *Creative Communication: Teaching the Language Arts.* New York: McGraw-Hill Book Co., Ryerson Ltd., 1972. p. 34.

McCall, Adeline. "Improvising on the Black Keys," in *Music for Kindergarten and Nursery School.* Boston: Allyn and Bacon, Inc., 1966. pp. 84-85.

McFee, Oralie et. al. *Learning Activities Book 1.* New York: General Learning Corporation, 1969. p. 8.

Michel, P. "The optimum development of musical abilities in the first years of life." *Psychology of Music,* June 1973, I, 14-20.

Mussen, P. H., J. J. Conger, and J. Kagan. *Child Development and Personality.* New York: Harper & Row, Publishers, 1969.

New Dimensions in Music: Music for Early Childhood. New York: American Book Company, 1970.

Nimnicht, Glenn et. al. *The New Nursery School.* New York: General Learning Corporation, 1969. pp. 81-82, 84.

Peters, Martha L. "A Comparison of the Musical Sensitivity of Mongoloid and Normal Children." *Journal of Music Therapy,* Vol. 7, No. 4, 1970.

Piaget, Jean et. al. *The Child's Conception of Geometry.* London: Routledge and Kegan Paul Ltd., 1960.

———. *The Child's Conception of Number.* New York: Humanities Press, 1952. p. 125.

Pillsbury Foundation Studies. *Music of Young Children*, 5th printing. Santa Barbara, Calif.: Pillsbury Foundation for Advancement of Music Education. Reprint of research 1941-1951.

Pitcher, Evelyn et. al. *Helping Young Children Learn*, 2nd ed. Columbus, Ohio: Charles E. Merrill Publishing Co., 1974. p. 50.

Pratcher, Mary. *Teaching in the Kindergarten*. New York: Exposition Press, 1968. p. 77.

Read, Katherine H. *The Nursery School: A Human Relationships Laboratory*, 5th ed. Philadelphia: W. B. Saunders Company, 1971. p. 230.

Rudolph, Marguerita, and Dorothy Cohen. *Kindergarten: A Year of Learning*. New York: Appleton-Century-Crofts, 1964. p. 233.

Sample, Robert E. "Are You Teaching Only One Side of the Brain?" *Learning Magazine*, February, 1975. pp. 25-28.

Shumsky, Abraham. *Creative Teaching in the Elementary School*. New York: Appleton-Century-Crofts, 1965.

Silberman, C. E. *Crisis in the Classroom*. New York: Random House, Inc., 1970.

Sinclair, Caroline B. *Movement of the Young Child Ages Two to Six*. Columbus, Ohio: Charles E. Merrill Publishing Co., 1973. p. 61.

Spodeck, Bernard, *Teaching in the Early Years*. Englewood Cliffs, N.J.: Prentice-Hall, Inc., 1972. pp. 270-71.

Stafford, Philip L. *Teaching Young Children with Special Needs*. Saint Louis: The C. V. Mosby Company, 1978. p. 255.

Stevens, S. Lillian. *The Teacher's Guide to Open Education*. New York: Holt, Rinehart and Winston, 1974. p. 29.

Smith, Robert M. *Clinical Teaching: Methods of Instruction for the Retarded*. New York, McGraw-Hill, 1968.

Sutton-Smith, B. *Child Psychology*. Englewood Cliffs, N.J.: Prentice-Hall, Inc., 1973.

Taylor, Harold. "Music as a Source of Knowledge." *Music Educators Journal*, September, 1964. p. 36.

Todd, Vivian E. and Helen Heffernan, *The Years Before School: Guiding Preschool Children*, 2nd ed. New York: The Macmillan Company, 1970. p. 494.

Wheeler, Lawrence, and Lois Raebeck. *Orff and Kodaly Adapted for Elementary School*. Dubuque, Iowa: Wm. C. Brown Company Publishers, 1972. p. 2.

Whitehead, Robert. *Children's Literature: Strategies for Teaching*. Englewood Cliffs, N.J.: Prentice-Hall, Inc., 1968. p. 145, 175.

Winn, Marie and Mary Ann Porcher. *The Playgroup Book*. Baltimore, Md.: Penguin Books, Inc., 1967. p. 102.

Young, William T. "Musical Development in Disadvantaged Children." *Journal of Research in Music Education*, Fall, 1974.

Zimmerman, Marilyn P. *Musical Characteristics of Children*. Washington, D.C.: Music Educators National Conference, 1971. p. 28.

Appendix A
Exemplary Teaching Plans

Exemplary Teaching Plans

The following plans all state music objectives first because teaching music is the primary purpose of this book. The featured songs can serve to motivate interest in other areas of instruction that deal with and share the subject matter of those songs with the music objectives. These plans are designed to be adapted for use either to teach music as an independent subject or music as integrated with other subjects.

Teaching Plan No. 1
Performance Objectives in Music
The child should
1. Sing in a low-pitched 5-note range.
2. Sing repeated pitches and to match them.
3. Feel the pulse (beat) sufficiently so that the child is able to clap or stamp when there are rests in this song.
4. Recognize that the rhythm pattern of the first measure repeats in the second measure (is the same) and the remainder of the song is rhythmically different (simple form concepts).

Learnings in Related Areas (Safety Education)
1. Pronounce and learn the words of the song.
2. Concepts of stop, go, wait.
3. Concepts of red, green, yellow.
4. Following directions.

Materials
Song: "Traffic Lights," page 144 in this book.
Recordings: *Health and Safety Through Music* (available from Lyons); *Learning Basic Skills Through Music: Health and Safety,* by Hap Palmer.
Finger Plays and Poems: Select from sources listed at end of chapter 6.

Procedures
The following activities are not stated in order of presentation. Read, discuss, demonstrate or learn finger play, poem. Utilize appropriate parts of the recordings, wih pupil participation. When the song is taught, the teacher sings the entire song, perhaps several times, then asks children to echo her singing of the first measure, then the second measure (tone matching), and so on. After the

entire song is learned, different children or groups can sing measures one and two while all join in singing measures three and four.

Teaching Plan No. 2

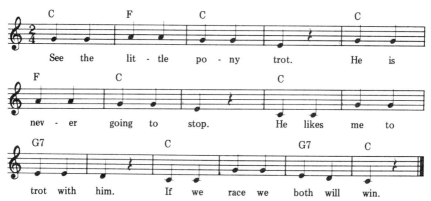

Performance Objectives in Music

Children should

1. Demonstrate understanding of high and low pitches at the end of the first two phrases, the beginning of the last two phrases, and the last three pitches of the song by using hand levels.
2. Identify obvious skips and steps in the melody (measures 9, 13, 16) by use of hand levels.
3. Interpret 2/4 meter through use of the body in trotting.
4. Play simple parts on the bells (phrases one and two).
5. Discuss and demonstrate the sounds a pony makes as he walks, trots, and gallops.

Performance Objectives in Related Areas

Language and poetry

Listen to and repeat the words in the following poems, then interpret them through rhythmic pantomime; also select a percussion instrument to add interest to the poems "Trot, Trot, Horsie," and "Shoe the Pony Shoe," both found in *This Little Pig Went to Market,* ed. by Norah Montgomerie.

After listening to the finger play "I Have a Little Pony," by Edith Leonard and Dorothy Van Deman, the children should be able to repeat the finger play using appropriate rhythm of words, pronunciation and enunciation, and follow directions and dramatize with hands.

Art and language	Discuss pictures of ponies and pictures showing what they eat (science). Draw pictures of ponies. Be a member of a herd of wild ponies and create original rhythm and movement.

Teaching Plan No. 3

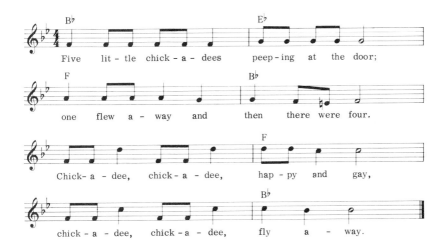

Five Little Chickadees — Traditional *Spritely*

Five lit-tle chick-a-dees peep-ing at the door; one flew a-way and then there were four. Chick-a-dee, chick-a-dee, hap-py and gay, chick-a-dee, chick-a-dee, fly a-way.

Performance Objectives in Music

Children should

1. Discuss how they think the chickadees feel in the song (mood). Explain how they know the chickadees are happy. (Relate to "chickadee, chicka-dee" pitches in measures 5 and 7).
2. Discover and show through appropriate movement how tempo (fast, moderate, slow) affects the mood when the teacher establishes those different tempos.
3. Listen to the teacher as she plays the song on the piano and be able to indicate when repeated notes, steps, and skips appear in the melody.

Performance Objectives in Related Areas

The child should

Language arts and counting	1. Dramatize the song. Choose groups of five children. Be sure all children have the opportunity to participate.
	2. Select a number (printed on cardboards) from one to five, and children will arrange themselves in sequential order.

	3. Count from one to five.
	4. Subtract as one, two, three, four, and all of the chickadees fly away.
	5. Demonstrate that they understand "less" and "more" by increasing or diminishing the proper number of chickadees.
Art	6. After viewing a picture of a chickadee, discuss the picture as to its artistic appeal—colors, mood, patterns, etc. Watch a live bird and explain it as to shape, size, color, and movement.
Language and writing	7. Create and dictate their own story, poem, rhyme, or song about birds as the teacher records it for them.
Health	8. Explore what birds eat, how they keep clean, where they sleep, and how they stay safe; demonstrate their understanding of these activities through pantomime or dramatic interpretation.
Science	9. Examine a bird and discuss its body covering and the different parts of its body; how it protects itself from weather, man, and other animals.

Additional Materials

Literature	Finger Plays: "Two Dickey Birds," and "Robin Redbreast." See references at end of science section of chapter 6. Poems: see anthologies listed at end of chapter 6.
Music	Related songs: "Little Bird," and "There Came to My Window," from *New Dimensions in Music: Music for Early Childhood.* "Little Bird" has very interesting meter changes. Related recordings for listening, discussion, and dramatization: *Birds, Beasts and Bigger Fish,* by Pete Seeger, Folkways Records.
Science	Related filmstrips: "Filling the Bill," "You Don't Look Like Your Mother," both from Bowmar, and "Learning About Birds," from EBF. Books: *What's Inside, I Can Fly, Listen to the Birds,* and *All About Eggs.* See references at end of science section, chapter 6. *Birds in the Sky,* by John Hawkinson and Lucy Hawkinson. Chicago: Childrens Press, Inc., 1965.

Children need the opportunity to use a variety of sources of information and then to have time and freedom to interpret the information through the use of both verbal and nonverbal activities. Audiovisual materials will be needed as an aid to the children's learning in each of the above situations, but their bodies become the most accessible and meaningful tool for self-interpretation and communication.

Teaching Plan No. 4 for Kindergarten

Performance Objectives in Music

The child should

1. Identify phrases that sound almost alike.
2. Demonstrate by appropriate body movement that two parts of phrase two are almost the same.
3. Demonstrate by appropriate body movement "same" and "different" in the melody (preparing for recognition of ABA form).
4. Indicate descending scale lines in any way they can invent.
5. Use hand levels to indicate the presence of steps and skips in the melody.

Performance Objectives in Related Areas

The child should

Language
1. Demonstrate ability to identify and name letters by clapping only when singing an alphabet name.
2. Hold up the card he has with a letter of the alphabet printed on it when that letter is sung in the song.

3. Listen to the record *ABC, 1 to 10,* then sing back the alphabet songs and rhymes he hears. The teacher uses additional materials: a song, "Marching Around the Alphabet," by Hap Palmer, from *Learning Basic Skills Through Music,* Vol. 1; finger plays and poems from the sources at the end of chapter 6; books from the list of books about ABCs at the end of chapter 6.

Creative production

4. After singing and dramatizing songs, hearing and dramatizing records, poems, rhymes, and stories about ABCs, he should create his own song, poem, or story about them.

Appendix B
How Early Childhood
Record Albums Relate to
the Curriculum

How Early Childhood Record Albums
Relate to the Curriculum

(The Early Childhood Albums cited below are from the catalog of Educational Activities, Inc., Freeport, New York.)

Mathematics	Album K 7010—*Stories and Songs about Numbers.* 1 to 10 taught by singing along, acting out, and finger games.
Music-Science	*Instruments of the Orchestra.* Each is individually introduced and later combined into an orchestra. *Sounds of the City.* Audio discrimination is developed by listening to sounds of milk trucks, garbage trucks, truck, bus, train, airplane, fire engine, policeman, ambulance.
Science	*Jungle Animals and Farm Animals.* Discrimination between domesticated and wild animals.
Language Arts	*Nursery Rhymes.* Familiar rhymes set to music to sing along with, act out, and listen to.
Mathematics	Album K7012—*Stories and Songs about*: *Sizes.* Animal and insect size is compared to that of a child; advantages and disadvantages of small and large size are presented. *Shapes.* Mike and his magic glasses teach round and square shapes.
Language Arts and Art	*Colors.* Taught through the story of a little bird who changes colors and later becomes a canary.
Social Science	*Houses.* A giraffe's search for a home illustrates many types; tent, igloo, grass hut, etc. *Feelings.* Love, happiness, sadness, anger, etc., in story form.

Album K7013—*Stories and Songs about*:

Mathematics	*Distance.* A family trip reaches concepts of near and far; comparison of means of transportation; different points of view; boy, kangaroo, crocodile, ant.
Social Science (feelings)	*The Dark.* Helps children overcome fear of the dark by a story in which "the dark" is afraid of the child.
Mathematics	*Measuring.* The importance of measuring is shown through an amusing story of a king and his inchworm.
Social Science	*Feeling Shy.* An elephant who overcomes his shyness by developing confidence helps children to do the same.

Album K7014—*Storis and Songs about*:

Social Science	*Manners.* A dog wins the manners contest by thinking of others instead of himself.
Language Arts, Social Science, Science	*Guessing Sounds.* Ducks, cats, horses, mice, clocks, etc., in an interesting story; children develop sound discrimination through identifying their sources.
Social Science	*Families.* Kindness between brothers and sisters.
Health and Safety	*Safety.* The owl selects a "traffic cop" to keep things safe and teaches important safety lessons.
Science	*Tastes.* Sour, bitter, salty, and sweet are taught.

Appendix C
Sources

Catalogs

Suppliers of Early Childhood Material

Bowmar, 622 Rodier Drive, Glendale, Calif. 91201. Request *Early Childhood Catalog*. Records, filmstrips, books, etc.

Children's Music Center, Inc., 5373 W. Pico Blvd., Los Angeles, Calif. 90019. Catalog: *Best Records, Books, Rhythm Instruments for Early Childhood*. This catalog is classified in helpful ways.

Educational Activities, Inc., Freeport, N.Y. 11520. Records, filmstrips, cassettes and instructional media. Publisher of Hap Palmer materials.

Golden Records Educational Division catalog. Michael Brent Publications, Inc., Port Chester, N.Y. 10573.

Lorraine Music Co., Inc. 23-80 48th St., Long Island City, N.Y. Records and cassettes for music and other subjects.

Lyons, 530 Riverview Ave., Elkhart, Ind. 46514. Music learning materials for all areas of early childhood through primary. Catalog: *Learning Materials for the Early Years*. Includes materials of Hap Palmer, Ella Jenkins, Mary Helen Richards, Lou Stallman and Bob Susser, Grace Nash, and others. Also percussion instruments, Autoharp, etc.

Magnamusic-Baton, Inc., 6394 Delmar Blvd., St. Louis, Mo. 46514. Early childhood musical instruments.

Music Education Group, 1234 Sherman Ave., Evanston, Ill. 60202. Early childhood musical instruments. Autoharp.

Playtime Equipment Co., 808 Howard St., Omaha, Neb. 68102. A catalog for kindergarten and primary, including books for all areas of early childhood through primary.

Rhythm aBnd, Inc., P.O. Box 126, Fort Worth, Texas 76101. Early childhood musical instruments.

Scientific Music Industries, 823 S. Wabash Ave., Chicago, Ill. 60605. Bells, rhythm instruments and more.

World of Peripole, Inc., P.O. Box 146, Browns Mills, N.J. 08015. Early childhood musical instruments.

Sources

Films and Filmstrips

Audio-Visual Enterprises (AVE), c/o Virginia Smith, 911 Laguna Road, Pasadena, Calif.

Audio-Visual Division, Inc., 355 Lexington Ave., New York, N.Y.

Bowmar, 622 Rodier Drive, Glendale, Calif. 91201.

Bro-Dart, Inc., Williamsport, Pa. 17701

Coronet Films, 65 E. South Water St., Chicago, Ill. 60601

DCA Educational Products, Inc., 4895 Stenton Ave., Philadelphia, Pa.

Education Activities, P.O. Box 392, Freeport, New York, N.Y. 11520

Encyclopedia Britannica Films, 1150 Wilmette Ave., Wilmette, Ill.

Eye Gate House, Inc., 146-01 Archer Ave., Jamaica, N.Y.

Film Associates of California, 11559 Santa Monica Blvd., Los Angeles, Calif.

International Communications Foundation, Communications Films Division, International Communications Films, 870 Monterey Pass Road, Monterey, Calif.

McGraw-Hill Book Company, Inc., 330 West 42nd St., New York, N.Y.

Prentice-Hall Media/Jam Handy, 150 White Plains Rd., Tarrytown, N.Y. 10591.

Society for Visual Education, Inc., 1343 West Diversey Parkway, Chicago, Ill.

Sources

Recordings

Angel Records, 1960 Avenue of the Americas, New York, N.Y.

Bowmar, 622 Rodier Drive, Glendale, Calif. 91201

Capital Records, Inc., 1290 Avenue of the Americas, New York, N.Y.

CBS Records Division, 51 West 52nd St., New York, N.Y.

Columbia Records, 51 West 52nd St., New York, N.Y.

Decca Records Company, 445 Park Ave., New York, N.Y.

Disneyland Records, 477 Madison Ave., New York, N.Y.

Educational Activities, P.O. Box 392, Freeport, N.Y. 11520.

Educational Record Sales, 157 Chambers St., New York, N.Y.

Elektra Records, 1855 Broadway, New York, N.Y.

Eye Gate Happy Time Records, Eye Gate House, Inc., 146-01 Archer Ave., Jamaica, N.Y.

Folkraft Record Company, 1161 Broad St., Newark, N.J.

Folkways Record Corporation, 701 7th Ave., New York, N.Y.

Franson Corporation (Children's Record Guild, Young People's Records), 225 Park Ave. South, New York, N.Y.

Golden Records, 250 West 57th St., New York, N.Y.

Honor Your Partner Records, P.O. Box 392, Freeport, N.Y.

Kimbo Educational, P.O. Box 477, Long Branch, N.J. 07740.

Liberty Records, Inc., 1776 Broadway, New York, N.Y.

Lyons, 530 Riverview Ave., Elkhart, Indiana 46514.

Mercury Record Production, Inc., 110 West 57th St., New York, N.Y.

RCA Victor Records, Educational Dept., 1133 Avenue of the Americas, New York, N.Y.

Stanley Bowmar Company, Inc., 4 Broadway, Valhalla, N. Y.

Vanguard Record Sales Corporation, 71 West 23rd St., New York, N.Y.

Vox Productions, Inc., 211 East 43rd St., New York, N.Y.

Publishers of Music Book Series

Addison-Wesley Publishing Co., Reading, Mass. *Comprehensive Musicianship Through Classroom Music.*

Allyn and Bacon, Inc., Boston, 02210. *This Is Music for Today.*

American Book Co., New York 10003. *New Dimensions In Music.*

Follett Publishing Co., Chicago 60607. *Discovering Music Together.*

Ginn and Co., Boston 02117. *The Magic of Music.*

Holt, Rinehart & Winston, Inc., New York 10017. *Exploring Music.*

The Macmillan Co., New York 10022. *The Spectrum of Music.*

Prentice-Hall, Inc., Englewood Cliffs, N.J. 07632. *Growing With Music.*

Silver Burdett Co., Morristown, N.J. 07960. *Making Music Your Own.*

Silver Burdett Co., Morristown, N.J. 07960. *Silver Burdett Music.*

Summy-Birchard Co., Evanston, Ill. 60204. *Birchard Music Series.*

Index of Songs

Index